Financial Politics in Contemporary Japan

STUDIES OF THE EAST ASIAN INSTITUTE
COLUMBIA UNIVERSITY

D1364217

STUDIES OF THE EAST ASIAN INSTITUTE
COLUMBIA UNIVERSITY

The East Asian Institute is Columbia University's center for research, teaching, and publication on modern East Asia. The Studies of the East Asian Institute were inaugurated in 1962 to bring to a wider public the results of significant new research on China, Japan, and Korea.

Financial Politics in Contemporary Japan

Frances McCall Rosenbluth

Cornell University Press

Ithaca and London

First published 1989 by Cornell University Press.

International Standard Book Number 0-8014-2274-4
Library of Congress Catalog Card Number 89-30074
Printed in the United States of America
*Librarians: Library of Congress cataloging information
appears on the last page of the book.*

*The paper in this book is acid-free and meets the guidelines for permanence
and durability of the Committee on Production Guidelines
for Book Longevity of the Council on Library Resources.*

Contents

Acknowledgments

In the process of researching and writing this book I incurred large debts of gratitude to many people. I acknowledge those debts here without hope of repaying them. I am especially grateful to my teachers of Japanese politics, Gerald Curtis and James Morley, who encouraged me through every step of my graduate education and whose high standards of research and analysis I am still striving to achieve. Hugh Patrick gave unselfishly of his time and intellect in trying to educate me on the Japanese economy and perhaps more than anyone else deepened my understanding of the political economy of Japanese finance.

My research in Japan was funded by a Fulbright Fellowship and a Social Science Research Council Fellowship. I am grateful to these institutions for making my fieldwork possible and for the many kindnesses of their staff members, which made my stay in Japan more enjoyable.

Many people in Japan generously assisted my research efforts. Although I can name only a few of them here, I am grateful to all who assisted me. Professors Koichi Hamada and Akiyoshi Horiuchi served as my academic advisers at the University of Tokyo Faculty of Economics and helped me in innumerable ways. I am grateful to Professor Tachi Ryuichiro and the staff of the Ministry of Finance Institute for Fiscal and Monetary Studies for hosting me as a visiting scholar, Yuichiro Nagatomi and his staff for hosting me at the Foundation for Advanced Information and Research, and Hisao

Acknowledgments

Kanamori and his staff for hosting me at the Japan Economic Research Center. Each of these institutions gave me introductions and access to important resource materials. Many Ministry of Finance officials, bankers, and journalists spent much time providing me with valuable information.

Many mentors and colleagues in the United States read various versions or parts of this manuscript and helped improve it: Jonathan Aronson, Theodore Bestor, John Conybeare, Jeff Frieden, David Friedman, Peter Gourevitch, Jennifer Holt, Charles Lipson, Helen Milner, Mike Mochizuki, Richard Nelson, Frank Packer, Louis Pauly, Mark Ramseyer, John Ruggie, Jack Snyder, Takaaki Suzuki, Robert Uriu, and Kozo Yamamura. Special thanks go to T. J. Pempel, who waived his anonymity as a reviewer and made helpful suggestions for revising the manuscript, and to Roger Haydon of Cornell University Press, who steered the book through reviews and production. Finally, I thank my family and friends, who offered endless encouragement, and especially Jim Rosenbluth, whose cooperation and willingness to make numerous personal compromises made this project possible.

FRANCES MCCALL ROSENBLUTH

New York, New York

Financial Politics in
Contemporary Japan

1

Why Financial Reform
in Japan?

Japan is in a historic process of deregulating its financial markets. That financial institutions and practices in Tokyo bear a growing resemblance to those of New York and London testifies to strong international market pressures. And yet marked national differences remain, both in the process of deregulation and in important aspects of Japan's financial markets and institutions. For as undiscriminating and relentless as market forces may be, they generate policy changes only to the extent that they incite important players in the domestic polity to alter the regulatory framework in Japan's financial system.[1] We need to understand who those players are and what other factors constrain their behavior.

The central argument of this book is that politics matters, even in the seemingly arcane area of financial regulation, where overt politicization of policy making is infrequent. Financial regulation is changing in Japan not because the Ministry of Finance (MOF) now deems Japanese financial institutions ready to compete globally but because the institutions themselves find much of the protective regulation no longer useful. Frequently politicians are not directly involved in discrete instances of policy change. But the process is inherently political in that the MOF's responses to financial interest groups anticipate intrusion by politicians should the financial in-

[1] For a similar point in a different context, see Peter Gourevitch, *Politics in Hard Times: Comparative Responses to International Economic Crises* (Ithaca: Cornell University Press, 1986), p. 54.

1

stitutions be dissatisfied with the MOF's bureaucratic solution. My principal focus is on the actors and institutions in one segment of the financial system, the banking industry. Banks, as financial intermediaries between small depositors and corporate borrowers, figured centrally in Japan's economic development, particularly in the years of postwar recovery and rapid growth. As new changes have swept through the Japanese economy in recent decades, the banking industry has been transformed as well.

What follows is not an analysis of market forces; that work is already being undertaken by economists.[2] Rather, I use Japan's banking deregulation as a vehicle for addressing the political questions "Who gets what?" and "By what process?" An examination of policy outcomes against a backdrop of market stimuli affords us a closer look at the structure of influence within Japan's political system, the filter through which market forces must penetrate.[3]

Although few recent studies of Japanese financial deregulation focus on the political dynamics of change, one might devise a threefold categorization extrapolating from the three major competing explanations of Japanese policy making in general. The first explanation is that Japan is basically a reactive state and that the United States, in conjunction with several European states, has gradually forced open Japan's tightly closed financial door.

[2] Excellent studies on the economics of Japanese financial deregulation include Robert Feldman, *Japanese Financial Markets: Deficits, Dilemmas and Deregulation* (Cambridge: MIT Press, 1986); Yoshio Suzuki, *Kinyū Jiyūka to Kinyū Seisaku* (Tokyo: Tōyō Keizai Shimpōsha, 1985); Shōzō Tanida, ed., *Kinyū Jiyūka to Kinyū Seido Kaikaku* (Tokyo: Ōtsuki Shoten, 1986); Bunji Kure and Kinsō Shima, *Kinri Jiyūka* (Tokyo: Yūhikaku, 1985); Shinichi Gotō, Bunji Kure, and Ryūtarō Hizume, *Nihon no Kinyū Kakumei* (Tokyo: Yūhikaku, 1982); Kazuo Tatewaki, *Kinyū Daikakumei* (Tokyo: Tōyō Keizai Shimpōsha, 1982); Ryūichirō Tachi, *Kinyū Saihensei no Shiten* (Tokyo: Tōyō Keizai Shimpōsha, 1985); Shōichi Rōyama, *Kinyū Jiyūka* (Tokyo: Tokyo Daigaku Shuppankai, 1986); and Thomas Cargill and Shōichi Royama, *The Transition of Japanese Finance and Monetary Policy in Comparative Perspective with the United States* (Stanford, Calif.: Hoover Institution Press, 1987).

[3] Only one in-depth study of the politics of private finance in Japan exists in English, and none in Japanese. James Horne, in *Japanese Financial Markets* (London: Allen & Unwin, 1985), examined developments in Japan's financial markets from 1970 to 1980 to reach broader conclusions about the Japanese decision-making process. This book, while building on Horne's enlightening description and analysis, differs from Horne's work in three respects: the case studies, the time frame, and the conceptual framework.

Why Financial Reform in Japan?

International pressure on Japan to deregulate its financial markets continues a long history of foreign pressures for market opening in Japan, at least since the mid-1960s, when Japan began to post chronic balance-of-payments surpluses. The United States in particular is faced with a secular decline in American competitiveness in world markets and thus has less tolerance for Japan's continued reluctance to open its own markets to American goods and services. The United States has, and indeed should, some argue, abandoned its unqualified commitment to free trade in favor of a policy of specific reciprocity against countries such as Japan which have not shown a willingness to play by the rules of free international exchange.[4] The battle lines according to this type of reasoning are essentially international versus domestic, and the dominant scenario is that of Japan reluctantly but ineluctably opening in response to sharp foreign prodding.

A second explanation attributes the major stimulus for change to the Japanese government. Just as the Ministry of International Trade and Industry (MITI) forced Japanese industry to do what the wise bureaucrats knew was good for it, so the Ministry of Finance (MOF) has compelled Japanese banks and securities firms to conform to changing world conditions. The Ministry of Finance, in this view, is opening Japan's financial markets because it deems Japanese corporations and financial institutions now competitive enough on a global scale to take advantage of freer financial markets.

The conviction that bureaucrats dominate Japanese policy making has a venerable tradition and in fact is still espoused with a few modifications by some of the sharpest analysts of Japanese politics.[5]

[4]See Stephen D. Krasner, "Asymmetries in Japanese-American Trade: The Case for Specific Reciprocity," University of California-Berkeley Institute of International Studies, Policy Papers in International Affairs no. 32 (1987), and Krasner, "A Trade Strategy for the United States," *Ethics and International Affairs* 2 (1988), 17–35. For the view that Japan *is* willing to play a supporting role in the free trade system, see Takashi Inoguchi, "Japan's Images and Options: Not a Challenger, but a Supporter," *Journal of Japanese Studies* 12 (1986), 95–119; Kent Calder, "Japanese Foreign Economic Policy Formulation: Explaining the Reactive State," *World Politics* 40 (July 1988), 517–41.

[5]Chalmers Johnson subscribes to a belief in a strong Japanese bureaucracy, but one that often works to maximize its own more than national interests. See his "MITI, MPT, and the Telecom Wars: How Japan Makes Policy for High Technology," BRIE Working Paper no. 21 (Berkeley, Calif., September 1986), p. 8, and

3

Financial Politics in Contemporary Japan

In the purer form of the bureaucratic dominance model the main
battle lines are state versus society, and the state often wins. If this
conception is valid, we would expect the bureaucracy to remain
internally coherent as well as autonomous from political parties and
interest groups.

A third explanation of Japan's financial deregulation holds that
politicians are the key players. Ever ready to do what is needed to
win reelection, Liberal Democratic party politicians have pushed
the banks and the bureaucrats in the directions necessary to make
constituents happier, to keep themselves in office longer, and to
secure extra campaign funds along the way.

In recent years a number of Japan specialists have noted the
growing prominence of LDP involvement in policy making since the
mid-1970s. Slower economic growth has engendered sharper conflicts of interest in the private sector which are less amenable to bureaucratic solutions than the largely allocative decisions of Japan's
rapid growth era.[6] Although most scholars are careful not to exag-
gerate the role of politicians in Japan, a purely pluralist model of
policy making would have politicians spearheading challenges to
the financial system's status quo on behalf of competitive sectors
that are willing to use financial resources in exchange for political
favors.

MITI and the Japanese Miracle (Stanford: Stanford University Press, 1982); for a
more explicitly historical study, see Johnson, Japan's Public Policy Companies
(Washington, D.C.: American Enterprise Institute, 1978). The rational-actor model
of the Japanese state is well articulated in the work of John Zysman, who writes of a
powerful state bureaucracy that is to a considerable extent insulated from parliamentary and interest-group pressure. See Zysman, Governments, Markets, and
Growth (Ithaca: Cornell Unversity Press, 1983), p. 296. In this view, the bureaucracy is largely free to devise economic policies that promote its perceptions of
the national interest.

[6]For example, Michio Muramatsu, Ichirō Miyake, Yasushi Yamaguchi, and
Elichi Shindō, Nihon Seiji no Zahyō (Tokyo: Yūhikaku, 1985); Seizaburō Satō and
Tetsuhisa Matsuzaki, Jimintō Seiken (Tokyo: Chūō Kōronsha, 1986); Michio
Muramatsu and Ellis Krauss, "The Conservative Policy Line and the Development
of Patterned Pluralism," in Kozo Yamamura and Yasukichi Yasuba, eds., The
Political Economy of Japan, vol. 1: The Domestic Transformation (Stanford,
Calif.: Stanford University Press, 1987), pp. 516–54; T. J. Pempel, "The Unbun-
dling of 'Japan, Inc.': The Changing Dynamics of Japanese Policy Formation," in
Kenneth Pyle, ed., The Trade Crisis: How Will Japan Respond? (Seattle, Wash.:
Society for Japanese Studies, 1987), pp. 117–52.

4

Why Financial Reform in Japan?

A close examination of the factual record in Japan's financial deregulation presented in the following chapters suggests that none of these explanations is entirely adequate. Although American policy makers might like to think that the Yen-Dollar Committee was largely responsible for Japan's financial opening, in fact international political pressures were absent for many of the regulatory changes. The Ministry of Finance would welcome credit for leading the liberalization, but in fact the MOF has been more of an enforcer of private bargains than a major proponent of change. The politicians would like to claim that the LDP dictated the flow of events, but financial institutions involve political allies only when negotiations with the Ministry of Finance break down. Moreover, politicians are as likely to come to the aid of uncompetitive sectors resisting change as they are to champion the reformist efforts of the competitive sectors. I submit, rather, that deregulation has been propelled by financial institutions, acting in cooperation with the Ministry of Finance and sometime politicians, to construct a new set of rules they need to compete in a changing economic environment.

The Political Context of the Japanese Financial System

The Japanese financial sector comprises several well-organized interest groups that have successfully employed their political resources to influence financial policy in Japan. Rules governing private finance are changing because shifts in Japan's economic environment have rendered the initial regulatory structure no longer beneficial to these groups. A careful distinction between what is being deregulated and what is not, who is benefiting and who is not, will help illuminate the structure of interest representation in Japan.

The principle of collective action explains the paradox of how a relatively small number of organized groups could maintain an advantage over the vast general public in the policy-making process of representative democracies by way of a public goods problem: because the per capita gain to each individual resulting from policy change tends to be small, there is less incentive for a voter to expend the time, money, and energy mobilizing for political action than

5

there is for interest groups that have a larger stake in the resolution of a given issue.[7] The larger and more dispersed the group, the greater the expense of learning of their common interests, of becoming organized, and of deciding on a plan of action. According to the supply-and-demand theory of regulation, there is an intrinsic bias in favor of smaller groups with large per capita stakes.[8] Business groups have an added advantage because, as Charles Lindblom notes, "Government needs a strong economy just as much as business does. . . . Business simply needs inducements, hence a privileged position in government and politics, if it is to do its job."[9]

A stream of political scientists, starting with Arthur Bentley at the turn of the century, have emphasized the importance of interest groups in the formulation of public policy.[10] Political scientists thus preceded their economist colleagues by many decades in questioning the public interest explanation of regulation.[11]

The corporatist literature has added another dimension to the analysis of policy process and outcomes by focusing on the institutionalization of particular state-society relationships.[12] Alan Cawson defines corporatism as a political process "in which organizations representing monopolistic functional interests engage in

[7]Mancur Olson, *The Logic of Collective Action* (Cambridge: Harvard University Press, 1982), and *The Rise and Decline of Nations* (New Haven: Yale University Press, 1982); George Stigler, "The Theory of Regulation," *Bell Journal of Economics and Management Science* 2 (1971), 3–21; Richard A. Posner, "Theories of Economic Regulation," *Bell Journal of Economics and Management Science* 5 (1974), 337–52; Sam Peltzman, "Toward a More General Theory of Regulation," *Journal of Law and Economics* 19 (1976), 211–40.

[8]R. G. Noll, "Government Regulatory Behavior: A Multidisciplinary Survey and Synthesis," in Noll, ed., *Regulatory Policy and the Social Sciences* (Berkeley: University of California Press, 1985), p. 44.

[9]Charles E. Lindblom, *Politics and Markets* (New York: Basic Books, 1977), p. 175.

[10]A. F. Bentley, *The Process of Government* (Chicago: University of Chicago Press, 1908); D. Truman, *The Governmental Process* (New York: Knopf, 1951); G. A. Almond, "Corporatism, Pluralism, and Professional Memory," *World Politics* 35 (1983), 245–60.

[11]Marxist economists had, in a sense, gotten there first; but I am referring specifically to the notion that interest aggregation, not only ownership of the means of production, is a key factor in influencing policy.

[12]See, for example, P. C. Schmitter, "Models of Interest Intermediation and Models of Social Change in Western Europe," *Comparative Political Studies* 10 (1977), 2–38; Schmitter and G. Lehmbruch, eds., *Patterns of Corporatist Policy-Making* (Beverly Hills, Calif.: Sage, 1982).

political exchange with state agencies over public policy outputs which involve those organizations in a role which combines interest representation and policy implementation through delegated self-enforcement."[13]

Peter Katzenstein has rendered the vague, sprawling concept of corporatism somewhat more useful by distinguishing among types of democratic corporatism. Social corporatism, for example, he characterizes by centralized labor organization and decentralized business associations, liberal corporatism by the reverse situation in which labor is decentralized and business organization is centralized.[14] Other scholars have made further categorizations, such as T. J. Pempel and Keiichi Tsunekawa's "corporatism-without-labor" depiction of Japan, and Cawson's formulation of meso or sectoral-level corporatism.[15]

The problem with most corporatist analysis, however, is its failure adequately to consider the nature of the political system in which this institutionalization of state-society relationships takes place.[16] In representative democracies, parliaments have the constitutionally granted capacity to circumscribe the actions of the state's administrative apparatus through legislation, budget appropriations, and other oversight mechanisms. Even if the bureaucracy and peak organizations from the private sector are intertwined in mutually beneficial institutional arrangements, it is the parliament that, to a considerable extent, determines which groups are represented and on what terms. The political arena is bypassed only to the extent that extraparliamentary arrangements reflect the influence the peak organizations wield over the elected representatives in the political system.

As an examination of Japan's financial regulation bears out, both

[13] Alan Cawson, *Corporatism and Political Theory* (Oxford: Blackwell, 1986), p. 38.

[14] P. J. Katzenstein, *Small States in World Markets: Industrial Policy in Europe* (Ithaca: Cornell University Press, 1985).

[15] T. J. Pempel and Keiichi Tsunekawa, "Corporatism without Labor? The Japanese Anomaly," in Philippe C. Schmitter and Gerhard Lehmbruch, eds., *Trends toward Corporatist Intermediation* (Beverly Hills, Calif.: Sage, 1979), pp. 231–70; Cawson, *Corporatism and Political Theory*.

[16] Peter Hall also makes this point. See his *Governing the Economy: The Politics of State Intervention in Britain and France* (New York: Oxford University Press, 1986), p. 271.

the bureaucracy and the financial sector benefit from the institutionalization of their ties which limits the range and intensity of demands on the state: in exchange for policies that satisfy the politically powerful financial sector, the bureaucracy is able to minimize the intrusion of politicians into financial policy making. In the event of conflicting interests among different types of financial institutions, the financial regulators engage in "preemptive equilibration" of these interests before overt politicization occurs. This saves financial institutions potentially exorbitant sums in political lobbying costs. In game theoretic terms, the bureaucracy monitors and enforces compromises within the financial sector to prevent cheating by any financial institution. Should the financial authority attempt to implement policies against the perceived interests of the financial sector, however, the disgruntled group has the option of invoking the power of political representatives at the expense of the bureaucracy's procedural autonomy. The possibility of politicization serves as a check on the bureaucracy and ensures that policy outcomes are consonant with the respective political resources of the various groups in the financial sector. Not surprisingly, the most common policy-making pattern that results is one of stable negotiations between the bureaucracy and groups of financial institutions.

The characterization I present here of Japan's financial policy making is consistent with the broad conclusions of a growing number of Japan specialists. Richard Samuels states that "the Japanese bureaucracy does not dominate, it negotiates" with the private sector in a pattern of policy making he calls "reciprocal consent."[17] Daniel Okimoto calls Japan a "network state" or "societal state," noting that the bureaucracy's power derives largely from its ability to operate collaboratively with the private sector.[18] Ellis Krauss and Michio Muramatsu call the policy-making process in Japan "patterned pluralism," stating that lobbying is not open-ended because interest groups are usually allied over time with the same bureau-

[17]Richard Samuels, *The Business of the Japanese State: Energy Markets in Comparative and Historical Perspective* (Ithaca: Cornell University Press, 1986), pp. 260–62.

[18]Daniel I. Okimoto, "Political Inclusivity: The Domestic Structure of Trade," in Takashi Inoguchi and Okimoto, eds., *The Political Economy of Japan*, vol. II: *The Changing International Context* (Stanford: Stanford University Press, 1988).

cratic agencies and political parties.[19] Seizaburō Satō and Tetsu-hiko Matsuzaki use a similar expression, "channeled pluralism," to depict how private-sector groups influence both bureaucrats and politicians in vertically segmented policy arenas.[20] John Haley's phrase "governance by negotiation" and Michael Young's "private ordering" also capture the notion that the bureaucracy does not control or direct the private sector but negotiates with it, relying heavily on the private sector's collaboration in the formulation and implementation of policy.[21]

Placing the Theory of Regulation in Context

Given what we know from collective action theory about the systematic advantage of producer groups in achieving favored policy outcomes in any representative democracy, it is hardly remarkable that so many Japan specialists speak of stable negotiations between the public sector and peak associations of private interests. When collective action barriers operate as predicted by George Stigler's elegant, simple supply-and-demand theory of regulation (hereafter "the theory of regulation"), producer groups always win and consumers always lose. The only variation within and across countries should be in which producer groups prevail over the others by virtue of their industrial concentration and intensity of interest in given policy outcomes.

The supply-and-demand theory of regulation distinguishes between politicians' "primary constituencies" and the general electorate. Primary constituencies are those that, by virtue of their superior organization, information-gathering capabilities, and campaign-

[19] Michio Muramatsu and Ellis S. Krauss, "The Conservative Policy Line and the Development of Patterned Pluralism," in Yamamura and Yasuba, *The Political Economy of Japan*, vol. 1: *The Domestic Transformation*, p. 537.

[20] Seizabuō Satō and Tetsuhiko Matsuzaki, *Jimintō Seiken* (Tokyo: Chūō Kōron-sha, 1986).

[21] John O. Haley, "Governance by Negotiation: A Reappraisal of Bureaucratic Power in Japan," in *The Trade Crisis: How Will Japan Respond?* Kenneth B. Pyle, ed. (The Society for Japanese Studies, 1987), pp. 177–91; Michael K. Young, "Judicial Review of Administrative Guidance: Governmentally Encouraged Consensual Dispute Resolution in Japan," *Columbia Law Review* 84 (1984), 943–45.

funding power, wield direct influence on politicians' perceived chances for reelection and hence on policy outcomes. In Japan the most powerful of these constituencies are agriculture, big business, and the small- and medium-sized business sector. Organized labor, too, has a voice through the opposition parties, though that voice is muted because of the LDP's longstanding majority in the Diet. The general voting public is periodically given an opportunity to reward or sanction politicians at the polls but is less motivated to stay informed, let alone take an activist stance on issues in which each voter has a small per capita interest. The expected rewards simply cannot justify the necessary expenditure of time, money, and effort. In the supply-and-demand theory of regulation, then, primary constituencies exert influence in the policy-making process through their superior will and ability to affect electoral outcomes on the basis of specific policy outcomes.

Applying the theory of regulation to Japanese finance, we would expect regulation clearly in favor of financial institutions at the expense of the unorganized public in retail banking. Interest rate yields on small savings deposits should be low and unchanging. Wholesale banking is more complicated, because corporate customers are also well-organized in producer groups. Moreover, to the extent that corporate customers have access to competitive foreign suppliers of banking services, Japanese banks must offer attractive deposit yields and loans to retain their clients. The comprehensiveness of Japanese wholesale banking should therefore correlate with the degree to which Japanese corporations can do business with foreign banks as an alternative to domestic banking.

Though appealing because of its simplicity, the supply-and-demand theory of regulation must be placed within a broader institutional and geographical context in order to explain the full range of possible policy processes and outcomes. First, constitutional rules establish centralization or division of authority in state institutions. Second, the nature of the electoral and political party systems shapes which interests in society are best represented and by what means. Third, the degree of centralization or fragmentation of private-sector groups has an important bearing on industries' collective action advantage over consumers.[22] Finally, the theory of

[22]These structural features are adapted from Robert A. Dahl, *Dilemmas of*

10

regulation assumes an insulated domestic market. Once national boundaries are penetrated and domestic firms must compete against foreign firms operating under different rules, domestic production may become impossible to sustain. We should expect the domestic firms to seek changes in domestic regulation that will allow them to retain competitiveness under the changed circumstances.

An examination of Japanese financial policy in light of these structural features indicates that, at least for the time being, stable bargaining between the Ministry of Finance and the financial sector is likely to remain the dominant mode of regulatory policy making and adjustment. First, on the dimension of state structure, the Japanese Ministry of Finance has a broad mandate to regulate nearly the entire financial sector and is indeed capable of limiting competition among financial subsectors. This point is important because politicians typically delegate policy formulation and implementation in instances when taking sides between competing constituents is a political liability. They generally prefer skirting contentious issues to hurting their chances for re-election. A bureaucratic agency with broad jurisdiction, however, can contain the conflict with an administrative settlement. But if the bureaucracy is fragmented into discrete competitive agencies, the contest between constituents for favorable regulation will spill over into the judicial system or into the political arena for jurisdiction.

An important qualification to the MOF's broad mandate, however, is that when policy issues fall between the jurisdictions of two or more ministries, the policy-making process becomes significantly more contentious. The battle between the MOF and the Ministry of Posts and Telecommunications over the postal savings system is an example, explored in detail in Chapter 6. Although historically most issues have been managed in vertically integrated issue areas, there have always been some interministerial disputes, and international pressures for market opening have added to these. The centralization of state authority therefore varies with issue area and seems to be changing with time.

Japan's judiciary system is independent of the Diet and the bureaucracy, but "outsiders" such as consumers have not frequently

Pluralist Democracy: Autonomy vs. Control (New Haven: Yale University Press, 1982), especially p. 65; and Hall, *Governing the Economy*.

used the courts to challenge regulation detrimental to their interests. Japanese courts' power to review administrative actions is seriously circumscribed and is largely limited to instances of criminal liability or a disputed private right.[23] Consumers face this institutional barrier to legal redress, as well as additional disincentives to challenge administrative regulation: the Japanese code of civil procedure does not permit class action suits and allows few means of effective discovery either before or during trial. As Mark Ramseyer has pointed out, a widely dispersed group of plaintiffs is disadvantaged by the first circumstance, and the second bestows enormous advantages on defendants who possess greater access to information.[24]

Second, in Japan's political party system strong voting discipline within the governing Liberal Democratic party inhibits would-be mavericks from capitalizing on latent voter dissatisfaction with established policy. The flexibility of opposition politicians is also limited when it comes to championing consumer causes because of their strong ideological and institutional bonds to more explicitly labor-related issues. Although the LDP as a whole has shifted its platform over time in response to electoral challenges from opposition parties, its primary constituencies continue to be business and agriculture. There are many consumer issues, such as yields on savings, which neither the LDP nor the opposition parties have addressed.

In Japan's electoral system for the House of Representatives (the most powerful of the two houses of the Diet), two to six politicians are elected from each district on the basis of a plurality in which each voter has a single nontransferable vote. This electoral system, which Arendt Lijphart calls "semiproportional," shares with proportional representation systems the characteristic that numerous parties rather than two dominant parties are likely to survive each

[23] See John O. Haley, "Toward a Reappraisal of the Occupation Legal Reforms: Administrative Accountability," manuscript, November 1986. Also useful is Morris Fiorina, "Group Concentration and the Delegation of Legislative Authority," in Roger Noll, ed., *Regulatory Policy and the Social Sciences* (Berkeley: University of California Press, 1985).

[24] See Mark Ramseyer, "The Costs of the Consensual Myth: Antitrust Enforcement and Institutional Barriers to Litigation in Japan," *Yale Law Journal* 94 (1985), especially pp. 631–34.

election.[25] The Liberal Democratic party has used the fragmentation of its opposition to stay in power since 1955 and has appropriated their policy initiatives to the extent perceived necessary to avoid electoral defeat. The LDP's longevity as the ruling party, attesting to its successful electoral strategy in the semiproportional system, has unquestionably contributed to the stability of the government–private sector process of negotiation.

Third, industrial concentration varies across industries in Japan but is quite high in wholesale finance. A small number of commercial banks and securities firms dominate the market and, in concert with the Ministry of Finance, have devised competition-inhibiting measures and mechanisms. At the national level, peak associations are less than encompassing. Labor, as Pempel and Tsunekawa have pointed out, is not part of the ruling coalition though it has benefited along with the rest of society from Japan's economic growth. Consumer interests, to the degree they differ from producer and labor interests, have even less extra-electoral national representation.

The bureaucracy plays a key role in policy making, even if its function is more one of mediating and equilibrating the interests of politically powerful interest groups than of formulating policy objectives or controlling policy outcomes. The politicians also play a central if sometimes unobserved role: they determine which groups are given a voice in policy making and the terms on which bureaucracy–private sector settlements are reached. The bureaucratic-dominance model and the politician-led model of Japanese politics outlined earlier each capture only a part of the entire policy-making process.

Japan in the International Arena

The discussion so far has focused on the domestic features that shape Japan's political process and policy outcomes. Japan is also a

[25]See A. Lijphart, R. L. Pintor, and Y. Sone, "The Limited Vote and the Single Nontransferable Vote: Lessons from the Japanese and Spanish Examples," in B. Grofman and A. Lijphart, eds., *Electoral Laws and Their Political Consequences* (New York: Agathon Press, 1986), pp. 154–79; a proportional representation

country dependent in significant measure on foreign sources for raw materials, export markets, investment opportunities, and even national security. Considering the huge costs Japan would incur in foregoing any aspect of its interdependence, the external environment imposes compelling constraints on Japan's policy choices. The theory of regulation does not consider the possibility that, even if domestic regulation benefits domestic industry, foreign threats or competition may nullify much of that benefit. The exponents of the foreign-pressure model of Japanese policy making are undoubtedly correct in stressing Japan's international vulnerability.

The rise in size and competitiveness of the Japanese economy, particularly relative to that of the United States, has heightened Japan's exposure to two kinds of international pressures. First, foreign countries exert greater *political* pressure because they are more likely to retaliate against what they perceive to be Japan's protectionism when Japanese success in foreign markets is increasingly conspicuous. Japanese firms' penetration of foreign markets also increases the potential costs of retaliation in terms of curtailed opportunities for Japanese firms abroad.[26] As we shall see, the lucrative business Japanese financial institutions engage in abroad has increased their sensitivity to retaliatory threats against closure of market segments in the Japanese financial system.

Second, international market pressures also press hard against Japan, although these too are in a sense politically derived. In order to compete effectively abroad, producers need to keep their cost structure in line with the global competitive standard. Exporters will therefore look for cheaper inputs to substitute for factors that protectionism renders expensive. Consider the case of finance. In the 1970s Japanese corporations discovered they could raise funds in the Eurobond market more cheaply and easily than in the domes-

---

system is typified by large electoral districts in which politicians and/or parties are elected in proportion to the votes they receive. G. Bingham Powell, Jr., *Contemporary Democracies* (Cambridge: Harvard University Press, 1982), pp. 58–59.

[26]For analysis of the effects of interdependence on the foreign economic policies of other countries, see J. Frieden, "Sectoral Conflict and U.S. Foreign Economic Policy, 1914–1940," *International Organization* 43 (Winter 1988), 59–90; and Helen Milner, "Resisting the Protectionist Temptation: Industry and the Making of Trade Policy in France and the United States During the 1970s," *International Organization* (Autumn 1987), 639–65.

tic bond market. Their sourcing shift reduced the utility to Japanese banks of limiting domestic bond issuance and set in motion the deregulation of the bond market in Japan. This market pressure is politically derived in the sense that the Japanese government theoretically could cut off Japanese corporations from external funding sources but politically could not. The Japanese securities industry would have joined the nonfinancial business sector, both of which are competitive globally and politically powerful domestically, in a campaign to block any such move. Market forces enter through chinks in the political armor of protected groups.

The Japanese state's administrative apparatus is unified only in the sense that areas of regulation are vertically organized with one bureaucracy generally possessing jurisdiction over one issue area. Threats of retaliation and international market forces in some instances render traditional forms of market segmentation difficult to maintain, resulting in more frequent jurisdictional disputes among different bureaucratic agencies. Bureaucracy–private sector negotiations therefore break down or are inconclusive, and politicians are drawn in as mediators. This, however, typically means a change in the policy-making process rather than in policy outcomes, since politicization does not necessarily open access to other interests that are normally bypassed in negotiations between the bureaucracy and primary constituency groups.[27]

A second effect of the growing interdependence of certain segments of Japanese business with the rest of the world is that interests and relative strength within the business sector are increasingly divergent. Bureaucracy-business negotiations will become more complex and intractable, and politicians will intervene more frequently. As with interministerial disputes, however, the difference between the bureaucracy-mediated agreements and politicized ones is largely in the process rather than in terms of who benefits.

The bureaucracy, the politicians, and international pressures are all pieces of the Japanese policy-making puzzle. Financial deregulation provides an excellent vehicle for exploring in detail how the

[27]Katzenstein points out that, in general, state structure shapes the policy-making process, whereas outcomes are shaped by the ruling coalition and policy networks in domestic politics. "Conclusion" in Peter J. Katzenstein, ed., *Between Power and Plenty* (Madison: University of Wisconsin Press, 1978), pp. 306–8.

15

pieces fit together. Financial institutions respond to changes in the international environment by seeking from bureaucrats, and if necessary from politicians, amendments in financial regulation which would allow Japanese financial institutions to remain competitive enough to retain their client base. Although the financial institutions prefer to keep domestic markets closed to foreign penetration if possible, threats of retaliation and the escape of domestic clients to foreign markets chisel away at remaining pockets of domestic protection.

Chapter 2 examines more closely the major players in Japanese financial policy making, how they interact, and how the financial institutions respond to shifts in the international environment by pressing for selective financial deregulation in Japan.

2

The Regulatory Framework
and the Process of Change

The most salient actors in Japan's financial policy making are the Ministry of Finance, the financial institutions, and the politicians. In the first three or four decades after World War II these three groups coexisted in a comfortable and self-reinforcing triangular relationship. In recent years, however, major shifts in Japan's external and domestic economic environment have thrown the postwar financial regulatory structure off balance and are forcing financial institutions in a number of instances to press for changes in regulations they initially favored.

The Institutional Structure of Japanese Finance

The Bureaucracy

Bureaucrats, maximizing their personal success, will behave in a variety of ways depending on who is assessing their performance and by what criteria. In Japan, what constitutes bureaucrats' success is largely determined by the bureaucracy itself. In the Ministry of Finance in particular, bureaucrats stay with their agency for their entire government career of about thirty years with a view to moving up the ladder before parachuting into a comfortable private-sector job upon retirement.[1] Only the minister and two vice-ministers are

[1]See, for example, Tuvia Blumenthal, "The Practice of Amakudari within the Japanese Employment System," *Asian Survey* 25 (March 1985), 310–21; also

17

political appointees. The cabinet minister, moreover, generally represents the interests of the ministry as a means of building networks of political support and financial backing among the ministry's clientele. So unlike in the United States, where the top ranks of the bureaucracy are filled with political appointees and where there is a considerable amount of lateral entry into and exit from the bureaucracy, in Japan the ministry sets its own rules of the game.

A Ministry of Finance official's job proceeds most smoothly, and hence the official's chances of success are best, when (a) politicians and courts stay out, allowing the MOF to preside over the delicate balancing of interests, and (b) the financial institutions believe the MOF can enforce the compromises over which it presides. Contrary to William Niskanen, I argue that a bureaucracy tries to maximize its jurisdiction only when its more important goal, ease of regulation, is also attained.[2] J. Q. Wilson makes a similar point about careerist bureaucrats as opposed to political appointees, suggesting that careerists are more averse to risk than imperialistic, and more concerned with security, autonomy, and stability than with growth, competition, and change.[3] The Ministry of Finance, in fact, will on occasion voluntarily cut back its "territory" to avoid politicization or unenforceability.

What is "ease of regulation" for a central and wide-reaching bureaucracy such as the Ministry of Finance? The ministry is made up of seven bureaus, three of which are responsible for public finance, three for private-sector finance, and one for tariffs and customs administration. In addition, a ministry secretariat manages personnel, handles official communications with the Diet, and oversees the Salt and Tobacco Monopoly. Because each bureau has its own jurisdiction, the Ministry of Finance is sometimes described in journalistic literature as a loosely aligned cluster of bureaus (*kyoku atte, shō nashi*). The Budget Bureau, which has traditionally been the most prestigious bureau because of its power over the other

Chalmers Johnson, *Japan's Public Policy Companies* (Washington, D.C.: American Enterprise Institute for Public Policy Research, 1978), pp. 101–17.

[2] William A. Niskanen, *Bureaucracy and Representative Government* (Chicago: Aldine, 1971), cited in J. A. C. Conybeare, "Competition: A Critical Analysis of the Budget Maximizing Model of Bureaucracy," manuscript, June 1983.

[3] J. Q. Wilson, "The Politics of Regulation," in Wilson, ed., *The Politics of Regulation* (New York: Basic Books, 1980), pp. 375–76.

ministries, is most concerned with maintaining sound government finances on the expenditure side. The Tax Bureau's charge, and hence its preoccupation, is to bring in government revenue. The Finance Bureau's job is to manage smoothly the issuance of government debt. The Customs Bureau brings in customs duty. The Banking Bureau is responsible for a stable and globally competitive banking sector. The Securities Bureau has the same responsibility for the securities sector. And the International Finance Bureau oversees the foreign operations of Japanese financial institutions and shares responsibility with the Banking and Securities Bureaus for the operations of foreign financial institutions in Japan.[4]

Despite the disparate and sometimes conflicting goals of the bureaus, there are several factors that facilitate interbureau cooperation or at least compromise. Perhaps most important is the rotation of personnel, generally every two years. A Banking Bureau official this year may be in the Securities Bureau the next. The MOF is willing to sacrifice some degree of technical specialization to the higher goal of intraministerial coordination.[5] A second important factor is the prestige Japanese society attaches to a position in the MOF, which contributes to high morale in the ministry.[6] The Japanese bureaucracy is highly prestigious, with 85 percent of civil servant elite being graduates of the two top-ranking universities in Japan, the University of Tokyo and the University of Kyoto. Many of the best students traditionally have sought careers in the bureaucracy, and of all the ministries, the MOF has been the first choice.[7] Third, once in the ministry, bureaucrats still face fierce competition for the highest administrative positions and are thus

[4] *Ōkurashō no Kikō* (Tokyo: Ōkura Zaimu Kyōkai, 1984).

[5] The loss of efficiency is minimized, however, by the presence of more or less permanent staff in each bureau, those who have passed not the "high class civil service exam" but a lower-grade qualifying exam, who accumulate technical knowledge as the career bureaucrats come and go.

[6] Mitsuo Takamoto, *Ōkura Kanryō no Himitsu* (Tokyo: Chōbunsha, 1982), pp. 10–19; Akihiko Morita, *Ōkurashō Ura no Ura* (Tokyo: Dōyūkan, 1983), pp. 53–61; Yoshimitsu Kuribayashi, *Ōkura Shukeikyoku* (Tokyo: Kodansha, 1986), pp. 19–25.

[7] Michio Muramatsu and Ellis Krauss, "Bureaucrats and Politicans in Policymaking: The Case of Japan," *American Political Science Review* 78 (1984), 130–31; Daniel I. Okimoto, "Political Inclusivity: The Domestic Structure of Trade," in Takashi Inoguchi and Okimoto, eds., *The Political Economy of Japan*, vol. 2: *The Changing International Context* (Stanford: Stanford University Press, 1988).

highly motivated to measure up to the ministry's standards. Although all bureaucrats who passed the highest civil service exam and have entered the ministry are ensured of positions for the entirety of their careers, only one in each class of twenty-five to thirty makes it to the top post of administrative vice-minister, and only seven can hope to become a director general of a bureau, the next highest position. The promotion policy appears to penalize bureaucrats who fail to compromise in the service of the MOF's greatest good—ease of regulation. Bureaucrats who push too hard for sectional interests at the expense of the MOF's integrity can expect to be bypassed for important positions.[8] The best postretirement positions, moreover, go to those who have made it the farthest in the ranks of the ministry.

Because the MOF is a single institution, it is able to forge decisions that take into account its various parts.[9] Although the various bureaus do often have conflicting interests and individual officials have differing views, there is a high premium placed on resolving differences internally. If directors general of bureaus cannot agree on a given issue, their dispute is referred to the Coordination Bureau or, if necessary, to the administrative vice-minister, who may confer with retired MOF officials. Final arbitration takes place within the MOF itself.[10]

In the United States, by contrast, financial regulation is spread among numerous agencies, including the Federal Reserve Board, the Securities and Exchange Commission, the Department of the Treasury, the Federal Deposit Insurance Corporation, and the Federal Savings and Loan Deposit Insurance Corporation, not to mention all of the state bureaus that oversee private finance. Lacking coordinating mechanisms, differences among them are settled by the courts, politicians, or by default the marketplace.[11]

In this study, the Banking Bureau and, secondarily, the Securities Bureau, figure most prominently since they are directly involved in

[8]Interviews with Ministry of Finance bureaucrats.

[9]For an interesting exploratory piece on the importance of institutional structure, see J. G. March and J. P. Olsen, "The New Institutionalism: Organizational Factors in Political Life," *American Political Science Review* 78 (1984), 734.

[10]Interviews with MOF officials, Tokyo, October 1985 through September 1986.

[11]Although the Bank of Japan is in charge of implementing monetary policy, the Ministry of Finance dominates the Bank of Japan Policy Affairs Committee, which sets the interest rates and monetary targets.

the regulation of financial institutions and markets. The Banking Bureau alone deals with issues purely of banking administration, and both become involved when policy decisions affect the well-being of both the banking and securities industry. Why are well-organized groups, in this case the banking and securities industries, better represented in regulatory policy than are the interests of the general public? MOF regulation may affect consumers as adversely as it benefits the producers of financial services, but the consumers are, first, less likely to know about it, or at least the full truth about it; and second, even if they knew something they would be less likely to organize a campaign to chastise the regulators. The financial sector, on the other hand, is well positioned to reward or punish the Ministry of Finance. The regulated groups constitute the most salient "theater of external judgment."[12]

The Ministry of Finance, like other ministries in the Japanese bureaucracy, relies to a considerable extent on "administrative guidance" (gyōsei shidō), injunctions without coercive legal effect, to "encourage" regulated groups to behave in certain ways.[13] The MOF's extralegal directives extend far into the affairs of the financial institutions beyond the strict confines of legislation. But bureaucratic discretion must not be exaggerated, for as Michael Young has pointed out, regulated groups that are dissatisfied with the bureaucracy's administration have three alternatives to quiescence: the courts, noncompliance, or resort to the political process.[14]

Recourse to courts in administrative policy matters in Japan is infrequent, even when agreement between the bureaucracy and the regulated group breaks down. There is a strong incentive for the private-sector group to cooperate with the ministry with which it must continue to deal over the long run.

Beyond the general usefulness to both the bureaucracy and the

[12]R. G. Noll, "Government Regulatory Behavior: A Multidisciplinary Survey and Synthesis," in Noll, ed., Regulatory Policy and the Social Sciences (Berkeley: University of California Press, 1985), p. 41; "There are not many economic objectives that democratic governments can accomplish without relying on private or semi-private groups outside their direct control." A. J. Heidenheimer, H. Heclo, and C. T. Adams, Comparative Public Policy (New York: St. Martin's Press, 1983), p. 128.
[13]Michael K. Young, "Judicial Review of Administrative Guidance: Governmentally Encouraged Consensual Dispute Resolution in Japan," Columbia Law Journal 84 (1984), 923.
[14]Ibid., p. 946.

regulated parties of "legal informalism," however, there are institutional barriers to litigation in Japan.[15] As noted earlier, the Japanese judicial system adopted the continental principle from German, Swiss, and French law of judicial restraint on disputes of administrative law, on the premise that the bureaucracy should retain flexibility in the implementation of legislation.[16] As Frank Upham writes, "Plaintiffs seeking judicial review of administrative action face the initial problem of whether the challenged agency behavior constitutes . . . administrative acts that immediately and directly create or delimit private rights and duties." Under this definition, much industrial and regulatory policy is beyond judicial review since only legally formal acts, not administrative guidance, create legal rights and duties.[17]

Nor is noncompliance a frequent choice of disgruntled groups, lest the ongoing ties with the ministry be jeopardized without even redress from another authoritative body such as a court. Financial institutions have, at times, challenged the MOF's mandates, such as during the 1960s and 1970s, when banks repeatedly failed to meet the MOF's ceilings on compensating balances.[18] But the MOF has chosen to deal with these episodes quietly and in consultation with the banks themselves. Indeed, in what Michael Young calls "private ordering," the MOF and other ministries minimize disobedience by deferring much of the actual formulation and implementation of guidance to the regulated groups themselves, and by encouraging compliance by rewarding those who do comply more often than by punishing those who do not.[19] Rather than rely on its limited array of sanctions, or worse yet, succumb to the intrusion of politicians who may take up the regulated group's cause, the bureaucracy seeks to maintain close working relations with the sector under its juris-

[15]"Legal informalism" is the term with which Frank Upham characterized the Japanese judicial system. See Frank Upham, *Law and Social Change in Postwar Japan* (Cambridge: Harvard University Press, 1987).

[16]John Haley, "Toward a Reappraisal of the Occupation Legal Reforms: Administrative Accountability," manuscript, November 1986. See also Shokitsu Tanakadate, "A Summary of the Limitations on Administrative Adjudication under the Japanese Constitution," J. Rosenbluth, trans., *Law in Japan* 18 (1985), 108–17.

[17]Upham, *Law and Social Change in Postwar Japan*, pp. 170–71.

[18]Tables provided by the Federation of Bankers Associations.

[19]Young, "Judicial Review of Administrative Guidance," pp. 934, 940.

diction, building up the credibility necessary to secure voluntary compliance.[20]

Even in Japan, where stable ties between the state and segments of society take on characteristics of an iterated game, the MOF has not been entirely successful in securing the cooperation of the financial institutions it oversees. The MOF's desire has always been to have a strong, highly concentrated, easily regulated financial sector: the fewer and stronger the banks, the less likelihood of bank insolvency or other troublesome problems. And most of the MOF's friction with the financial sector has arisen when the MOF has sought additional regulatory authority with which to implement its goals or when it has attempted, even without that authority, to eliminate smaller, weaker institutions through mergers with larger banks.[21] To avoid the incursion of politicians into the details of financial administration, the MOF time and again has had to shore up politically influential small banks with loans or take other emergency measures.[22] As economic growth began to decelerate in the mid-1970s, Japanese corporations began paring down their bank loans, and weak banks have become even weaker. Because weak financial institutions still have recourse to politicians, tension between an MOF in search of efficiency and financial institutions in search of survival will likely intensify and spill over into the political arena with increasing frequency.[23]

The Regulated Groups

The Banking Industry

"Big finance" in the postwar era primarily refers to the twelve city banks, with close ties to large industrial enterprises and with a

[20] Okimoto, "Political Inclusivity," p. 17.

[21] As we will see later, smaller banks have generally been successful in resisting the MOF's merger stratagems.

[22] The MOF often uses indirect means, such as inducing other financial institutions in various ways to help an ailing institution maintain liquidity or even solvency through troubled times. See, for example, Nihon Keizai Shimbunsha, ed., *Ginkō: Chihō Kinyū Sensō* (Tokyo: Nihon Keizai Shimbunsha, 1985), pp. 202–5; Nikkei Bijinesu, ed., *Ginkō: Fuyu no Jidai* (Tokyo: Nihon Keizai Shimbunsha, 1981), pp. 153–61; Sankei Shimbun Keizai Bu, ed., *Sōgō Ginkō no Konwaku* (Tokyo: Kou Business, 1978), pp. 62–67.

[23] See P. J. Katzenstein, "Small Nations in an Open International Economy," in

23

nationwide network of deposit-taking branches. Five commercial banks—Sumitomo, Daiichi Kangyō (the product of a 1971 merger between Daiichi and Kangyō), Fuji (formerly of the Yasuda zaibatsu), Mitsubishi, and Mitsui—rotate the chairing of the National Federation of Bankers Associations annually among themselves.[24] An informal grouping of all twelve city banks, the City Bank Roundtable (Toshi Ginkō Konwakai), is a more important forum for forging common positions vis-à-vis the MOF on matters of financial administration.[25] But "big finance" also includes the three long-term credit banks, which are permitted to issue five- to seven-year debentures in exchange for lending long-term to industry; the trust banks, which accept large-denomination trust accounts and pension funds from business, issue long-term debentures, and make long-term loans to industry; and the Bank of Tokyo, which issues three-year debentures and specializes in foreign exchange and international finance.

At the other end of the scale are the smaller banks, including (1) the approximately 130 regional banks, (2) the 456 even smaller credit associations (shinkin), (3) the smaller yet 448 credit cooperatives (shinyō kumiai), and (4) the agricultural cooperatives (nō-kyō).[26] Though capitalized at much lower ratios, these small financial institutions have political influence by virtue of their strong ties to the local elite in politics, government, and industry. Their pri-

---

P. Evans, D. Rueschemeyer, and T. Skocpol, eds., *Bringing the State Back In* (New York: Cambridge University Press, 1985), pp. 237–41, for a fascinating account of how two political parties in Austria have neutralized the authority of the nation's financial bureaucracy.

[24]Sumitomo Bank is the only bank based outside of Tokyo which is in this inner circle of city banks. Sanwa Bank and Tokai Bank, which actually outrank Mitsui in terms of assets, do not take turns chairing the Federation of Bankers Associations. The leadership that attends the position, in any case, is largely nominal. The other four city banks are Daiwa, Saitama, Kyowa, and Taiyo-Kobe.

[25]Shinichi Gotō, *Toshi Ginkō* (Tokyo: Kyōikusha Shinsho, 1985), pp. 13–31.

[26]Until January 1989, there were sixty-nine "mutual banks" that specialized in loans to medium-sized and local businesses. The mutual banks were recategorized as regional banks in 1989 since their business was virtually indistinguishable from that of the regional banks and they wanted to get rid of the title "mutual bank," which connotes smaller-scale business. See "Sōgin no Fugin Tenkan," *Kinyū Bijinesu*, October 1988, pp. 18–27; "Japanese Banks 1986," Federation of Bankers Associations of Japan, 1986; Masao Miwa, *Kinyū Jiyūka to Nōkyō Kinyū* (Tokyo: Zenkoku Kyōdō Shuppan, 1984), pp. 112–15.

mary clientele are two of the bulwarks of LDP support: small- and medium-sized business and, in the case of the agriculture cooperatives, the still-powerful agricultural sector.

The National Federation of Bankers Associations (Zenkoku Ginkō Kyōkai) is the umbrella organization for the banking industry, but each subgroup of banks has its own association with its own distinct interests. In its disputes with the "outside," such as with the securities industry, the postal system, or the MOF, the banking industry attempts to forge a unified stance under the federation's auspices when possible. But in the slower growth years since the mid-1970s, differences among the groups have widened on issues affecting the distribution of market share within the banking industry itself. Small financial institutions, for example, opposed the introduction of automatic teller machines, which were championed by the larger banks in the early 1980s as a way to meet the competition from the postal system. The expense would be felt more heavily by the smaller, weaker institutions. Ultimately, the small institutions bought time for themselves by means of an MOF-enforced compromise delaying the timetable for mechanization.

The Securities Industry

The industry is dominated by "Big Four," as Nomura Shōken, Daiwa Shōken, Nikkō Shōken, and Yamaichi Shōken are collectively known. The largest, Nomura Shōken, had been the securities division of Nomura Bank before World War II. Nomura Bank's commercial banking division became Daiwa Bank upon the enactment of the 1947 Securities Exchange Act. The other securities houses were much smaller and only began to develop strong ties to politicians in defense against the banks' assault on the separation of banking and securities activities during the Occupation period.

Nomura, Daiwa, Nikkō, and Yamaichi together account for three-fourths of all stocks and bonds underwriting and are also the largest traders and retailers of securities.[27] These four securities firms set the agenda for the rest of the industry in policy matters as well. The Big Four have numerous joint working committees, and

[27]Kikuo Iwata, "Kisai Chōsei ni kansuru Shomondai," *Jōchi Keizai Ronsō*, 24, no. 2 (1982), 12–16.

no decision is made by the Council of Securities Organizations (Shōken Dantai Kyōgikai) without their prior agreement.[28]

The Politicians

In one sense, politicians simply maximize their chances for reelection.[29] Because they are concerned with their *net* support, they are not likely to champion a cause, for whatever promised number of votes or sum of campaign money, if they would lose more potential support from an aggrieved group than they gained from the beneficiary of their efforts. Representatives will favor a policy if they believe the benefits to their constituencies are more visible than the costs, and/or they can claim credit while evading responsibility for the costs.[30] Thus if the interest group's only opponent is an unorganized or unaware public, politicians will likely attempt to increase their margin of support by using the redistributive powers of regulation.[31]

The LDP

Japan's ruling political party, the Liberal Democratic party, has influence over the MOF's financial policy administration by virtue of its potential for intervening on behalf of disgruntled groups in the financial sector. But politicians prefer, if possible, to avoid taking sides if favoring one group of supporters invites the wrath of another. William Riker's minimum winning coalition, the notion that politicians target their group of supporters as narrowly as possible in order to minimize the policy payoffs to these groups which are necessary in return for support, did not consider politicians' uncertainty over the size of their coalitions and thus the desire for political "insurance."[32] Indeed, the LDP shows a strong preference for

[28]Keizō Ōnuma, "Yonsha Shūdō de Seijiryoku o Jiku ni Gyōeki no Kakuhō ni Binsō," *Kinyū Jānaru*, May 1987, pp. 74–77.

[29]Anthony Downs, *An Economic Theory of Democracy* (New York: Harper and Row, 1965), p. 11.

[30]M. P. Fiorina, "Group Concentration and the Delegation of Legislative Authority," in Noll, *Regulatory Policy and the Social Sciences*, p. 180.

[31]Fiorina calls the rewarding of concentrated costs at the expense of diffuse benefits "legislative sins of omission" in ibid., p. 182.

[32]K. A. Shepsle and B. R. Weingast, "Political Preferences for the Pork Barrel," *American Journal of Political Science* 25 (February 1981), 96–111.

delegating to the MOF delicate balancing operations between Japanese banks and their rivals, the securities houses, for fear of alienating either group. Delegation to the bureaucracy avoids or disguises political responsibility for the consequences of policy measures that may inflict some damage on supporters.

As we have noted, the MOF is, for its own reasons, eager to preside over its own compromises between groups in financial policy formulation and implementation. And it is only because the MOF has a widely encompassing mandate over the various parts of the financial sector that the ministry is *capable* of equilibrating interests before any group approaches the politicians for favorable intervention. But not all aspects of financial policy are under the MOF's jurisdiction; the notable exceptions are foreign financial markets and the domestic postal savings system. First, foreign financial markets have exerted pressures on Japan that are sometimes beyond the MOF's control, increasing the cost to the MOF of maintaining a protective regulatory blanket around Japanese financial institutions. Second, the postal savings system has claimed a growing share of the nation's deposits since the mid-1970s, at least in part because of the depositors' ability to evade taxes on interest income more readily through the postal system. As will be discussed more fully in Chapter 6, until recently savers have been able to avoid the 3-million-yen ceiling on tax-free postal deposits by opening multiple accounts in different post offices. The banks have always viewed the postal savings system as a menace, but the slow-growth environment has accentuated that sense of threat. These two issue areas in the financial sector reflect more generally the growing redistributive demands on the LDP in a slower-growth economy which it cannot delegate back to any bureaucracy, regardless of how politically costly some of the choices might be. The direct involvement of politicians, primarily of the LDP, in policy formulation has risen inexorably since the first oil shock in 1973.[33]

To say that the LDP has become more directly involved in policy formulation in the last fifteen years may sound like a strange way to speak of a party that has been in power since 1955. And the statement should not be misinterpreted, because the relative infre-

[33] M. Muramatsu, *Sengo Nihon no Kanryōsei* (Tokyo: Tōyō Keizai Shimpōsha, 1981), pp. 211–18; T. Inoguchi, *Gendai Seiji Keizai no Kōzu* (Tokyo: Tōyō Keizai Shimpōsha, 1983), pp. 178–80.

quency of the LDP's direct involvement in the earlier postwar years masked the party's substantial influence and indeed satisfaction with how matters were proceeding. There is ample evidence of politicians' readiness to intervene in financial policy making when necessary, even in the early 1950s, as we shall see in Chapter 4. The important point is that slower economic growth has intensified the competition among groups in the private sector for a smaller pie during a time when the formal levers of bureaucratic powers are being reduced in the process of opening up the Japanese economy.[34]

Much of the LDP's policy deliberation takes place in the Policy Affairs Research Committee (PARC), which is actually a system of formal divisions (*bukai*), numerous issue-specific commissions (*chōsakai*), and special committees (*tokubetsu iinkai*). The function of these PARC units is to review bills drafted by the bureaucracy and, more generally, to formulate policy. Because politicians tend to invest most of their efforts, at least in their early years, in the activities of one or two policy areas, they become identified as members of a particular policy caucus, known colloquially as "tribe" (*zoku*).[35] For the LDP members, belonging to a policy caucus is important as a means of gathering information relevant to their constituents and for attracting campaign contributions from affected groups.

Membership in the PARC divisions is voluntary, meaning that the size of the divisions reveals much about the composition of the LDP's "conservative coalition" of supporters as well as about the LDP's policy priorities.[36] Agriculture, with 195 members in 1983; Construction, with 191; and Commerce, with 144, have traditionally been the most popular divisions and retain their rank as the largest. The relevance of these divisions to votes and money is

[34]Gerald L. Curtis, "The Domestic Roots of Japanese Foreign Policy," Working Paper no. 27, University of Toronto–York University Joint Centre on Modern East Asia, March 1984, p. 15.

[35]Michio Muramatsu and Ellis Krauss, "The Conservative Policy Line and the Development of Patterned Pluralism," in K. Yamamura and Y. Yasuba, eds., *The Political Economy of Japan: The Domestic Transformation* (Stanford: Stanford University Press, 1987), pp. 540–42; Takayoshi Miyagawa and Kenichi Takemura, *Jimintō no Yomikata* (Tokyo: Sun Publishers, 1984), pp. 170–71.

[36]"Conservative coalition" is T. J. Pempel's well-chosen phrase to characterize the "conservative nature of the support-base of government in Japan." See his *Policy and Politics in Japan: Creative Conservatism* (Philadelphia: Temple University Press, 1982), p. 11.

obvious. Divisions more remote from constituents' interests are considerably smaller, such as Science and Technology, with 55 members in 1983; Environment, with 63; and Foreign Affairs with 75.[37]

Most relevant to this study is the Finance Division (Zaisei Bukai), a medium-sized body in the PARC (118 members in 1983) which presides over an LDP consensus on financial policy matters as well as the government budget. Bills or administrative orders drafted by the Ministry of Finance are reviewed in the Diet's Finance Committee (Ōkura Iinkai) or Budget Committee (Yosan Iinkai) only after they have been reviewed first by the PARC Finance Division and then formally submitted by the cabinet to the Diet.[38] A second, less formal LDP committee, the Financial Affairs Research Commission (Kinyū Mondai Chōsakai), distinguishes itself from the PARC Finance Division in its focus on issues of private finance, including those broached directly by the financial sector. The membership of the LDP's Finance Division and that of Financial Affairs Commission overlap, and their senior members collectively make up what is known as the LDP's "finance tribe," or Zaisei Kinyū Zoku.[39] Because the LDP has numerically dominated the Diet Finance Committee, this committee has tended to be a forum for the opposition parties to express their views, whereas the LDP's policy caucuses (zoku) have been the real locus of decision making.[40]

As in the LDP in general, leadership within the policy caucuses is

[37]Takashi Inoguchi and Tomonobu Iwai, "Jimintō Rieki Yūdō no Seiji Keizai Gaku," Chūō Kōron, August 1985, pp. 138–39.

[38]Within the Finance Policy Group there are overlapping subgroups of experts in private finance and in the public finance areas of tax and budget. The discussion here focuses on the private finance segment of the Finance Policy Group, though clear distinctions are just beginning to emerge as the policy caucuses (zoku) become increasingly specialized. See Takashi Inoguchi and Tomoaki Iwai, Zokugiin (Tokyo: Nihon Keizai Shimbunsha, 1987), pp. 205–9.

[39]Public finance—budgeting and taxation—cuts across all sectors of the economy and therefore encompasses a broader swath of the LDP than does private finance, for which the financial sector is the primary audience. The chairpersons of all the PARC divisions, for example, are automatically members of the LDP Tax Policy Research Committee (Zeisei Chōsakai). See Seizaburō Satō and Tetsuhisa Matsuzaki, Jimintō Seiken (Tokyo: Chūō Kōron Sha, 1986), pp. 160–61.

[40]Of course the LDP often incorporates opposition amendments in some measure, to blunt the opposition's publicity campaigns, which can be damaging to the LDP at elections. See M. M. Mochizuki, "Managing and Influencing the Japanese Legislative Process" (Ph.D. diss., Harvard University, 1982).

largely a function of seniority. In the case of the "finance tribe," a Diet member may become a political vice-minister in the Ministry of Finance after two or three terms in the House of Representatives (which means roughly four to eight years in the Diet). After three or four terms, the Diet member may be appointed by the LDP leadership chair of the PARC Finance Committee. After five to seven terms, a Diet member is in line for a cabinet position, though the Ministry of Finance position, being key to administration policy, is generally reserved for a more senior core of LDP leaders.[41] Indeed, to advance to the highest ranks of LDP leadership, a Diet member must move beyond a narrow focus of attention on a single policy area. The real power elite within the LDP is made up of those who have mastered the skill of forging compromises across the range of interests represented by the party.

That policy specialization beyond a certain point works against an LDP Diet member's career is a key point in understanding the policy-making process in Japan. It helps explain why there are not more would-be mavericks who try to capitalize on potential voter dissatisfaction with established policies. Theoretically, after all, producer-oriented policies are vulnerable to attack by political entrepreneurs who owe no political debt to the special interests that seek to use regulatory policies for their own purposes. The more a policy favors a special interest at the expense of the public, the more support from consumers/voters a politician has to gain by exposing it. In the United States, for example, Senator Edward Kennedy made a campaign issue of the investigation he launched in 1974 of the Civil Aeronautics Board, which led eventually to deregulation of the airline industry.[42] But in Japan, for one LDP politician to contest party policies openly is to invite sanctions of various sorts, and possibly ostracism.[43] Alternative views are incorporated into policy

---

[41]S. Satō and T. Matsuzaki, "Jimintō Chōchōki Seiken no Kaikatsu," *Chūō Kōron*, November 1984, pp. 88–89.

[42]R. G. Noll and B. M. Owen, eds., "Conclusion," in *The Political Economy of Deregulation* (Washington, D.C.: American Enterprise Institute, 1983), pp. 158–59.

[43]In a relatively rare example, a few LDP Diet members who were under heavy fire from their small-business constituents dared to challenge openly the value-added tax pushed by the LDP in 1986–87. Once one LDP politician from a certain district expressed opposition to the tax, the other LDP man from the same district

decisions when the party as a whole is convinced that certain measures against a special interest are necessary to prevent serious disaffection at the polls.

How are compromises forged within the LDP? As in the U.S. congressional committee system, disproportionate influence over policy in a given area is given to the overseeing (PARC) division and its members. A degree of specialization allows committee members to maintain a greater voice in an area of concern to their constituents.[44] But when there is a strong difference of views between or among committees, responsibility for the decision rises through higher levels of the party hierarchy until, if necessary, it rests with the top four positions in the party: the president of the party (also the prime minister), the secretary general of the party, the chairman of the PARC, and the chairman of the Executive Council. These leaders measure the strength of the various positions and the consequences for the LDP's overriding concern to maintain a parliamentary majority, before forcing concessions to the minority view to the extent necessary to prevent noncooperation or retaliation.[45]

The Opposition Parties

If LDP politicians are impeded from expression open defiance of established policies that may be hurting a pool of voters, the opposition parties are similarly beset, but for different reasons. The largest opposition party, the Japan Socialist party (JSP), is heavily dependent on the nation's largest labor organization. The General Council of Japanese Trade Unions (Nihon Rōdō Kumiai Sōhyōgikai or Sōhyō) represents about one-third of Japan's union membership, is the JSP's largest single supporter both in terms of funding and votes,

---

soon followed suit lest he be chastised in the following election. The party discussed various sanctions, but ultimately found its hands tied because of the strength of public sentiment in favor of the defecting politicians. Even these "mavericks," however, would vote for the LDP's tax platform when it came to the Diet floor.

[44]Barry Weingast, "Rational Choice Perspective on Congressional Norms," *American Journal of Political Science* 23 (May 1979), 245–63; Weingast, "Regulation, Reregulation, and Deregulation: The Political Foundations of Agency-Clientele Relationships," *Law and Contemporary Problems* 44 (Winter 1981), 147–77.

[45]Miyagawa and Takemura, *Jimintō no Yomikata*, pp. 39–41.

and has considerable influence over the JSP. (In November 1987 most of the private-sector unions that had belonged to Sōhyō, including the powerful Steel Workers' Union, left Sōhyō to join the new National Federation of Private Sector Unions (Rengō). Many of the public-sector unions remaining in Sōhyō are expected to join Rengō in 1989.) But demographics have hurt the JSP. Unionization has been on the decline in Japan since the 1970s—down to 27 percent of the working population in 1986—and instead of moving in tandem with shifts in the composition and preferences of the voting public, the JSP has declined along with unionization.[46] Indeed, the composition of the JSP electoral base shows that the JSP's dependence on labor has actually increased even as labor as an organized force has waned. At the same time, labor's support for the JSP has been decreasing. In 1955 33 percent of the JSP voters were wage earners, 26 percent were salaried workers, 25 percent farmers, 13 percent self-employed, and 3 percent other. By 1975 42 percent were labor, 31 percent salaried workers, 10 percent farmers, 10 percent self-employed, 6 percent managerial, and 2 percent other.[47] The JSP's share of Diet seats has dropped from its peak of nearly 25 percent in the mid-1950s to about 10 percent in the mid-1980s.[48]

The Kōmeito, the second largest opposition party, is the political arm of the religious organization, Sōkagakkai.[49] With no institutional link to the labor unions, the Kōmeito relies instead on the backing of its highly motivated, well-organized religious supporters. But the Kōmeito's organizational strength is also its weakness;

[46]The opposition parties have never been able to claim the loyalty of all organized labor. Most unions are organized at the level of the enterprise and more than a third of them are not members of any national federation of unions. This was true even when unionization was slightly over 30 percent in the 1960s and early 1970s. See Walter Galenson and Konosuke Odaka, "The Japanese Labor Market," in H. Patrick and H. Rosovsky, eds., *Asia's New Giant* (Washington, D.C.: Brookings, 1976), pp. 627–33.

[47]Ichiro Miyake, Yasushi Yamaguchi, Michio Muramatsu, and Eiichi Shindō, *Nihon Seiji no Zahyō* (Tokyo: Yūhikaku, 1985), p. 120.

[48]Jirō Kamishima, *Gendai Nihon no Seiji Kōzō* (Tokyo: Hōritsu Bunkasha, 1985), pp. 171–72; the JSP's seats were down to under 10 percent following the devastating defeat in the July 1986 elections.

[49]Despite breaking its formal ties with the Sōkagakkai in 1969, the Kōmeito continues to rely on the Sōkagakkai (which is itself a lay organization of the Buddhist sect of Nichiren Shōshū) for electoral support and indeed has relatively little voter appeal outside the Sōkagakkai. See Gerald L. Curtis, *The Japanese Way of Politics* (New York: Columbia University Press, 1987), pp. 24–25.

linked in the public's mind to religious zeal, the party has been unable to increase its support base much beyond its principal following in the Sōkagakkai. The Kōmeito has not captured more than about 10 percent of the popular vote since its inauguration in 1967.[50]

The Democratic Socialist party, formed by a conservative wing of the JSP which broke off in 1960, has been supported largely by a segment of labor (Zen Nippon Rōdō Sōdōmei or Dōmei, Japan Confederation of Labor). About one-fifth of Dōmei consists of union members, though it actually has far more private-sector workers than Sōhyō. In November 1987 Dōmei disbanded in order to take the lead in forming the larger, nonpartisan National Federation of Private Sector Unions (Rengō). Dōmei's joining with the smaller labor federations Chūritsu Rōren and Shinsambetsu, and private-sector unions from Sōhyō, reflected union leaders' dissatisfaction with their level of influence in the national policy-making process. Although most of the constituent enterprise unions will continue to support the political parties they have supported in the past, the loss of Dōmei was a blow to the DSP. In addition to Dōmei, the DSP's support base includes a portion of the small-business sector (the Minsha Chūshō Kigyō Seiji Rengō, Social Democratic Small and Medium Sized Business Political League). Highly dependent on the organized electoral and financial support of these two groups, the DSP has failed to attract large groups of voters in the political center. The DSP has never commanded more than about 8 percent of the popular vote. It was reduced to 6.4 percent of the vote and captured only twenty-six Diet seats in the LDP landslide elections of 1986.[51]

The Japan Communist party is both the most staunchly ideological of the parties and the least beholden to any particular group for campaign contributions because it publishes a lucrative newspaper, the *Akahata* (Red Flag), with readership well beyond party adherents. The JCP holds only 5 percent of the Diet seats.[52]

Some analysts have gone so far as to call the opposition parties' organizational lassitude and indifference to the demands of the

[50]Miyake, Yamaguchi, Muramatsu, and Shindō, *Nihon Seiji no Zahyō*, p. 131.
[51]Curtis, *The Japanese Way of Politics*, pp. 21–24; Kamishima, *Gendai Nihon no Seiji Kōzō*.
[52]Kamishima, *Gendai Nihon no Seiji*; Miyake, Yamaguchi, Muramatsu, and Shindō, *Nihon Seiji no Zahyō*, p. 127.

electorate one of the LDP's greatest assets.[53] The opposition parties themselves are dependent on special interest organizations or constrained by ideological platforms that limit the parties' latitude in policy choices.[54] The Japan Socialist party, for example, almost always takes the position of the Federation of Labor Unions even at the cost of losing votes from a wider portion of the population. None of the opposition parties has challenged the LDP and the MOF on some key financial regulatory issues that affect wide segments of the population, such as low bank deposit yields and the unfavorable terms of consumer credit. There are too many bank workers who would lose jobs if the banking industry were to lose profits and fall upon harder times. Hence when one speaks of the "political" influence in financial policy making, one is thinking almost exclusively about the one dominant government party, not of its electoral competitors.

The LDP, though wed to various groups, has successfully incorporated a number of the opposition's initiatives into its own policy program rather than lose the electorate. Thus, the opposition's political entrepreneurship has had some, if indirect, effect. Riding the tide of demographic change, the LDP has managed to hold on to its dominance in the Diet despite the decline of the population engaged in agriculture. In 1955, when 42 percent of the population was engaged in the primary sector, the LDP's electoral base consisted of 43 percent agriculture, 25 percent self-employed, 15 percent labor, 13 percent salaried workers, and 4 percent other. By 1975, with only 17 percent of the population in farming, 19 percent of the LDP's support base were farmers, 27 percent salaried workers, 25 percent labor, 25 percent self-employed, 4 percent other.[55]

The Political Influence of Financial Institutions

Though hardly significant in terms of votes, the financial sector is an important contributor of political funds. From unequal points of

[53]Satō and Matsuzaki, "Jimintō Chōchōki Seiken no Kaikatsu," *Chūō Kōron*, November 1984, p. 66; Gary Allinson, *Suburban Tokyo: A Comparative Study in Politics and Social Change* (Berkeley: University of California Press, 1979), p. 223.

[54]Mancur Olson, *The Rise and Decline of Nations* (New Haven: Yale University Press, 1982), pp. 43–47.

[55]Miyake, Yamaguchi, Muramatsu, and Shindō, *Nihon Seiji no Zahyō*, p. 110.

origin, the banking and securities industries have become interest groups of roughly equal political strength. Although their political resources and strategies continue to differ, making precise comparison impossible, there has been a noteworthy degree of convergence in political strategies in recent years, as we shall see.

Banks have been consistent contributors to conservative politicians, dating back to the close relationship in the prewar era between Mitsui and the Minseitō, and Mitsubishi and the Seiyūkai. Although the Minseito had a slightly more pro-business orientation and the Seiyūkai was perhaps more closely tied to the local elites, the two parties were actually not very different and competed for funds from the same businesspersons and landed gentry.[56]

Banks, at least the big banks, have made large contributions to the Liberal Democratic party since its formation in 1955. Traditionally in Japanese politics the banking industry has been among the "Big Three" (*Gosanke*) private-sector funders of the annual contributions to political parties, nearly all of the money going to the LDP.[57] All banks' publicly reported political contributions consistently have amounted to about 20 percent of private industry's combined (reported) contributions, and in 1983, for example, the banks accounted for 18.4 percent, construction and real estate for 13.3 percent, and steel for 6.3 percent of political funding, together giving 31.7 percent of the total. A caveat, however, is that because a large portion of political campaign contributions are never reported, these figures are only rough indicators of financial support to the LDP by these groups.

Politician friends can be expensive to cultivate, however. Not only do politicians have exorbitant campaign needs themselves, but

[56]For differences between the Minseitō and Seiyūkai on private finance, see for example *Ginkō Tsūshinroku,* March 20, 1927, pp. 95–97; April 20, 1927, pp. 106–7; and October 20, 1927, pp. 63–65. For variance between the postwar Minshutō and Jiyūtō, see Mitsuo Takamoto, ed., *Sengo Kinyū Zaisei Rimenshi* (Tokyo: Kinyū Zaisei Jijō, 1980); and Takamoto, ed., *Sengo Kinyū Gyōseishi* (Tokyo: Kinyū Zaisei Jijō Kenkyūkai, 1985).

[57]Based on report by the Home Ministry (*Asahi*), September 4, 1984; the *Gosanke* is not a stable configuration. The electric power companies, which used to be in the triad with the steel and banking industries, were replaced by construction and .real estate only in the mid-1970s. The steel industry's contribution has dropped off substantially since its more prosperous and generous days during the rapid growth period, and reported contributions of life insurance companies and securities firms are on the rise. See Curtis, *The Japanese Way of Politics*, pp. 183–87.

35

they also have friends who want loans at low cost. As long as the Ministry of Finance was capable and willing to protect banks from domestic and foreign competition, banks could afford to remain politically aloof. The large banks pay a retainer's fee, as it were, through lump-sum contributions to the LDP. But at the same time, banks generally have avoided becoming too close to individual politicians. Only when the MOF has been unable to protect them have the banks switched to a strategy of giving to individual influential politicians.[58]

The distinction between lump-sum contributions to the LDP and support for individual politicians is important for two reasons. Because there are usually two, three, or four LDP members running from the same election district for one, two, or three slots, the toughest battle for LDP politicians is at the faction and individual level.[59] Second is the increasing division of labor within the LDP, as reflected in the *zoku* (policy caucus) phenomenon mentioned earlier. Much as in the United States, ranking committee members have more authority in their chosen areas of specialization, though in Japan it is the LDP committees rather than the parliamentary ones that wield the greatest influence. At several junctures in the postwar years, when the MOF attempted to introduce financial reform, banks did resort to giving funds to individual politicians.

More important, this change in banks' political strategy toward funding individual politicians and smaller groups within the party has become more abiding. Small banks have always given the bulk of their contributions to Diet members from their districts, since much of their concern was at the local level. As Japan's changing economic environment fundamentally weakens MOF's ability to protect banks, even the city banks have called on the LDP for more special favors, beyond the generally "favorable environment" provided by the LDP's conservative, stable rule. Rather than continue contributing large lump sums to the LDP, banks have begun giving more to individual politicians for three reasons. First, the rise in importance of policy caucuses enhanced the rule of individuals or

[58]Interviews with bankers, MOF officials, and LDP politicians, June 1985 through September 1986 in Tokyo.

[59]Most electoral districts in Japan are three-member, four-member, or five-member districts; one, Amami Ōshima, is a single-member district.

small groups of politicians in the disposition of issues in their respective areas of policy specialization. Second, banks had to match the effective lobbying of the securities industry, which already, by virtue of the securities firms' means of donating funds, was largely aimed at individual Diet members. Third, the 1975 revision of the Political Contribution Law (Seiji Shikin Seihō Ichibu Kaisei An) placed lower ceilings on the sum private-sector corporations or other groups could contribute to political organizations. As a result, LDP politicians began raising a sizable portion of their financial support by selling tickets to campaign parties (*hagemasu kai*). Most businesses, including banks, have taken the liberty of reporting the cost of these tickets as business expenses rather than as political campaign contributions.[60]

The securities firms are relative newcomers to the political scene. Unlike small banks, the small securities houses are not rooted in local communities but center in urban areas. This accounts in part for the lesser political power of the small securities houses relative to their counterparts in the banking industry. The large securities firms gained in political influence during the Occupation years because of their ability to make sizable political contributions, but the small houses were less well positioned. The evidence is clear: the MOF's success in reducing the number of securities companies from 1,152 in 1949 to 212 in 1986 through mergers stands in stark contrast to the MOF's inability to do the same in the banking sector.

Because the banking community had long been a major source of political contributions, it would have been difficult for politicians to take the side of the securities houses in the battle over the boundary line between banking and securities activities had it not been for the clear directive of the Supreme Commander of Allied Powers to build up the securities industry. Viewed from the (Occupation) General Headquarters, the banks' grip on finance was anticompetitive and therefore inured to the detriment of corporations and depositors alike. The stock and bond markets should be developed into viable alternatives for fund raising and investment. From the Japanese politicians' point of view, particularly those in the Jiyūtō (one of the two forerunner parties of the LDP) who had distanced themselves

[60]Hiroaki Fujita, *Nihon no Seiji to Kane* (Tokyo: Keisō Shobō, 1980), pp. 116–22; Curtis, *The Japanese Way of Politics*, pp. 185–87.

37

from big banks, Occupation policy provided a convenient "inevitability" argument.[61] To the banks, the politicians could disclaim any responsibility for the separation of banking and securities businesses; to the securities firms, they could accept credit and, of course, campaign contributions.

Securities firms give less than banks in publicly reported annual donations, but probably more through the "back door." Although there is no official record of back-door giving, it is widely alleged in Japan that securities companies tip politicians off on good stock purchases, then effect a price increase through concentrated sales efforts and tell the politicians when to sell for a handsome capital gain before the stock drops back down. There are several pieces of circumstantial evidence of this type of activity.[62]

What Is Being Deregulated?

Banks dominated private finance in prewar Japan. Like universal banks in Germany, Japanese commercial banks engaged in a wide range of financial activities, including securities transactions. Securities firms were left with the small niche of retailing stocks and bonds and trading on secondary markets.[63]

In 1927, two years before the disaster on Wall Street, one of the largest Japanese banks, the Bank of Taiwan, failed. This in turn set off a serious run on other banks in Japan. Many banks were too weak to recover and had to close their doors permanently. In Janu-

[61]For the Jiyūtō's policies toward private finance, see, for example, issues of *Kinyū Zaisei Jijō* between 1950 and 1955; and Mitsuo Takamoto, ed., *Sengo Kinyū Gyōseishi* (Tokyo: Kinyū Zaisei Jijō Kenkyūkai, 1985).

[62]Larry Repeta, "Declining Public Ownership of Japanese Industry," *Law in Japan* 17 (1984), 153–84; Katsuhiro Hirota, *Seibi Jiken: Kōhan Dokumento* (Tokyo: Koju Jisha, 1984); Kei Tsugawa, *Kabutochō no Chibu to Hibu* (Tokyo: Sanichi Shobō, 1979); "Japan's Drug Stocks Fluctuate on Rumor," *Asian Wall Street Journal*, May 3–4, 1985. See also news reports of the Recruit Cosmos stock incident which surfaced in July 1988, in which at least eighty politicians and journalists were found to have purchased unlisted Recruit stock and subsequently benefited from the quadrupling of their shares in a relatively short period; David Sanger, "Insider Trading the Japanese Way," *New York Times*, August 10, 1988.

[63]Kamekichi Takahashi, ed., *Nihon no Kōshasai Shijō* (Tokyo: Diamond, 1963), p. 128; Junichi Senda, ed., *Henkakuki no Ginkō to Shōken* (Tokyo: Yūhikaku, 1986), pp. 164–68.

ary 1928 a new Banking Law (Shin Ginkō Hō) went into effect, facilitating mergers in the banking sector and restricting new entry. Instead of imposing a wall between banking and securities activities as in the United States—because in Japan the problem had been more one of bad loans than risky stock market speculation on the part of the banks—the MOF allowed banks to "clean up" the bond market.[64]

In 1933, with the MOF's blessing, the banks formed a Bond Arrangement Committee (Kisaikai) to determine which firms could issue bonds, when, and on what terms. The Bond Committee established a collateral requirement for all bond issues and determined that banks would serve as "trustees" of the required collateral, for a handsome fee. A trustee bank (*jutaku ginkō*) is not technically a guarantor of the issue but has the more limited burden of "managing" the collateral—that is, ensuring that it is of suitable quality and holding some of the issue until the bonds reach maturity and the creditors have been paid. In cases of default, banks have indeed presided over the liquidation of the collateral and distributing the returns to the bond holders, on occasion making up the difference from their own coffers. But few firms, particularly in the early years of postwar reconstruction, could meet the strict requirements for bond issuance, resorting instead to bank loans.

The American Occupation forces arrived in Japan after World War II with a mind to recast Japan's institutions on the American model. A number of the proposed reforms did not take root, in part because the Occupation officials themselves softened the "democratization campaign" in 1947 and 1948 in the interest of speeding Japan's economic recovery, and in part because the Japanese "re-interpreted" some of the reforms as soon as the Americans left in 1952. Banks were ultimately exempted from strict application of

---

[64]The U.S. Banking Act of 1933, popularly known as the Glass-Steagall Act, drew a sharp jurisdictional boundary between commercial banking and investment banking because the overlap between these two types of activities was believed to be a cardinal reason for the 1929 U.S. stock market crash and hence a contributing factor to the Great Depression. Congress sought to restore public confidence in the commercial banking system through the institution of the Glass-Steagall "Wall." See Joseph J. Norton, "Up against 'The Wall': Glass-Steagall and the Dilemma of a Deregulated ('Reregulated') Banking Environment," *Business Lawyer* 42 (February 1987), pp. 327–68.

39

the antitrust measures, for example. SCAP did, however, effect one significant change in Japan's financial system when it required a separation of banking from securities activities. Following the American Glass-Steagall example, section 65 of the Securities Exchange Act of 1948 forbade banks from henceforth engaging in securities and investment banking activities, except as a small percentage of their own investments.

This was a startling piece of legislation. In 1948 banks were indisputably the premier force in the private sector. By contrast, securities firms were lilliputian in strength and could never have overturned bank dominance without SCAP's decree. Not surprisingly, banks battled the restrictive legislation, and they did obtain some concessions.[65] Banks regained the right to deal in securities upon a client's orders, as part of a trust contract, and banks could hold up to 10 percent of the shares issued by a corporation.[66] But they lost the securities business. At that time, their interest in securities was in any case more a matter of principle than immediate concern.[67] With the postwar economy in ruins, the stock and bond markets were weak, leaving the loan market as the keystone of corporate finance. Firms, in fact, were willing to pay a premium for a steady line of credit, further enhancing the power of banks.[68]

In postwar Japan the bank-dominated Bond Committee continued to control the bond issuance market as it had in the prewar period. The interest rates were low, and the quantity was kept small and rationed; the government and municipal bonds received first priority, followed by electric power companies. In 1961 the MOF permitted the securities firms to issue bond fund instruments to the

[65] Nihon Shōken Keizai Kenkyūjo, *Sengo Shōkenshi o Kataru* (Tokyo: Ōkura Insatsu, 1984), pp. 360–62; interview with an ex-MOF bureaucrat, June 1986, Tokyo.

[66] Yasuji Abe, *Ginkō Shōken Kakine Ronsō Oboegaki* (Tokyo: Nikkei, 1980), p. 59; the 10 percent rule was lowered to 5 percent by the Antimonopoly Law of 1976. The MOF gave banks ten years to get below the limit, but in 1986 city banks were over by 2–4 percent for many firms in their conglomerate.

[67] Takuji Matsuzawa, *Watakushi no Ginkō Shōwashi* (Tokyo: Tōyō Keizai Shimpōsha, 1985), pp. 108–9.

[68] Koichi Hamada and Akiyoshi Horiuchi, "The Political Economy of the Japanese Financial Markets," in Kozo Yamamura and Yasukichi Yasuba, eds., *The Political Economy of Japan*, vol. I: *The Domestic Transformation* (Stanford: Stanford University Press, 1987).

general public (*shasai tōshin*); but they became too popular, competing with the banks for small savings. The MOF ordered that the accounts be longer term to keep them out of reach of the average depositor. This effectively held down the size of the bond market and increased the lending power of the banks.[69]

Another pillar of postwar financial regulation was introduced in the Interest Control Law of 1948.[70] It authorized the MOF to set low deposit and loan ceilings in order to promote economic growth.[71] But banks, independently of any MOF directive, required customers to keep balances, not subject to immediate withdrawal. Banks used these compensating balances to increase their effective interest rate spreads, thus retaining a portion of the income transferred from savers rather than passing it along to the borrowers as the MOF had intended. If, for example, a bank lent 100 million yen to a corporation at the prime rate of 5.25 percent and required that 40 percent of that be kept in a bank deposit getting 4 percent interest, the corporation was in effect borrowing only 60 million yen for a net interest payment of 3.65 million, or an effective interest rate of 6.08 percent.[72] Banks were able to do this because of

[69] Abe, *Ginkō Shōken Kakine Ronsō Oboegaki*, p. 43; *Sengo Shōkenshi o Kataru*, p. 429; Yukio Noguchi and Eisuke Sakakibara, "Ōkurashō—Nichigin Ōchō no Bunseki," *Chūō Kōron*, August 1977, p. 119.

[70] Deposit rates were not subject to regulation until the mid-1930s, when the military imposed controls. But banks had maintained interest rate ceilings among themselves to limit competition since at least 1902. See Keimei Kaizuka, "A Comparative Study on Financial Development," Research Institute for the Japanese Economy, University of Tokyo, March 1986, p. 29.

[71] The mechanics of a change in the interest rate are begun by the minister of finance, who commissions the Interest Rate Adjustment Council (*Kinri Chōsei Shingikai*) to study the matter and make a recommendation to the Bank of Japan Policy Committee (*Nihon Ginkō Seisaku Iinkai*). The fifteen-member Interest Rate Adjustment Council is composed of the director general of the MOF Banking Bureau, the director general of the Economic Planning Agency (EPA) Adjustment Bureau (usually on leave from the MOF), deputy governor of the Bank of Japan, *seven* representatives from the financial sector, three representatives from industry, and two academics. The Bank of Japan Policy Committee is composed of the governor of the Bank of Japan, one representative each from the MOF and the EPA, and one each from the city banks, regional banks, industry, and agriculture. In fact, the MOF has veto power over any interest rate decision, subject, of course, to pressure from the cabinet. See Asahi Shimbun Keizaibu, ed., *Ginko* (Tokyo: Asahi Shimbunsha, 1976), pp. 90–91.

[72] Tadao Morimoto, *Ginko Daisensō: Hakaisuru Nihon no Kinyū Kōzō* (Tokyo: Daiyamondo Sha, 1979), pp. 165–67.

41

the high demand for funds in the recovery and rapid growth years. Corporations were willing to pay a premium for a steady stream of credit to fuel their ambitious investment programs. These balances, then, enabled banks to profit from the low deposit-rate ceilings. Indeed, banks' profitability through the 1960s was significantly higher than that of the nonfinancial-sector industries.[73]

While borrowing from a number of banks, most corporations maintained closest ties to one particular bank, their "main bank." Corporations valued these close ties because of the main banks' implicit commitment to bail out its firms when hit by hard times.[74] For banks, continuous dealings with firms compensated for the weak corporate disclosure rules by reducing the costs of monitoring the creditworthiness of borrowers.

The Unraveling of the Postwar Structure of Benefits

Over the decades since the end of World War II, market forces have gradually rendered the postwar regulatory structure less palatable to one of its greatest beneficiaries, the banking industry.[75] First, bank borrowers now have stronger bargaining power when

[73]Toshihiko Yoshino, *Sengo Kinyūshi no Omoide* (Tokyo: Nihon Keizai Shimbunsha, 1985), pp. 144–47.

[74]There are at least two alternative explanations for stable, long-term relationships between banks and firms. The view that these ties reflect an implicit insurance scheme is espoused by Paul Sheard, "Corporate Organisation and Structural Adjustment in Japan" (Ph.D. diss., Australian National University, 1986); Hisahiko Okumura, "Kinyū Shisutemu no Henkaku to Kigyō no Zaimu Kōdō no Kakushin, *Business Review* 33, no. 1 (1984), 36; Sadahiko Suzuki and R. W. Wright, "Financial Structure and Bankruptcy Risk in Japanese Companies," July 15, 1983. The revisionist hypothesis, tested with better results by Akiyoshi Horiuchi and Frank Packer, focuses on information asymmetries. Banks value continuing ties with firms for the knowledge they gain and will seek to maintain those ties only to the extent that the value of that knowledge exceeds the cost of supporting the firm in bad times. See Horiuchi and Packer, "The Function of Financial Institutions: What Role Has the 'Main Bank' Played in Japan?" University of Tokyo, unpublished manuscript, December 1986; also Horiuchi, "Kinyū Kikan no Kinō: Riron to Genjitsu," September 1986, to appear in Tachi Ichiro and Shōichi Rōyama, eds., *Nihon no Kinyū* (Tokyo: University of Tokyo Press, 1987).

[75]The securities industry also has benefited from financial regulations such as fixed commissions for underwriting and brokering stocks and bonds.

Table 1. Profitability of Japanese banks and other industries, 1953–1982 (after-tax current profits per capital account)

Year	All banks	City banks	All industries	Manufacturing
1953–57	13.6%	12.0%	7.6%	n.a.
1958–62	12.4	10.5	9.1	10.9%
1963–67	14.5	12.8	10.7	9.9
1968–72	15.8	15.8	13.8	10.7
1973–77	10.6	10.0	9.5	8.8
1978–82	8.1	8.4	9.8	9.8

Source: Akiyoshi Horiuchi, "Economic Growth and Financial Allocation in Postwar Japan." Research Institute for the Japanese Economy, University of Tokyo, August 1984, p. 22.

seeking loans. Second, government bonds became more costly for banks to hold passively. And third, bank depositors now have attractive alternatives to bank accounts and are demanding better terms. Gone are the days of unchallenged bank dominance.

The Stronger Bargaining Power of Bank Borrowers

Borrowers are in a stronger position relative to banks for a number of reasons. As Japan's brisk rate of economic growth tapered off after the first oil shock, corporations have become less eager to borrow, since for most firms there are fewer investment opportunities that warrant a high debit-financing cost. Retained earnings are enough to cover much of the lower investment needs of many firms.

Even for strong companies that continue to have large investment needs, there are alternatives to bank debt; these firms are therefore no longer willing to pay a high premium for a credit line with a bank. As corporations have become stronger, their concerns have shifted from solvency to flexibility and cost, and cultivating relations with the main bank is less crucial to the firm's well-being. For the increasing number of Japanese firms that have access to cheaper funds in the Eurobond market, there is little reason not to pare down their bank loans at home.

Banks have fought to keep their best customers by cutting their loan margins and by demanding smaller compensating balances, because they did not have good loan alternatives. As will be discussed later in greater detail, banks have also agreed to ease the

43

conditions for domestic corporate bond issuance rather than lose altogether the business associated with the corporate bond market.[76]

Changes in the Government Bond Market

Japan maintained a balanced government budget until 1965, and ran only a small deficit from 1965 to 1975. To combat the post-oil-shock recession and also to meet the vast increase in social welfare expenditures mandated under new laws in 1971–73, the LDP opted for heavy government spending in 1975.[77] The large government deficit that ensued grew unabated in the subsequent years, peaking at 40 percent of total spending in 1979.[78] This became a serious problem for banks, because banks are the largest underwriters in a syndicate of financial institutions for government debt issued below the market price. The syndicate system operated smoothly as long as the size of issuance was small enough to be reabsorbed by the Bank of Japan a year after each issuance, and at little cost to the banks. But with the surge in government bonds since 1975, the Bank of Japan could no longer provide adequate compensation to the banks.

Dissatisfied with the progress in their negotiations with the MOF, banks boycotted government debt underwriting for three consecutive months in 1978. The MOF gave an inch: banks could change their accounting practices in order to hide from the public and their shareholders the losses banks were taking on government bonds. Still unhappy, banks demanded freedom to sell government bonds to bank customers and the additional right to buy and sell government bonds for their own account to profit on short-term price fluctuations. In the Banking Act of 1982, the MOF granted these

[76]The pools of surplus funds which large corporations began amassing in the 1970s resulted in the sharp growth in demand for short-term financial instruments such as Gensaki, which in turn injected more flexibility into the entire interest rate structure. See Robert Feldman, *Japanese Financial Markets: Deficits, Dilemmas and Deregulation* (Cambridge: MIT Press, 1986).

[77]Yukio Noguchi, "Public Finance," in Kozo Yamamura and Yasukichi Yasuba, eds., *The Domestic Transformation*, vol. 1 of *The Political Economy of Japan*, ed. Yasusuke Murakami and Hugh T. Patrick (Stanford: Stanford University Press, 1987), pp. 186–222.

[78]Michihiko Matsuno, *Kokusai* (Tokyo: Okura Zaimu Kyokai, 1983), pp. 2–13.

requests. For the first time since World War II, MOF redrew the lines between the banking and securities industries.

The Depositors' Stronger Bargaining Power

Since the mid-1970s large depositors, such as corporations with case, are no longer willing to place funds in low-yield compensating deposits. In the 1960s securities firms offered high-yield securities with a repurchasing agreement (*gensaki*), but twenty years ago few firms could afford to refuse the banks' requirement for compensating balances. As firms began to feel freer to take their money elsewhere, banks had to raise the effective yields on large deposits at the expense of their own profit margins.

Small depositors still have not tasted the fruits of deregulation. Postal savings are an alternative to bank accounts, and unfortunately for the banks, the Ministry of Posts and Telecommunications allows the post offices to offer slightly better terms than do the banks. If the banks raise their rates, the postal system will match the increase and maintain the gap in deposit yields.[79] Deregulating small deposits would therefore favor the postal savings system. Banks are still hoping to gain a political settlement that would bring the postal system more closely in line with the bank rates. The problem for the banks is that the postal system is politically powerful. There are nearly twenty thousand commissioned postmasters around Japan who, at least in the minds of many politicians, have sway over a large number of votes at election time. Banks have only recently begun to lobby with the LDP against what they perceive to be the post offices' encroachment on their deposit base.

The Case Studies

Chapter 3 deals with the overt influences of the international system on Japanese economic policies. Although it is easy to assume that foreign political pressures were a key source of Japanese finan-

[79]Toshihiko Hayashi, "The Postal Savings System in Japan: A Roadblock to Deregulation?" Hoover Institution Working Paper on Economics no. E-85-10, 1985, pp. 7, 15.

cial deregulation, American demands to open financial markets were successful where domestic interests were already moving in that direction. The MOF readily opened the Euroyen bond market to foreign and domestic use; the greatest beneficiaries were probably Japanese city banks and securities firms, since they possess the advantage of investing and raising yen. It was the MOF and Bank of Japan (BOJ) that picked up the tab: more yen in the hands of foreigners would make monetary control somewhat more difficult. Foreign demands also succeeded in opening the Tokyo Stock Exchange and the trust bank business to foreign firms, principally because the Japanese securities firms and trust banks that thereby lost some market share stood to lose even more in their overseas operations if they were targeted for retaliation by their foreign hosts.

More instructive than the instances in which foreign demands seemed to "work" are those in which they did not. The Japan Offshore Market (JOM) remains smaller than its huge potential because the bank-securities standoff over section 65 limited the JOM to a strictly banking center. And the complaints of foreign banks that the low ceiling on bank deposits is disadvantageous to their commercial bank operations in Japan, since foreign banks have fewer of these deposits, have resulted in only incremental change. Small-denomination deposits will be tied to a market instrument, with a fixed spread, but only at a pace that the politically powerful but economically weak financial institutions will tolerate and only within the context of a joint solution with the postal savings system.

The problem of regulatory change left in the wake of foreign pressure is fully consistent with the theory of regulation. Markets or instruments were deregulated only when the domestic financial industry no longer benefited from the old rules. The Ministry of Finance successfully presided over the deregulation without intrusion by politicians, the courts, or any group outside the small circle of regulated institutions.

Chapter 4 focuses on two aspects of the Banking Act of 1982: the MOF's unsuccessful attempt to strengthen bank disclosure rules, and the MOF's successful modification of the postwar boundary line between the banking and securities industries. In the first in-

46

stance, the policy-making process became politicized as soon as the banks realized the MOF would not withdraw its draft bill. The prospect of additional disclosure was onerous to the banks, since it would involve additional administrative costs and the loss of valuable privacy. Small banks fought even harder because they were objects of the MOF's hidden agenda: stricter disclosure rules would forceably weaken small banks' resistance to merger, thus facilitating the MOF's efforts to streamline the banking industry and reduce its own exposure to financial disturbances. Banks circumvented the MOF and took their case to the LDP, whereupon the politicians stepped in and withdrew the objectionable disclosure clauses from the banking bill. This was a rare case in which the Ministry of Finance, failing to anticipate the political response, invited unwelcome intervention. The theory of regulation does not prepare us for this failing, but it correctly predicts its result.

In the same law was a highly contentious section that permitted banks to deal in, trade, and sell government bonds over the counter. The securities industry was bitterly opposed to the banks' entry into this area of finance, not only because they would lose some of their share of a lucrative market but also because they viewed this as a precedent for further amendments to section 65 of the Securities Exchange Act, which heretofore barred banks' participation in the securities markets. Indeed, it was both loss of share and precedent for further redrawing of the boundaries between the securities and banking industries. Nor were banks entirely satisfied, however, because the compromise was that they would have to wait several years before beginning the government securities business.

Neither the securities nor banking industry brought in politicians to skew the MOF's plan in their favor. Although both industries could have done so, they knew that competitive bidding for political services would have been more costly than the income foregone in the MOF's proposal. That was because to win, the LDP would demand a large enough sum from the winner to compensate for the lost support of the losing side. Or, more likely, the LDP would have ultimately arrived at a similar compromise, but both sides would be short a princely sum in "campaign contributions." A political decision, in other words, would be unlikely to alter significantly the terms of the compromise. Many policy decisions are, of course, politicized in this way, but in this case the MOF was able to equilibrate preemptively because (a) it had the *will* to avoid political intervention; and (b) its comprehensive mandate, over both banking and securities sectors, gave it the *capacity* to do so. These are key attributes if the policy-making process is to function as the theory of regulation leads us to expect.

Chapter 5 explains how corporate access to the cheaper funds and greater flexibility of the Eurobond market indirectly induced Japanese banks to allow the domestic bond market to develop more fully. If banks were as loath as ever to lose their domestic lending business to the domestic bond market, these were no longer the only alternatives. The international market was readily accessible to those large Japanese firms regarded as world-class borrowers. Rather than lose all business related to domestic bond issuance, the banks agreed to a more lenient standard for domestic issuance. But this was only after assurances from the MOF that, instead of letting the new domestic bond business feed the profits of only the securities industry, the MOF would expand the ceilings for the private placement market from which the banks could profit. It is important to note, however, that only corporate clients, no individual depositors and borrowers, have ready access to foreign markets. The theory of regulation therefore leads us to expect deregulation only in wholesale markets where there is international competition but not in retail markets where the customers have no alternative to domestic financial services.

In Chapter 5 the LDP never appears in the foreground. As with the government securities issue in the Banking Act of 1982, the MOF was able to find a solution that, if not pleasing to both sides, at least left them equally disgruntled. And the MOF's ability to monitor compliance to the spirit of the agreement minimized the chances of either side trying to take advantage of possible loopholes.

Chapter 6 examines a case that does not square well with the theory of regulation. Unlike the previous chapters, which show the MOF acting in a rational way to guard its own interests and those of its primary clients, Chapter 6 describes the MOF and the banking industry battling a politically potent rival, the postal savings system. Although the tax bill of 1987 eliminates the exemption for interest on most postal savings, thus closing a loophole that had benefited the postal system at the expense of banks, the differential in deposit rate still favors the postal system. As a negative example of how the institutional structure of government shapes or constrains the policy-making process, the absence of a bureaucratic organ overseeing both the banks and the postal savings system leaves LDP intervention as the only option. Though forced to decide, the LDP has chosen so far to abide by the status quo.

These four case study chapters examine significant episodes in Japan's financial administration in recent years to determine why deregulation is taking place. In most cases the financial deregulatory process follows the predictions of the theory of regulation: financial institutions have abandoned protective regulations selectively, and only when failure to do so would have resulted in greater losses. In Chapter 7 we make further generalizations that help us address the broader subjects of Japanese politics and the role of Japan in the international arena.

3

Foreign Pressure
to Liberalize

A cynic might summarize the postwar history of U.S.-Japan economic relations as Japanese success met with American rancor. Beginning in the 1960s, when the Japanese textile industry first threatened the security of its American counterpart, a steady stream of Japanese exports has reached American shores and blighted uncompetitive American industries. As the U.S. trade deficit with Japan has grown steadily, few American politicians have taken solace in the neoclassical doctrine of comparative advantage.

The trade debate has intersected with finance at several points. In the 1970s foreign corporations and governments began to seek access to low-interest-rate funds in Japan, charging Japanese firms with an unfair capital cost advantage in international competition. Second, in the early 1980s trade in services, including finance, was added to the agenda for bilateral economic negotiations as the service sector came to represent a large portion of both nations' gross national product (GNP). Third, since the late 1960s, when Japan began chalking up successive trade surpluses with the United States, attention was focused on the exchange rate between the yen and dollar as a determinant of relative competitiveness of the two economies. In 1971 the United States took the dollar off the gold standard, forcing the yen as well as European currencies to appreciate against the dollar. But American trade deficits with Japan continued unabated, and by the 1980s the U.S. government determined that a "fair" exchange rate could only be achieved if Japan opened its financial markets.

Because this triad of complaints leveled at Japan's financial system came from different groups in the American economy, there was no coordinated plan until the early 1980s to act on them. Indeed, the goals were sometimes at cross-purposes. American financial institutions wanted maximum freedom to operate in Japan, even if "national treatment" had to be interpreted in the broadest way possible. They had little interest in the increased attractiveness of the yen as an investment currency, however, since American financial intermediaries reap greater gains from the international use of the dollar. It was American industry that hoped internationalization of the yen would cause the yen to appreciate against the dollar and thereby make Japanese goods more expensive relative to American products. But even industry had conflicting goals, insofar as greater access to Japanese capital markets would increase the outflow of capital from Japan and put downward pressure on the yen.

Within Japan, too, were contending interests. Banks for the most part fiercely defended their protected environment, just as securities firms fought to exclude new entrants and keep the fixed commission system. But market forces had already begun to drive a wedge between the strong and the weak financial institutions in Japan, across jurisdictional lines, and foreign pressure heightened their differing concerns. The foreign assault on Japan's closed trust banking system, for example, became a convenient vehicle for top Japanese city banks and securities firms to attempt a break into the private preserve of trust banks. Small financial institutions continued to resist change across the board.

The regulators also had mixed interests. The Bank of Japan, as implementor of monetary policy decisions, has long resisted the expanded role of the yen in international markets since sudden, large shifts in the foreign demand for yen would affect the domestic money supply, interest rates, and exchange rates. As long as the Ministry of Finance opposes the development of a short-term government bill market that could be employed in the central bank's open market operations, the BOJ has to rely on the increasingly less

51

dependable window guidance and operations in the interbank market. The Ministry of Finance, on the other hand, is less concerned about the yen's internationalization and has even gained some mileage with the "inevitability" argument in forcing the Japanese financial system to conform in some degree to market discipline.

Japan in the International System

Japan, like any country, faces the spector of foreign retaliation against attempts to protect domestic industries from foreign competition. The perceived theat of retaliation increases with what is judged to be the likelihood of punitive measures and the extent of damage expected by those measures. It is perhaps ironic that Japan's spectacular economic achievements in the past three decades have actually increased the country's vulnerability to such retaliation. For now that Japan competes as an equal with the other industrialized economies in world markets, there is greater fear of Japan's market power and hence a greater inclination to retaliate against its domestic closure. At the same time, Japan's economic successes abroad increase the cost to Japanese firms of having those business opportunities foreclosed through retaliation.

In the past decade top Japanese banks and securities houses have joined the ranks of the world's largest financial institutions. Initially following in the wake of Japanese corporations that established operations overseas, Japan's financial institutions have in more recent years profited enormously from their role in channeling Japan's large pool of savings into foreign markets. Furthermore, Japanese banks, through their foreign securities subsidiaries, engage in lucrative securities operations that are denied them in their own country. A sharp curb on their foreign activities could hurt Japanese banks severely.

Japan has not been able to act "rationally" in the global arena to the extent that the protection of small, inefficient financial institutions requires adherence to policies that invite foreign hostility. Moreover, fierce rivalries among different types of financial institutions, most notably that between securities firms and commercial banks, limit the range of action available to the Ministry of Finance

52

in pursuing its efficiency and stability goals. For both the securities and banking industries possess strong ties to politicians in the Diet who would interfere in financial policy were the MOF to aggrieve either industry.

Foreign diplomatic pressure is effective only when market forces have already altered domestic costs and benefits or when there is a perceived threat of retaliation. Furthermore, whereas external pressure may alter the pace and to some extent the nature of change in the Japanese financial system, the domestic factors are primary in determining how foreign demands should be met and how the costs of change are allocated within Japan. As we shall see, the case of the Japan Offshore Market is a superb example of how an idea, originally conceived to assuage foreign pique at financial market closure, has been denied full fruition until the domestic alignment of interests is favorable. Restrictions on the Euroyen market, by contrast, seemed to yield more readily to foreign pressures. In fact, domestic interests had been moving toward a liberalized Euroyen market for some time, and foreign pressure merely speeded the timing. In both the offshore and Euroyen markets, domestic factors shaped the contour of change.

Access to Japanese Capital Markets

Japan emerged after World War II with a system of stringent credit, trade, and foreign exchange controls designed to maximize the small pool of foreign currency for the purchase of necessary imports. No loans could be made into or out of Japan without specific permission, foreign trade financing worked within precise limits as to final maturity and settlement arrangements, and residents were prohibited from holding foreign currency or dealing directly in external markets without prior permission. The presumption that all transactions were prohibited unless authorized by the government mirrored the postwar British system, which functioned until 1976.[1]

[1]Lawrence Krause and Sueo Sekiguchi, "Japan and the World Economy," in H. Patrick and H. Rosovsky, eds., *Asia's New Giant* (Washington, D.C.: Brookings, 1976), pp. 410–13; A. R. Prindl, "Japan Is Liberalizing the Wrong Things," *Euromoney*, March 1980, p. 96.

Financial Politics in Contemporary Japan

In the early 1950s the Ministry of Finance allowed selective and limited borrowing from foreign sources to speed economic reconstruction and growth, careful all the while not to generate a cumbersome repayment burden.[2] Foreign direct investment was even more strictly circumscribed lest profit remittances exacerbate Japan's balance-of-payments problem or giant foreign firms engulf large portions of Japan's convalescing industry.[3]

For the first two decades of postwar recovery, capital outflows from Japan, in the form of loans, portfolio investment, or direct investment, were minimal. The government was eager to minimize an effluence of capital became Japan's balance of payments was frequently in deficit. But perhaps more important than government restrictions on capital outflows was the lack of excess funds in Japan. The demand for funds to finance profitable domestic investment was very high. Banks were heavily indebted to the Bank of Japan during the recovery and rapid growth years and overcommitted to corporate borrowers. There was not much liquidity in the economy which could have spilled overseas. The only creditor sector in the economy, individual savers, would have benefited from the opportunity to lend abroad at better yields, but it was in no other group's interests to channel these savings overseas.

Capital inflows, too, were very low and were mainly in the form of trade credit by Japanese banks. Japan's achievement of creditworthiness in the early 1960s coincided with the American government's imposition of the Interest Equalization Tax designed to keep capital from flowing out of the United States and hurting the U.S. balance-of-payments position.

The year 1965 was a watershed for Japan. Despite brief interludes of deficit after the two oil crises in the 1970s, Japan had overcome its chronic balance-of-payments problem. Less concerned about deficit-induced deflation or currency depreciation, the Ministry of Finance began to take a more liberal stance toward foreign lending. At the same time, Japanese corporations had begun to expand their overseas operations, and Japanese banks were eager to

[2] Krause and Sekiguchi, "Japan and the World Economy," p. 414.
[3] Note that the Japanese government was actively protecting not only strategic, technologically advanced industries but politically influential small businesses as well. See Philip Trezise and Yukio Suzuki, "Politics, Government, and Economic Growth," in Patrick and Rosovsky, *Asia's New Giant*, p. 798.

continue doing business with firms' foreign subsidiaries. By 1969 Japan's long-term assets exceeded long-term liabilities for the first time since World War II, and Japan became a net creditor.[4]

By 1972 Japanese banks had become a presence in the international syndicated loan market. But in 1974, after the OPEC oil price hike hit Japan with a sizable balance-of-payments deficit, the Ministry of Finance limited foreign lending to $800 million annually from some $3 billion in 1973. Only in November 1976 did Japanese banks resume their long- and medium-term lending.[5]

Again in 1979, when the price of oil took another leap, Japan's balance-of-payments position deteriorated. And once again Japanese foreign loans plummeted. Not until June 1980, when Japan's balance of payments was once again in surplus, did banks return to the foreign loan market. Although syndicate loans represent only a small part of all capital outflows from Japan, the Ministry of Finance was eager to stop any further deterioration of the balance of payments.[6]

An obvious question, in light of bank truculence in other dealings with the Ministry of Finance, is why Japanese banks should be willing to sacrifice their international business for the sake of the MOF's balance-of-payments concerns. In fact, banks were not particularly victimized. In the aftermath of both oil crises, Japan's interest rates escalated sharply, and few potential borrowers were attracted to yen-denominated loans. In 1979, for example, the Bank of Japan raised the official discount rate in three successive rounds from 3.5 percent to 6.25 percent.[7]

Foreign access to the Japanese bond market parallels developments in the loan market, with the added complication of the Bond Arrangement Committee's strict criteria for corporate issues in Japan.[8] As discussed in Chapter 2, only corporations that meet the

[4]Krause and Sekiguchi, "Japan and the World Economy," pp. 441–42.
[5]Stephen Bronte, "The Restrictions Are Going," *Euromoney*, February 1978, p. 13.
[6]Stephen Bronte, "The Dilemma of Japan's City Banks," *Euromoney*, September 1979, pp. 28–39; Masaru Yoshitomi, "Adjusting the Yen to Japan's Role of International Creditor," *Banker*, January 1984, pp. 85–91.
[7]Stephen Bronte, "How Bankers in Tokyo Are Living through the Freeze," *Euromoney*, February 1980, pp. 122–33.
[8]Donal Curtin, "Zen and the Art of Yen Bond Syndication," *Euromoney*, December 1982, pp. 81–90.

committee's demanding asset criteria and are willing to provide the appropriate collateral, to be "managed" by the trustee banks for a fee, are qualified to issue bonds in Japan.

In 1970 the Asian Development Bank (ADB) became the first foreign entity to float yen bonds, more commonly known as samurai bonds, in Japan—but not before a heated exchange took place between the banking and securities industries over the fate of Japan's unique secured bond system. The problem was obviated by treating the ADB as a sovereign borrower and thus not obliging it to put up collateral.[9] In subsequent years a number of sovereign borrowers issued bonds in Japan, except for a twenty-month interruption, from 1973 to 1975, when the market was closed in response to the post-oil-crisis balance-of-payments deficit.

Because of relatively high interest rates in Japan in the mid-1970s, foreign borrowers did not approach Japan's bond market in earnest until April 1978, when Sears Roebuck requested permission to float unsecured bonds in Japan. Sears, since it was not a sovereign borrower, was asking what banks most dreaded. And the Ministry of Finance faced the problem only with reluctance, not wanting to jeopardize its good working relationship with the banking sector. A Japanese retailer, Ito Yokado, made untenable the MOF's predilection for the status quo when it announced its intention to issue unsecured dollar-denominated bonds in New York in June 1978.

The securities firms were as eager for the abolition of the collateral system as the banks were against it. But the arrangement had persisted because the securities industry was prospering despite the encumbrance, whereas drastic change might seriously undermine banks' profitability. As we have seen, Japanese corporations' access to the Euromarket was already putting pressure on banks to provide more favorable lending terms, but banks still felt they had something to lose by making the domestic bond market more attractive.

In characteristic fashion, the MOF hit upon a compromise that would meet with the basic satisfaction of the financial institutions involved. A set of conditions was drafted for eligibility of unsecured bond issuance such that forty foreign firms would quality and two Japanese firms, Toyota and Matsushita Electric. In March 1979 Sears Roebuck issued the first corporate bonds without collateral in

[9]For a more detailed account of the development of the yen bond market, see James Horne, *Japan's Financial Markets* (London: Allen & Unwin, 1985), chap. 8.

the Japanese market since 1933. One month later, Matsushita Electric became the first Japanese corporation to do so.[10] Banks held the line in practice, but the securities firms celebrated the successful assault on the collateral principle.

The Ministry of Finance responded to the OPEC oil price hike in 1979 as it had in 1973, placing a low annual ceiling of 50 billion yen on new yen bond issues in Japan. But again, high domestic interest rates repelled potential foreign borrowers, and the requests did not even meet the prescribed quota.[11]

In the early 1970s, by which time Japan had surmounted its chronic balance-of-payments problems, the Ministry of Finance had begun to relax the restrictions on capital flows in and out of Japan. Indeed, the new Foreign Exchange and Trade Control Law of 1980, which moved Japan's system of capital controls from one that was "closed in principle" to one that is "free unless prohibited," formally sanctioned rather than initiated the change in policy.[12] The Ministry of Finance reserved for itself the right to interdict capital flows in the event of (a) deterioration of Japan's balance of payments position, (b) drastic fluctuations in the foreign exchange market, or (c) disturbances of the money or capital market.[13] But by the 1970s the MOF already had made the flow of capital increasingly free in practice and was intervening in the market with less frequency.[14]

Foreign Banks and the Japan Offshore Market

When Andreas Prindl, the general manager of Morgan Guaranty's Tokyo office, learned of the new Foreign Exchange and Trade

[10]Richard Wise, "Corporate Debentures and the Internationalization of the Japanese Bond Market," *Columbia Journal of World Business* 17 (Fall 1982).

[11]Bronte, "How Bankers in Tokyo," pp. 122–33.

[12]Michèle Schmiegelow, "The Reform of Japan's Foreign Exchange and Foreign Trade Control Law," paper for the colloquium Japan's Response to Crisis and Change in the World Economy (Nice, France, November 7–9, 1984), pp. 9, 43; Hideo Nagakawa, "Shin Gaitamehō no Kōgeki," *Keizai Ōrai,* February 1981, pp. 142–51.

[13]Yukinobu Oguchi, *Gaitame Shijō no Sugao* (Tokyo: Monex, 1983), pp. 39–40; Hakuo Fukui, "Gaitamehō Kaisei ni tsuite," *Zaikei Shōhō,* February 25, 1980, pp. 2–7; Takeo Miyazaki, "Shin Gaitamehō no Shikkō ni saishite," *Kokusai Kinyū,* February 1, 1981, pp. 4–9.

[14]Ichirō Ōtani, "How Open Is the Tokyo Capital Market?" International Monetary Fund manuscript (December 1981); Ichirō Ōtani, "Exchange Rate Instability

Control Law, he wrote an article titled "Japan Is Liberalizing the Wrong Things." Rather than abandon controls on movement of the yen, Prindl argued, the Ministry of Finance should allow a Euroyen or, for that matter, a Eurodollar market to develop in Tokyo. By removing the withholding tax on interest paid to nonresidents, lifting the minimum reserve requirements imposed on borrowings from abroad, and permitting free offshore lending, the MOF would be giving Tokyo its natural place as a center of international finance without forfeiting the efficacy of domestic monetary policy. In short, financial institutions located in Tokyo would act as intermediaries between nonresident depositors and nonresident borrowers in a deregulated environment. Though money would change hands in Tokyo, at least on the books, there need be no leakage into the domestic financial system.[15]

Prindl spoke for many of the representatives of the seventy-six foreign banks in Japan who, despite years of hard work, together commanded less than 3 percent of Japan's banking business in 1980.[16] Responding to dissatisfied American banks that found themselves disadvantaged in many foreign markets, Congress had passed the International Banking Act in 1978. This act stopped short of invoking the terminology of "reciprocity," for indeed banking regulation was more restrictive in some respects in the United States than in foreign markets.[17] Nonetheless, the act strongly exhorted foreign countries to grant U.S. banks effective, not mere legal, national treatment. Congress also charged the Treasury to conduct periodic studies of American banking operations abroad to ensure that national treatment was being accorded U.S. banks.[18]

---

and Capital Controls: The Japanese Experience, 1978–1981," IMF manuscript (May 1982).

[15]Prindl, "Japan Is Liberalizing the Wrong Things," pp. 96–102.

[16]For an excellent account of foreign banks' attempts to break the Japanese market, see Louis W. Pauly, *Opening Financial Markets: Banking Politics on the Pacific Rim* (Ithaca: Cornell University Press, 1988), chap. 2; "Kinyū Sensō ni Hatten suru ka Gaigin no Sabetsu Teppai Yōkyū," *Kinyū Zaisei Jijō*, May 15, 1978, pp. 12–13.

[17]American banks are free, for example, to engage in securities activities in many foreign countries, whereas they are prohibited by the Glass-Steagall Act from doing so in the United States. Strict reciprocity would deprive U.S. banks of this highly valued freedom abroad. See, for example, E. Gerald Corrigan, "A Perspective on the Globalization of Financial Markets and Institutions," *FRBNY Quarterly Review*, Spring 1987, pp. 1–9.

[18]The first of the Treasury's "National Treatment" reports, released in 1979,

The foreign banks' problem was not that they were discriminated against by the regulators, but that, first, they lacked the network of branches that allowed them to tap low-cost savings deposits. Since foreign banks had to "buy" their money on the open market, their costs were higher and were thus at a competitive disadvantage. Second, they lacked the longstanding relationships with corporations on which the Japanese commercial banks thrived.

The foreign banks' dream was not that the yen be catapulted into a world-class currency, since much of their business derived from their expertise in marketing financial innovations often related to their own currencies. For American banks in particular, an offshore dollar market in Tokyo would support their comparative advantage.

The idea of an offshore banking facility was not new to the Ministry of Finance. An offshore market is a segregated set of accounts established by financial institutions to conduct international banking business with nonresidents.[19] Offshore banking centers already existed, mostly since the early 1970s, in Bermuda, the Cayman Islands, the Bahamas, Panama, London, the Isle of Man, Jersey, Guernsey, Luxembourg, Liechtenstein, Zurich, Bahrain, Singapore, Hong Kong, and Manila. For financial authorities, the rationale for removing restrictions on transactions involving only nonresidents, or in other cases only foreign currencies, was to increase the offshore centers' share of international bank intermediation without reducing the effectiveness of domestic financial regulation on residents. Presumably the center would also generate income from additional employment and the construction of physical infrastructure.[20]

The United States, too, had been considering the merits of an

---

concluded that American banks were experiencing difficulty in a number of countries, but that progress was being made through governmental negotiations. See Department of the Treasury, "Report to Congress on Foreign Government Treatment of U.S. Commercial Banking Organizations" (September 1979), especially pp. 134–35. As Louis Pauly points out, "An Administration seeking to head off further Congressional intervention [was pushing] ahead with financial diplomacy." Pauly, *Opening Markets*, chap. 2. Pursuant to congressional requests, the Treasury published subsequent "National Treatment" studies again in 1984 and 1986.

[19] U.S. General Accounting Office, "Supervisory Examinations of International Banking Facilities Need to Be Improved" (September 20, 1984), p. 1.

[20] Sydney J. Key (Division of International Finance, Board of Governors of the Federal Reserve System), "International Banking Facilities as a Free Economic Zone," *Aussenwirtschaft* 39 (May 1984), 57–74.

offshore banking center for some time. At least stronger American banks had good reasons for wanting to attract Eurodollar transactions to New York. Dollars had left the United States for Europe in vast quantities during the 1960s for a variety of reasons, but in large part because American interest-rate ceilings, maturity limitations, and reserve requirements on deposits at banks in the United States made it difficult for American banks to compete for dollar-based transactions. Rather than lose business, American banks followed the dollar abroad, but of course with the additional costs of maintaining large foreign offices.[21]

American banks first submitted proposals for an international banking facility (IBF) to the Federal Reserve Board in the early 1970s in the hope of circumventing the Voluntary Foreign Credit Restraint (VFCR) program, which set ceilings on nonresident deposits in American banks.[22] After the removal of the VFCR and other U.S. capital controls in January 1974, banks once again proposed the IBF as a way to reduce the encumbrance of domestic reserve requirements and interest-rate ceilings. Because transnational corporations had access to more competitive financing in the Euromarket, at least the top tier of the American banking industry wanted to lure them back with comparable service.

In June 1978 the New York State Legislature enacted a statute granting tax relief to IBFs under New York State and City law, under the condition that the Federal Reserve Board take action to exempt offshore transactions from interest-rate ceilings and reserve requirements. In 1980 Congress passed the Monetary Control Act, which broadened the Federal Reserve Board's authority to impose reserve requirements as well as to exempt IBFs from such requirements.[23] The board's final regulations permitting IBFs became effective December 3, 1981.[24]

---

[21]U.S. General Accounting Office, "International Banking Facilities Have Improved the Competitive Position of Banks in the United States," report to the Board of Governors of the Federal Reserve System (August 7, 1984), pp. 8–9.

[22]For a fascinating analysis of the politics of American credit policy during this period, see J.A.C. Conybeare, *United States Foreign Economic Policy and the International Capital Markets* (New York: Garland Publishing, 1988).

[23]Thomas F. Cargill and Gillian G. Garcia, *Financial Reform in the 1980s* (Stanford: Hoover Institution Press, 1985), pp. 60–62.

[24]Key, "International Banking Facilities as a Free Economic Zone," p. 59.

The goal of the New York offshore market was "to bring the United States a larger share of international banking activity and to make it more competitive with other international banking centers."[25] More than just New York banks would benefit, because the Clearing House Association granted non–New York banks direct access to their clearing system. In two years, 471 banks in 18 states had established IBF accounts, though the nature of tax relief varied from state to state.[26] A 1983 study by the U.S. General Accounting Office concluded that IBFs did indeed contribute to the competitiveness of American banks. The ratio of foreign dollar assets of banks in the United States to foreign dollar assets of banks elsewhere increased from 0.27 in September 1981 to 0.45 in June 1983.[27] But the facts are not altogether clear. The consensus in the American banking community is that IBFs have not attracted new business so much as drawn business from other offshore entities or their foreign subsidiaries.[28]

As implementer of domestic monetary policy, the Federal Reserve Board was anxious to minimize leakages into the domestic money supply. To prevent U.S. corporations from depositing domestic checking balances in IBF accounts by way of their foreign subsidiaries, foreign affiliates of U.S. firms were required to affirm in writing that IBF proceeds would be used outside the United States. Transactions were restricted to a minimum maturity of two business days, and the minimum transaction size was $100,000. As another measure to prevent leakage of offshore money into the domestic financial system, IBFs were not permitted to issue negotiable instruments such as certificates of deposit or bankers accep-

[25]Henry S. Terrell and Rodney H. Mills (staff, Board of Governors), "International Banking Facilities and the Eurodollar Market," report to the Board of Governors of the Federal Reserve System (August 1983), p. 2; see also U.S. General Accounting Office, "International Banking Facilities Have Improved the Competitive Position of Banks in the United States," especially pp. 14–20.

[26]Key, "International Banking Facilities as a Free Economic Zone," p. 65.

[27]The Government Accounting Office report states that the econometric results seem to attribute increased U.S. competitiveness in banking to the IBFs, even when accounting for the locational preference for the United States as a safe haven during the international debt crisis. U.S. General Accounting Office, "International Banking Facilities Have Improved the Competitive Position of Banks in the United States," p. ii.

[28]Key, "International Banking Facilities as a Free Economic Zone," p. 68.

tances, since the bearer of these notes could resell the instruments to a third party.[29]

The movement in America toward the establishment of international banking facilities provoked at least some interest from Japan. In 1978 a group of young bureaucrats in the International Finance Bureau, receiving cues from a particularly internationalist vice-minister for international affairs, Takashi Hosomi, quietly began studying an offshore market in Tokyo as a way to assuage foreign bankers' ire without having to dismantle the intricate web of domestic banking rules.

In April 1980, after having "parachuted" from his career in the MOF to become president of the Overseas Economic Cooperation Fund, Hosomi began publicly advocating the establishment of an offshore market in Tokyo. The Ministry of Finance set up a discussion group to examine the issue, comprising MOF section chiefs, department heads from Japanese banks and securities firms, and branch managers of foreign banks. Foreign bankers, in particular, met the initiative with enthusiasm, and chairman of Bankers Trust, Alfred Brittain III, endorsed a Tokyo offshore center in a Japanese financial journal in November 1980.[30] Eric Hayden, Bank of America's Asia division vice-president for economic and strategic planning, contributed to the debate in a lengthy paper on internationalizing Japan's financial system, published in December 1980 by the

[29]A study by the U.S. Government Accounting Office (GAO), however, concluded that "the federal bank regulatory agencies have not ensured that all IBFs are complying with regulatory restrictions. . . . variations [exist] in the scope and depth of examinations conducted by the Office of the Comptroller of the Currency, the Federal Deposit Insurance Corporation, and the Federal Reserve." The GAO urged the agencies to "work together to adopt more complete and uniform guidance to ensure compliance with the restrictions of IBF activities." "Supervisory Examinations of International Banking Facilities Need to Be Improved" (September 20, 1984), pp. 9–10; C. T. Conover replied, "The examination of IBF assets and liabilities does not need further refinement." William W. Wiles, secretary of the Federal Reserve Board of Governors, stated that the "discretion given to the Federal Reserve Banks to tailor the scope of examinations contributes to cost effective examinations." And R. V. Shumway, director of the FDIC, asserted, "The prospect of widespread high volume violations sufficient to undermine money supply analysis is highly unlikely and we believe this concern to be overstated." (Correspondence appears in the appendix to the GAO report.)

[30]Alfred Brittain III, "Tokyo Ofushoa Sentā no Sōsetsu o Teiansuru," *Kinyū Zaisei Jijō*, November 3, 1980, pp. 30–33.

Northeast Asia–United States Forum on International Policy at Stanford University.[31] In addition, the Banking and Financial Committee of the American Chamber of Commerce in Japan compiled its own report on the subject.[32]

Foreign interest notwithstanding, there was still considerable domestic resistance, from three different quarters, to the use of an offshore market as a buffer against foreign criticism. First, the Tax Bureau of the Ministry of Finance opposed lifting the 20 percent withholding tax on interest paid to nonresident depositors. The counterargument was that withholding taxes generate very little revenue income because most depositors go to the Singapore and Hong Kong offshore markets anyway.[33] But tax officials remained inimical, arguing that domestic firms, perhaps through their overseas subsidiaries, would find some way around domestic tax requirements.[34]

Second, the Bank of Japan objected on monetary policy grounds. The freedoms necessary for a viable offshore market would also pose a threat to the structure of domestic interest rates, warned BOJ officials. What in fact seemed to concern the Bank of Japan most was that the Ministry of Finance would be satisfied with the deregulation of offshore transactions and fail to proceed with domestic reforms such as allowing the development of a Treasury Bill (TB) market. The Bank of Japan's primary tools of monetary policy, such as the provision of credit to banks at the discount window and intervention in the interbank market, were becoming less effective as free interest rate instruments such as securities with repurchase agreements (*gensaki*) and certificates of deposit gained in importance. Far more convenient for the central bank would be a fully developed market in short-term government securities in which the BOJ could engage in open-market operations. But the Ministry of Finance continued to resist the TB market idea, both because the

[31] Later published as Eric Hayden, "Internationalizing Japan's Finance System," in Daniel I. Okimoto, ed., *Japan's Economy: Coping with Change in the International Environment* (Boulder, Colo.: Westview, 1982), pp. 89–122.

[32] Atsuko Chiba, "Will Tokyo Create an Offshore Banking Center?" *Institutional Investor*, June 1981, pp. 75–88.

[33] Ibid., p. 78; interviews in the Tax Bureau, Ministry of Finance, September 1986.

[34] "Kanjin na no wa Kinri Jiyūka," *Kinyū Zaisei Jijō*, February 22, 1982, p. 15.

placement of government debt would be more volatile if not more costly and because banks strongly opposed a new substitute for bank deposits.[35] Still hopeful that the MOF would have to acquiesce to a TB market as international interest rate arbitrage became more prevalent, the BOJ did not want to see international banking being cordoned off from Japan's domestic market.

A third and more significant source of resistance to a Tokyo offshore market was the banking sector itself, and particularly the long-term credit banks and trust banks. These institutions, led by the powerful Industrial Bank of Japan, were fearful that an offshore market would further erode their diminishing advantage in long-term lending in Japan by bringing Euromarket practices—including the lack of a long term–short term distinction—closer to home. City banks already effectively engaged in long-term lending by rolling over short-term credits as they became due. But since World War II only the long-term credit banks were allowed to raise long-term funds, in the form of five- and seven-year bank debentures, and thus minimize their interest rate risk.

Despite the lack of enthusiasm on the part of important groups, Hosomi embarked on a three-week overseas Offshore Banking Survey Mission in April 1982. With him was a mixed entourage, thirty-three strong, including both the convinced and the skeptical: officials from the Ministry of Finance and Bank of Japan, and representatives of nine leading commercial banks, five trust banks, two long-term credit banks, two short-term capital companies, three of the Big Four securities firms, and two foreign banks, Bankers Trust and Deutsche Bank.

The Tokyo IBF idea met with a more cordial welcome abroad than it had in Japan. Beryl Sprinkel, under secretary for monetary affairs in the U.S. Department of the Treasury, said, "The Japanese capital market has been growing and the U.S. Treasury welcomes the creation of a free international banking facility in Tokyo." E. Y. Whittle, chief executive officer of Lloyds Bank International in

[35]Takeshi Ōta (then director of the Foreign Department, Bank of Japan), "Offshore Money Market Proposal Calls for Caution," *Oriental Economist*, August 1982, pp. 27–28; Stephen Bronte, "This Is the Decade of the Conquering Yen," *Euromoney*, March 1982, pp. 71–81; K. Miyazaki, "Pros and Cons on Tokyo Offshore Market," *Oriental Economist*, September 1982, p. 6; interviews in the Finance Bureau and Banking Bureau, Ministry of Finance, 1986.

London, commented, "I have wondered for several years why you have not had such a facility." Although offshore markets already existed in Hong Kong and Singapore, Japan's domestic industrial and financial markets were much larger. A fully developed center of international finance in Tokyo would facilitate the efficient flow of funds around the clock, worldwide.[36]

By 1982, however, the center of gravity in international finance had already begun to shift away from deposit taking and lending, for two reasons. First, the Third World debt crisis had all but destroyed bank interest in joining loan syndicates for sovereign borrowers. In August 1982, when Mexico announced that it could not pay loans due, new lending to debtor nations ground to a virtual halt.[37] When banks later resumed their lending, they were guarded, favoring highly rated corporate borrowers over the desperate sovereigns. Second, corporations and banks alike responded to the increased interest rate and exchange rate volatility of the early 1980s with a preference for flexible financing arrangements, including floating interest rate instruments, various types of interest rate and exchange rate swaps, and short-term note issuance facilities. In other words, finance centered increasingly on highly liquid securities and less on the traditional bank deposits and loans. Regulatory environments such as in the United States and Japan, which demarcated banking from securities activities by a Glass-Steagall-type rule, were destined to remain second-tier financial centers unless they changed. American banks continued to book many of their transactions in Europe and were becoming less enthusiastic about the idea of another commercial banking center in Tokyo.

Hosomi's vision was for Tokyo to become a full-fledged financial market, like the City of London, where there were no legal boundaries among types of financial institutions and no wall between the

[36]Takashi Hosomi reported these foreign reactions in "Impressions from a Worldwide Survey Trip of International Banking Centers," *Money and Finance*, June 1982, pp. 1–2; bankers and officials in Hong Kong and Singapore were, however, concerned that the Tokyo IBF feature yen transactions lest their own dollar-based offshore operations be siphoned off by the Japanese (p. 3). See also Tōichirō Matsutani, "Moves to Establish Offshore Money Market," *Oriental Economist*, August 1982, pp. 18–24.

[37]Charles Lipson, "International Debt and International Institutions," in Miles Kahler, ed., *The Politics of International Debt* (Ithaca: Cornell University Press, 1985), pp. 233–34.

offshore and domestic markets.[38] "My personal opinion is that there should be no barrier to activities in the market," asserted Hosomi. "International financial activity is becoming more competitive, so why should Japanese financial institutions be under artificial restrictions? They should compete on the same ground with European institutions that can do both banking and securities business at the same time. Nobody can say what is investment and what is loan business any more."[39]

What Hosomi expressed as a private citizen the MOF would have liked to implement if it were capable of acting singularly in pursuit of Japan's competitiveness in international finance. For as we shall see later, the objections of the Bank of Japan and the Tax Bureau could be accommodated. The real problems now were the conflicting interests of the banking and securities industries and the disparate views within the banking industry, which blocked the MOF from moving ahead. City banks would have welcomed the introduction of securities activities in Tokyo's offshore market only if they could participate; the securities firms insisted that the IBF be limited to lending and borrowing unless they could retain their monopoly over the securities business.[40] And most of the long-term credit banks and trust banks saw only a threat. When the Hosomi survey mission stopped in Zurich halfway through their trip to discuss their tentative conclusions, one of the trust bank representatives insisted that they make no recommendations upon their return. As a result, the Hosomi group's official report was a descriptive account of various international banking centers and refrained from making any proposals.[41] But Hosomi drafted his own plan for international banking facilities in Tokyo, concluding that although a full-fledged securities and banking center such as London's would be ideal, the

[38]London had been a free market only in foreign currency transactions until 1976, when it removed its foreign exchange restrictions. And not until October 1986 was the City's fixed commission structure dismantled, clearing the way for cross-specialty mergers and consolidation.

[39]Takashi Hosomi, "Several Aspects of the Japanese Financial Market," speech at the Japan Society, New York (October 28, 1982).

[40]Donal Curtin, "What the Rising Yen Means for Tokyo," Euromoney, September 1982, p. 191.

[41]Ibid., p. 191; interviews with Hosomi and others, 1985–1986, Tokyo; Takashi Hosomi, ed., Kokusai Kinyū Sentā Gaikan (Tokyo: Kinyū Zaisei Jijō Kenkyūkai, 1982).

more immediate (because workable) arrangement should be for commercial banking activities only. New York was his suggested model.[42]

Hosomi's optimism, though tempered with a measure of pragmatism, was not shared by many others. Not even the strongest city banks saw enough potential gain from a Tokyo IBF to compensate the reluctant, vulnerable specialty banks. Nor were foreign banks much interested anymore, primarily because of changes in the nature of international finance. The general manager of Chase Manhattan's Japan operations warned, "I would not want the authorities to think the IBF will resolve the present earnings difficulties of the foreign banks, because it will not provide a source of significant earnings." Deutsche Bank's general manager in Tokyo contended that "an IBF in Tokyo would be more in the interest of Japanese banks than of foreign banks since Japanese banks will gain better access to foreign currency deposits."[43] Lacking a champion strong enough to overcome the resistance, discussion of the Tokyo offshore market faded from public view. But the idea continued to be discussed—in a special subcommittee of the Foreign Exchange Advisory Council (Gaikoku Kawase Shingikai) and in the International Finance Bureau's study group (Kokusai Kinyū Kihon Mondai Kenkyūkai).[44] And some MOF bureaucrats engaged in personal diplomacy. When Eisuke Sakakibara, director of the International Finance Bureau Research Division, attended a conference in New York on financial policy in 1982, he stopped by Washington to exhort the U.S. Treasury to put pressure on Japan to open an IBF.

[42]Takashi Hosomi, "A Draft Plan for the Establishment of International Banking Facilities in Tokyo," *Money and Finance*, January 1983, pp. 1–2. See also Hedeo Nagakawa, "1,500 oku doru o Toppashita Beikoku no IBF," *Kinyū Zaisei Jijō*, January 24, 1983, pp. 40–43; Takashi Hosomi, "Tokyo IBF Sōsetsu ni tsuite no Hosomi Shian," *Kinyū Zaisei Jijō*, January 24, 1983, pp. 30–36. Hosomi articulated his views in greater detail in *Tokyo Offshore Shijō* (Tokyo: Toyo Keizai Shimposha, 1985), especially pp. 246–70.

[43]Timothy McGinnis, "A Critical Step towards Realizing Full Liberalization," and Hans J. Beck, "Less Advantageous without Special Treatment of Corporate Tax," in *Money and Finance*, January 1983, pp. 2–4.

[44]Sō Nagaoka (assistant director general of the MOF International Finance Bureau), "Offshore Banking Center ni tsuite," *Zaikei Shōhō*, January 3, 1983, pp. 24–28; Hideo Nagakawa, "Offshore Banking Center no Ranyō Bōshi Taisaku," *Kokusai Kinyū*, April 15, 1983, pp. 28–33.

Only two years later, with new proponents, would the IBF debate reemerge.

The Exchange Rate Problem
and the Yen-Dollar Committee

If foreign banks were no longer clamoring for a Japanese offshore market, there were more Black Ships arriving in another port. America had been running a chronic trade deficit with Japan since the mid-1960s, but through the 1970s America's surplus on the invisibles account resulted in a bilateral current account surplus for the United States. In 1982 the U.S. overall current account went from a surplus of $6.4 billion for the previous year to a deficit of over $8 billion, over one-quarter of which was with Japan.[45] The figures for merchandise trade were even worse, and protectionist sentiment was sweeping through Congress, fanned by the raw winds of the 1981–82 recession in the United States. Moreover, the high consumer visibility of many of Japan's most successful export commodities increased American public awareness of the trade issue. It was ripe for politics. In early 1982 legislation to limit or exclude imports was introduced in the Congress in several forms.[46]

The Reagan administration, concerned to avoid domestic political fallout from what was touted to be the importation of unemployment and recession from Japan, but also eager to avert protectionist mudslinging across the Pacific, was in search of new solutions to the trade friction. Though not really an original idea, given the history of the post-Depression spate of competitive currency devaluations, some in Washington suggested a new focus on the yen-dollar exchange rate.

C. Fred Bergsten, one of the earliest proponents of the "misalignment" view, argued in the summer 1982 edition of *Foreign Affairs* that an improper bilateral exchange rate was responsible for much of the trade imbalance between the two nations. Bergsten's policy

[45] "Japan 1985: An International Comparison," Keizai Koho Center, Japan Institute for Social and Economic Affairs (Tokyo, 1985), p. 48.

[46] James F. Bere, "Enough Is Enough: New Realism in U.S.-Japan Trade," talk delivered at the Foreign Relations Council, Chicago (March 9, 1982).

suggestion was that, because the flexible exchange rate system had failed to prevent the serious overvaluation of the dollar which disadvantaged American goods on the international market, governments should work to realign the macroeconomic policies that lead to currency misalignments. Large U.S. government deficits should be cut, reducing the upward pressure on U.S. interest rates. Japan, by contrast, should apply the reverse policy mix, relaxing its fiscal stringency and easing credit on the monetary front. Bergsten's short-term recommendation was that Japan *restrict* the capital outflows that were reducing the aggregate demand for yen relative to the dollar, or in other words halt temporarily the process of capital liberalization.[47]

It is important to note, incidentally, that informed discussion of U.S.-Japan foreign exchange matters had moved beyond the earlier accusations of Japanese exchange rate manipulation to a less overtly castigating claim that the imbalance in capital flows was responsible for an inappropriately low yen value. In a statement before the House Ways and Means Subcommittee on Trade in April 1983, Under Secretary of Treasury Beryl Sprinkel testified: "We have found no evidence that the Japanese authorities were manipulating markets to weaken the yen. To the contrary, Japanese macroeconomic policy objectives, foreign exchange market intervention, and reluctance to lower the official discount rate all suggested that the Japanese authorities sought a stronger yen."[48]

Interest in the yen's valuation continued to grow in academic and policy-making circles. In a paper prepared in August 1982 for a National Science Foundation colloquium on international trade competitiveness, economists Lawrence B. Krause and Robert Z. Lawrence stated: "Since March 1973, the yen has gone through several periods when it was believed to have been seriously under-

[47]C. Fred Bergsten (assistant secretary of the Treasury for international affairs during the Carter administration, and at the time of writing director of the Institute for International Economics), "What to Do about the U.S.-Japan Economic Conflict," *Foreign Affairs*, Summer 1982, pp. 1059–75.

[48]"Statement of the Honorable Beryl W. Sprinkel, Under Secretary for Monetary Affairs, U.S. Treasury Department, Before the Subcommittee on Trade House Ways and Means Committee" (April 21, 1983), cited in Jeffry Frankel, "The 1984 Campaign for Liberalization of Japanese Capital Markets," unpublished manuscript (August 1984), pp. 68–70.

valued. Trade frictions with Japan seem to be closely related to the yen's undervaluation. . . . A study of the yen is desirable to establish the cause of the yen's volatility and what role policy plays in it."[49]

The idea of the yen's undervaluation relative to the dollar took on new political force in Washington when American industry seized on it as a way to meet Japan's productivity challenge. In a statement before the House Ways and Means Trade Subcommittee on November 30, 1982, Caterpillar chairman Lee L. Morgan called the undervalued Japanese yen "the single most important trade issue facing the United States. . . . American companies are losing sales to Japanese firms not because of cost, quality or service, but because of the unearned price advantage due to the undervalued yen." Morgan suggested several possible actions: Japanese measures to encourage capital inflows and to stimulate foreign investment in yen instruments in Japan, attachment of an import surcharge on Japanese manufactured goods, and intervention in foreign exchange markets. "These are strong actions we are talking about," said Morgan, "but this very important yen/dollar problem requires strong medicine, and requires it now."[50]

The strong medicine was not concocted as soon as Morgan would have liked, and he commissioned Stanford economist Ezra Solomon and Washington lawyer David Murchison to draft a report that would state his position in more convincing terms. Released in September 1983, the Solomon-Murchison Report reaffirmed that "United States manufacturing firms and workers are suffering substantial injury as a result of a significant misalignment of the Japanese yen and the dollar."[51] Although the authors conceded that other currencies had also depreciated significantly against the dollar, thus hinting that some policy problems might have been on the American side, they chose to stress exclusively the *result* of colliding

[49]Lawrence B. Krause and Robert Z. Lawrence, "Toward a Research Program for U.S. Trade Policy in the 1980s," paper prepared for the National Science Foundation's Colloquium on U.S. Policies in Response to Growing International Trade Competitiveness (September 24, 1982).

[50]Lee L. Morgan's statement as recorded in a telex sent to an American bank's Tokyo branch.

[51]David C. Murchison and Ezra Solomon, "The Misalignment of the United States Dollar and the Japanese Yen: The Problem and Its Solution" (September 19, 1983), p. 1.

70

national policies: "A large autonomous net flow of capital into dollar assets, a significant portion of which is from Japan."[52] The authors recommended that Japan, out of its own interest in preserving the free trade system, should take measures to remove all artificial curbs on the demand for yen, including interest rate controls on deposits, debentures, and government bonds and restraints on Euro-yen bond issues.[53] Rather than restrict their capital outflows to the United States, the report argued, the Japanese should contribute to a stronger yen by making the yen a more attractive investment currency. The idea of a Tokyo IBF also appeared on the agenda, not as a means of helping foreign banks to succeed in Japan but as a device to advance the use of the yen as a store of value and medium of exchange.

James Abegglen, then with the Boston Consulting Group K.K., agreed with the Solomon-Murchison view that a moderating of economic tensions between Japan and the United States could take place only through an adjustment of exchange rates, and that forcing Japan to deregulate its interest rate structure would increase the value of the yen by bringing yields on yen-denominated investments in line with American levels. Abegglen suggested that the U.S. government therefore focus more on Japan's financial deregulation, lending its support to those forces in Japan favoring liberalization, rather than persist in its earliest preoccupations with trade barriers.[54]

[52]Ibid., p. 10. Meanwhile, not only the Japanese but also the BIS, in its Fifty-third Annual Report (June 13, 1983), blamed the foreign exchange problem on high U.S. interest rates stemming from the large government deficit. Cited in Atshushi Hama, "The Yen-Dollar Relationship, Macro-Economic Policy, Financial and Capital Markets and Related Issues," *Keidanren Papers no. 10* (November 1983), p. 93.

[53]Murchison and Solomon, "The Misalignment of the United States Dollar," pp. 16–17. But H. T. Patrick has argued that the real problem, as a comparison with European currencies shows, is the dollar's overvaluation rather than the yen's undervaluation. And although it is doubtless true that the relative underdevelopment of Japan's financial markets do keep the value of the yen down, complete liberalization of financial flows would not necessarily prod the yen in the right direction. The more critical question, as Patrick sees it, is what would induce the dollar to depreciate against other world currencies.

[54]James Abegglen, "Economic Relations between Japan and the United States, 1983," *Journal of Japanese Trade and Industry*, no. 6 (1983), 53–55. Others, including Richard Freeman of the Federal Reserve staff, argued against the notion that "recent yen weakness has been induced by either regulation or selective liberal-

In the Senate Banking Committee, meanwhile, Republican senator Jake Garn introduced an amendment to the International Banking Act of 1978 which would explicitly authorize the Treasury Department "to consider reciprocity among other factors in acting on an application by a foreign bank to establish a Federal branch or agency, and for other purposes."[55] The amendment did not discard the concept of "national treatment" but broadened it to mean "equality of competitive opportunity" as measured, presumably, by profit and market share. Although the Senate Banking Committee eventually withdrew the bill, *Business Week* described it as "a bill that's packing a punch before it passes."[56] Even the threat of such legislation was powerful ammunition in Treasury's arsenal for its negotiations with Japan.[57]

The Japanese, of course, were unhappy about being held solely responsible for the U.S.-Japan currency misalignment and hence the trade imbalance. Even before the Solomon-Murchison Report was issued, the Ministry of Finance had been maintaining that the recent weakness of the yen was due to high interest rates in the United States, for which the large U.S. government budget deficit was primarily responsible.[58] The Japanese government was unwavering in this view and resented what it perceived as another instance of the American penchant for scapegoating.

The U.S. government was equally staunch in believing that the yen was undervalued and that the closure of Japanese financial

---

ization," in "Aspects of Recent Japanese Financial Market Liberalization," paper for conference at the Federal Reserve Bank of San Francisco (May 11, 1984), p. 14.

[55]S. 2193, 98th Congress, First Session, cited in "National Treatment of Banks," Hearings, U.S. Senate Committee on Banking, Housing, and Urban Affairs, September 1984, pp. 3–4.

[56]"A Bill That's Packing a Punch Before It Passes," *Business Week*, May 14, 1984.

[57]In committee hearings a year later, Senator Garn stated, "I think the best approach at this time is to continue to send the proper signals, but . . . if the signals are not sufficient, we may have to proceed with legislation." "National Treatment of Banks," Hearings, U.S. Senate Committee on Banking, Housing, and Urban Affairs, September 26, 1984, p. 75.

[58]Tomomitsu Oba (director general of the International Finance Bureau), "Tokyo Financial Market Ready for International Business," *Oriental Economist*, August 1982, p. 26. See also "The Yen-Dollar Relationship, Macro-Economic Policy, Financial and Capital Markets and Related Issues," *Keidanren Papers no. 10* (November 1983), pp. 93–96.

markets was at least partly to blame. The internationalization of Japan's financial markets and of the yen must be placed on the negotiating agenda, the Americans argued. Facing a presidential election year in 1984, Reagan could not afford to leave the U.S. trade deficit and dissatisfaction of American banks unaddressed. President Reagan and Prime Minister Nakasone agreed to meet in Tokyo in the fall of 1984 for a discussion of the exchange rate and other financial market issues.[59]

To lay the groundwork for a U.S.-Japan summit, Treasury Secretary Donald Regan and Finance Minister Noboru Takeshita met secretly in Honolulu in September 1983. Using the Solomon-Murchison Report as a basis for discussion, the Americans requested Japanese cooperation to boost the attractiveness of the yen as a means of correcting the bilateral trade imbalance. To concerns about the yen-dollar rate, the American government also added the plight of foreign banks and securities companies in Japan.[60]

Toward the end of October 1983, the Japanese cabinet announced a Comprehensive Economic Plan, obviously in anticipation of Reagan's visit. As measures to increase the international demand for yen, the Japanese government would (1) abolish the "real demand" principle in forward transactions in the foreign exchange market, to render the yen less risky for investors to hold (though the principle had not been enforced for some time); (2) establish a yen bankers' acceptances market; and (3) reexamine the barriers to foreign direct investment in Japan, such as the oft-cited exclusion of eleven "designated companies" from foreign investors. In addition, the government would study the problems of foreign financial institutions in the Japanese market.[61]

When President Reagan arrived in Tokyo in early November 1983, Treasury Secretary Regan was with him. And while Reagan

[59] *Kinyū Jiyūka to En no Kokusaika* (Tokyo: Kinyū Zaisei Jijō Kenkyūkai, 1985), p. 85. The MOF's International Finance Bureau Annual Report suggests that Reagan latched onto Japan's financial deregulation as a pre-campaign issue because Benigno Aquino's assassination in September 1983 destroyed the president's plans for a splashy Asia tour. *Kokusai Kinyū Kyoku Nenkan*, 1985, pp. 49–50.

[60] Morio Okazaki, "Nihon no Kigyō Kinyū—sono Kokusaika no Genjō," *Kikan Keizai Kenkyū*, Spring 1986, p. 17.

[61] *Kinyū Jiyūka to En no Kokusaika*; "Comprehensive Economic Measures," *Focus Japan*, December 1983, p. 10.

and Nakasone spoke mutually encouraging words, Secretary Regan and Minister Takeshita hammered out a detailed list of measures, in addition to those enumerated in the Comprehensive Economic Plan, designed to bolster the attractiveness of yen-denominated investment instruments. Perhaps the most concrete result of Reagan's Japan trip was the establishment of a bilateral team of officials to continue working on the exchange rate issue. This Joint Japan-U.S. Ad Hoc Group on Yen/Dollar Exchange Rate and Financial and Capital Market Issues would meet six times between January and June 1984.[62]

Although the Ministry of Finance had agreed at the outset to a number of liberalizing measures, the Japanese and American agendas were by no means identical. In a Diet statement in February 1984, Minister of Finance Noboru Takeshita averred that the dollar's excessive strength against a number of currencies including the yen—not the overvaluation of the yen—was a major cause of economic disputes between Japan and the United States.[63] The Japanese would press the United States to undertake efforts to pare down the U.S. government budget deficit as part of the yen-dollar negotiations.[64] Nonetheless, the Japanese knew they would have to take some sort of action to avert a rupture in economic ties with Washington.

The primary constraints on the Japanese bureaucrats were, as in the past, MOF and BOJ reluctance to forfeit some measure of control over the domestic money supply with the internationalization of the yen and the political strength of a large number of weak Japanese financial institutions.[65] MOF and BOJ reluctance to em-

[62]"En-Doru Mondai ga Shimesu Nichibei Masatsu no Kōzu," *Nikkei*, November 14, 1983, p. 2; "Bei Kinyū Kaikoku Unagasu," *Nikkei*, November 15, 1983, p. 1; *Kinyū Jiyūka to En no Kokusaika*, pp. 87–88.

[63]"Government Will Relax Restrictions on Financial Deals," *Japan Times*, February 22, 1984.

[64]"Report on Yen/Dollar Exchange Rate Issues," by the Japanese Ministry of Finance and the U.S. Department of the Treasury Working Group (May 1984), pp. 3–4.

[65]Mondo Ōkura, *Ōkurashō Ginkō Kyoku* (Tokyo: Pāru Shuppan, 1985), pp. 80–81. Tetsu Ueda, a JSP representative in the Diet, blamed U.S.-Japan economic friction on the LDP heel dragging; "Government Will Relax Restriction on Financial Deals," *Japan Times*, February 22, 1984; "Yuro-en Tōshi Shijō o," *Yomiuri*, February 25, 1984; "Gyōmu Han'i Nado Chōsei," *Nikkei*, February 25, 1984.

brace change, apparently, was not easy for Secretary Regan to bear. In a speech before the Keidanren in March 1984, he steamed, "I'm about to run out of patience. . . . How much more patience do you want? My response is: action, action, action [punctuating his words with a pounding fist], that's what I want now. I'm through with patience."[66]

American banks, for their part, did not want the U.S. government's concern with strengthening the yen to overshadow or work against the banks' interests. Increased use of the yen as an international trade-financing and investment currency, after all, would likely take some business away from the American banks whose global advantage was their ready access to dollar sourcing and investments. If all Japanese bank deposit rates were fully deregulated, then foreign banks in Japan would certainly have a smaller cost disadvantage in transacting business in Japan. But clearly the rates on small deposits, still the bulk of funds for most Japanese banks, would be the last to become market-based, and foreign banks wanted more immediate relief.[67]

Fortunately for American banks, one highly visible issue in Japanese finance was vulnerable to reciprocity threats: pension fund management. Though despairing of great possibilities in commercial banking in Japan in the near future, foreign banks eyed with undisguised enthusiasm the large pool of Japanese corporate pension funds that heretofore filled only the coffers of Japanese trust banks and insurance companies. The pension market's rapid expansion reflected an aging population and the shift from lump-sum retirement payments to annuity schemes. Amounting to some 10 trillion yen in 1982, the outstanding volume of pensions in trusts was expected to reach 60 trillion yen by 1996, a huge pension market second only to that in the United States.[68]

Foreign banks also had the good fortune to have ready-made

[66]Presentation by Secretary Donald Regan at the American Center, Tokyo (March 24, 1984), cited in Jeffrey Frankel, "The 1984 Campaign for Liberalization," p. 71. See also *Kinyū Jiyūka to En no Kokusaika*, p. 88; *New York Times*, March 25, 1984, which quotes Regan telling reporters, "We find it intolerable; . . . it has been all conversations and no action."

[67]Interviews with foreign bankers in Tokyo, July–September 1986.

[68]Eamonn Fingleton, "The Lure of Japan's Open Door," *Euromoney*, March 1986, pp. 71–82; interview with a Japanese trust bank officer, 7 November 1985.

allies in Japan. In the summer of 1982 Morgan Guaranty Trust Company and the Nomura Securities Company, Japan's largest brokerage house, proposed a joint venture to manage pension fund money.[69] This proposal was bolder than it sounds, because in Japan not even regular banks, let alone securities firms, were permitted to enter what had been since World War II the private preserve of eight licensed trust banks. Following this lead, three other pairs of American banks and Japanese securities firms put in their bids for joint ventures; Japanese city banks lost no time in requesting licenses for themselves. For the Japanese securities firms and city banks, foreign pressure was a boon of potentially giant proportions.[70]

By 1983 trust banking had made its way onto the American government's list of desired reforms in Japan's financial system, made possible by Congress's new rendering of "national treatment" to mean "equality of competitive opportunity." American bank access to Japan's pension fund market, if anything, would exert downward pressure on the yen since presumably much of the money would be invested in foreign instruments with which foreign banks had the greatest experience. But, then, consistency was not a U.S. government strength in the "yen-dollar" negotiations. The U.S. government, like the Japanese, was responding to domestic political pressures.[71] Four European banks gladly joined the fray, making nine foreign banks seeking trust banking licenses.

The success of Japanese banks abroad made them vulnerable to foreign threats. In London, for example, the Japanese have the largest foreign banking presence, with a 15 percent share of sterling deposits.[72] For when Japanese firms began to use the Euromarket,

[69]Pauly, *Opening Financial Markets,* gives a thorough account of the trust banking episode, so the discussion here will be brief.

[70]"Shintaku Sannyū Mondai no Shiten," *Kinyū Zaisei Jijō,* April 30, 1984, p. 21. A cartoon in a finance journal depicts a foreigner yanking on a closed door marked "Corporate Pensions." Tugging on the foreigner in hopes of getting in the same door are a Japanese banker and a securities man. "Kyōchō Shugi no Haigo ni Chiratsuku Kenkin Unyō Seido Henkaku e no Shiwaku," *Kinyū Bijinesu,* May 1986, p. 14.

[71]Jeffrey A. Frankel, in "The 1984 Campaign for Liberalization of Japanese Capital Markets," notes other examples of measures urged upon Japan, such as the yen bankers' acceptance market, which would not necessarily bolster the value of the yen (p. 40).

[72]Kevin Rafferty, "Will Japan Open up Its Pension Market?" *Institutional Investor,* January 1985, pp. 74–75.

Japanese financial institutions followed them there rather than lose the business to European or American competitors. Moreover, in Europe Japanese banks enjoy at least partial exemption from section 65 of the Securities Exchange Act, which keeps them out of the domestic securities market. The possibility of foreign-imposed restrictions on highly profitable overseas banking operations was enough to send chills through Japan's entire banking community.

Because the city banks and securities companies have vast networks within Japanese industry, the trust banks feared their assault more than the entry of the foreigners. Indeed, according to one American banker who advised his bank against the license, trust banking in Japan is labor-intensive, with high overhead, and would "require transaction volumes that would be hard to come by given Japanese corporate tendencies to value their Japanese bank connection regardless of the quality of the service."[73] Attention to yield may come more quickly than expected, and the nationwide Pension Fund Association (Kōsei Nenkin Kikin Rengōkai), representing the pension funds of over one thousand corporations, has already talked about unbundling the pension packages so that trusts and insurers would have to compete based on their performance records. But the competitive edge of the foreign trusts would have to be considerable to cut through the web of reciprocity ties that link company to bank.[74]

The final disposition in June 1984 of the trust banking controversy came as expected, though not before Secretary Regan levied sharp criticism at the slow pace of decision making. The MOF finally granted a license to all nine of the foreign banks that applied, under the condition that they establish separate trust banking subsidiaries rather than add the trust function to existing branch offices. But no Japanese banks or securities firms managed to use the foreign pressure to break into the pension market.[75]

[73]Robert L. Sharp, "Trust Banking in Japan: Less than Meets the Eye," *East Asian Executive Reports* 7 (March 1985), p. 8.

[74]Rafferty, "Will Japan Open up Its Pension Market?" pp. 73–78; interviews with Japanese and foreign bankers in Tokyo, 1986.

[75]Pauly, *Opening Financial Markets*; Isamu Sakurai (chairman of Sumitomo Trust and chairman of the Trust Banks Association), "Honrai no Shintaku Gyōmu Tenkai no Toki ga Kita," *Kinyū Zaisei Jijō*, April 21, 1986, pp. 22–26. As a quid for the trust banks' quo, legislation passed in May 1986 allowed the Japanese government (national, prefectural, local) to entrust its land to the trust banks. Every year

Controversy over membership of foreign securities firms in the Tokyo Stock Exchange generated a similar episode under the umbrella of the yen-dollar talks. To American annoyance, the Ministry of Finance took the position that the Tokyo Stock Exchange was "an autonomous membership organization, and that the government was not in a position to determine the terms and price of membership."[76] The Tokyo Stock Exchange (TSE) had already amended its rules in 1981 to permit, in principle, non-Japanese securities firms to become members.[77] Now the problem was unavailability of seats, as the TSE fixed its number at eighty-three and allowed new members only as space became available through a merger or the voluntary sale of a seat. But intransigence was a dangerous game for the securities industry to play, since they enjoyed expanding, profitable operations overseas. The Big Four, in fact, were eyeing membership on the London Stock Exchange and licensing in the United States as primary brokers of U.S. government bonds, but faced retaliatory exclusion if Japan remained closed. In June 1985 the Tokyo Stock Exchange announced the addition of ten new seats; in December six seats were awarded to foreign bidders, and the remaining four to Japanese securities houses.[78] In December 1986 seats were granted to sixteen more foreign securities firms.[79]

The Yen-Dollar Committee and the Euroyen Market

Although American financial institutions had managed to position themselves on the U.S. government's agenda, the primary task,

---

the trust banks receive a fee of 5–10 percent of the annual rental income in exchange for developing and administering the land and also are given a role in financing development projects. *Kinyū Jānaru*, June 1986.

[76] Report by the Working Group of the Joint Japan-U.S. Ad Hoc Group on Yen/Dollar Exchange Rate, Financial and Capital Market Issues (May 1984), p. 41.

[77] Office of the U.S. Trade Representative, "Japanese Barriers to U.S. Trade," pp. 41–42.

[78] Also in December 1985 foreign banks were permitted to open 50 percent-owned securities branches in Tokyo in recognition of Japanese banks' right to do the same in Europe; "Ōshūgin, Nihon ni Shōken Shinshutsu," *Nikkei*, February 2, 1986; "The Power of Reciprocity," *Economist*, December 7, 1985, p. 91; "Kinyū Shijō Sarani Kaihō Yōkyū," *Nikkei*, March 6, 1986; "Ōshū Kinyū Kaihō de Tainichi Kōsei," *Nikkei*, March 15, 1986.

[79] Cynthia Owens, "Fending Off the Foreigners," *Euromoney*, February 1988, p. 34.

as articulated in the Solomon-Murchison Report, was to increase the demand for yen by making capital inflows to Japan more attractive as the market was liberalized. Japan had already been moving in that direction for some time, since corporations had foreign currency alternatives to domestic bank deposits. But there were still pockets of rigidity, particularly in small deposits, and in certain market segments.

Rather than take on the Japanese domestic system in a frontal assault, the U.S. government decided on the indirect approach of liberalizing the Euroyen market. Enlarging the pool of market-based yen investment options outside Japan's borders presumably would help increase the value of the yen by increasing the foreign demand for yen-denominated financial assets. But beyond that it would increase the arbitrage opportunities between the international and domestic markets, and thus vitiate artificial restrictions on any financial instruments in Japan for which there were close substitutes overseas.[80]

Though indirect, the implications of this tack were not lost on the Japanese. The Bank of Japan's concern, as in the case of the International Banking Facility, was that monetary policy would be more difficult to implement effectively in the event of arbitrage between the domestic and Euroyen markets, as long as there was not a large short-term government bond market in which to conduct open market operations. If only the Ministry of Finance would stop trying to suppress the costs of government debt through an artificial interest rate structure, said BOJ officials, the central bank could cope more readily with internationalization.[81] Not so, said Ministry of Finance bureaucrats. Fears of runaway credit expansion are unfounded, they contended, since most of the yen returns to Japan for settlement of transactions.[82]

The Ministry of Finance had traditionally been wary of the expansion of yen transactions outside Japan's borders, because both the yen exchange rate and domestic interest rates would be increasingly

[80] Kinyū Jiyūka to En no Kokusaika, pp. 88–89.

[81] See, for example, Akira Oka (managing director, Bank of Japan), "Tanki Kinyū Shijō Jiyūka no Hōkō to Kinyū Seisaku," *Kinyū Zaisei Jijō,* April 20, 1981; Atsushi Fijiyama, "Kongo no Kinyū Seisaku to TB Shijō Sōsetsu no Igi," *Kinyū Jānaru,* June 1985, pp. 15–20.

[82] Kōzō Yamamoto (International Finance Bureau, Research Division), "Yuroen Shijō o Meguru Tsusetsuteki Kensai e no Gimon," *Nikkei,* September 20, 1984.

out of domestic control. Since the first yen bond issued outside Japan in 1977 by the European Investment Bank, only a few Euroyen bonds were placed each year by sovereign or public institutions. The Ministry of Finance barred Japanese and foreign private corporations from the Euroyen market altogether. Meanwhile, pointing to high U.S. interest rates instead of low Japanese yields, the MOF continued to disagree with the U.S. Treasury as to the reason for the yen-dollar misalignment. Hence, the MOF questioned the usefulness of the Euroyen market in correcting the problem.

Perhaps with the most to lose were the long-term credit banks and trust banks whose prosperity depended in substantial part on the jurisdictional division in Japan between long-term and short-term financing. These specialty banks' primary source of funding are fixed-interest, long-term debentures; they understandably feared contagion from the Euromarket, where no such distinctions hold.[83]

Japanese corporations, on the other hand, were the strongest domestic proponents of Euroyen market deregulation, since yen-denominated bond issuance in the Euromarket would both afford competitive financing terms and obviate the need for currency swaps or other devices used for hedging the foreign exchange risk entailed in foreign currency bonds. Moreover, once the yen had become accepted as a world-class investment currency, foreign importers and exporters would be more willing to denominate trade settlement transactions in yen, thus giving Japanese corporations an additional hedge against currency fluctuations.

Japanese securities firms also stood to gain from greater use of yen in the Euromarket, insofar as Japanese securities houses had a comparative advantage over their foreign counterparts in placing yen-denominated financial instruments.

The interests of even the city banks were too complicated to warrant a policy of simple obstructionism. In spite of the MOF's Three Bureaus Agreement, there were considerable profits to be made in securities transactions in the Euromarket, particularly as foreign corporations began to issue Euroyen bonds. Since the early 1980s, in fact, city banks had begun upgrading their international and securities sections into full divisions at the top level of bank

[83] Morio Okazaki, "Nihon no Kigyō Kinyū—Sono Kokusaika no Genjō," *Kikan Keizai Kenkyū*, Spring 1986, pp. 17–18.

management. But of course banks would fight to minimize the number of Japanese firms eligible to issue yen-based bonds in the Euromarket.[84]

In May 1984, after five meetings since its establishment in November 1983, the Working Group of the Joint Japan-U.S. Ad Hoc Group on Yen/Dollar Exchange Rate, Financial and Capital Market Issues (hereafter "Yen-Dollar Committee") issued a report on their agreements. Among various categories of liberalization measures to be taken, the Euroyen market would be further liberalized. Effective April 1, 1984, restrictions on Japanese corporate access to the Euroyen bond market had been relaxed to permit approximately thirty firms to issue straight, unsecured Euroyen bonds and one hundred firms to issue convertible Euroyen bonds. These firms accounted for over 70 percent of the straight bonds and 40 to 60 percent of convertible bonds issued in the domestic market.[85]

Under the new agreement, non-Japanese private corporations and foreign government bodies were authorized to issue bonds, on an unsecured basis, in the Euroyen market as of December 1, 1984. Qualification standards initially were to be those applied in the samurai market, which allowed access to corporations with a rating of A or better *and* which met certain strict financial criteria.

A further relaxation was scheduled for April 1, 1985, granting eligibility to Japanese corporations with a credit rating of AA or better as well as a "reasonable portion of the universe of world corporations whose outstanding debt would be rated A." This raised the number of Japanese companies eligible to issue Euroyen bonds to approximately 145. Moreover, both residents and non-residents would be able, without limitation, to swap nonyen bond issues into yen using either forward exchange markets or currency swaps. Later, in January 1985, the MOF agreed to exempt from

[84] For a description of Mitsubishi Bank's major restructuring effort, see Sei Serizawa, "Mitsubishi Ginkō Soshiki Kaisei no Nerai to Tokuchō," *Kinyū Zaisei Jijō*, November 3, 1986, pp. 47–51. Tellingly, the subtitle of the article translates, "Toward the Establishment of an International Universal Banking Structure." Other banks have adapted similarly.

[85] These numbers represented a compromise between the banks, which wanted fewer corporations to qualify, and the securities firms, which wanted two or three hundred corporations to be granted eligibility. "Kaikin Mokuzen Ginkō Shōken Tsubazeriai," *Yomiuri*, March 3, 1984; "Gaiatsu, Kokusai ni Osare," *Mainichi*, March 9, 1984; "Shikakenin wa Beizaikai," *Sankei*, April 3, 1984.

81

Japanese withholding tax all nonresident earnings from Euroyen bonds issued by residents.[86] But in order to shield the collateral principle in the domestic bond market from imminent demise, the proceeds from Euroyen bond issuance were not to be repatriated to Japan until 180 days after issuance.[87]

The Ministry of Finance did not give in to every American request. The Japanese government did not agree to institute a secondary Treasury Bill market, would not deregulate small-denomination deposits for the time being, and would not allow Euroyen lending for maturities longer than one year.[88]

In order to utilize pressure from abroad more selectively, the MOF had established a special Subcommittee on the Internationalization of the Tokyo Market, under the Foreign Exchange Advisory Council, to examine the matters under review by the Yen-Dollar Committee. This body was headed by the chairman of the Bank of Tokyo, Yūsuke Kashiwagi (formerly MOF vice-minister for international affairs), and included twelve other members from banks, securities firms, private corporations, and academe. Their recommendations, issued on May 30, 1984, only partially overlapped with the conclusions of the Yen-Dollar Committee.

The MOF's goal in invoking the subcommittee's study was not to stall on domestic deregulation but to take it beyond the scope of the Yen-Dollar Committee's concern. For although yen internationalization might weaken control of the domestic money supply, a competitive parallel market in Europe would aid the MOF in promoting efficiency and consolidation in the domestic financial system. "Foreign pressure" could be a convenient device for blunting a

[86]"Report of the MOF/Treasury Working Group on Withholding Taxes" (January 7, 1985); "Hikyojūsha Yuroensai Tekisai Kijun no Kanwa ni tsuite," *Kinyū Zaisei Jijō,* April 8, 1985, p. 43; "Ichiren no Kokusai Kaigi," *Kinyū Bijinesu,* July 1985, pp. 12–13.

[87]"Report by the Working Group of the Joint Japan-U.S. Ad Hoc Group on the Yen/Dollar Exchange Rate, Financial and Capital Market Issues" (May 1984), p. 49.

[88]Steven Cerier, "Overview of Japan's Financial Structure," Foreign Exchange Advisory Service, Manufacturers Hanover New York (June 20, 1984), pp. 3–4; Jay Yang, "Japan's Financial Liberalization and Yen Internationalization," *World Financial Markets,* June 1984, pp. 1–11.

domestic backlash against the MOF.[89] The subcommittee's most significant additions were (1) the category "market stability," which included familiar recommendations to bolster the deposit insurance scheme and to strengthen disclosure rules for financial institutions; and (2) a resuscitation of the Tokyo offshore banking market idea.[90]

In March 1985 the subcommittee issued a second report, endorsing yen internationalization for domestic as well as for foreign diplomatic reasons. Japanese financial institutions, it noted, would likely benefit from increased use of the yen in international transactions, and Japanese importers and exporters could hedge exchange rate risks by denominating in their own currency. As a way of encouraging use of yen in investment and trade financing, the report urged continued deregulation of Euroyen transactions and, again, the establishment of a Tokyo offshore market.[91]

The MOF continued to loosen the restrictions on the Euroyen market. The total outstanding amount of Euroyen bond issues had already surged from 70 billion yen in 1983 to 1.6 trillion yen in 1986. This amount surpassed that of yen bonds issued in Japan by foreign borrowers, because the Bond Arrangement Committee continued to move slowly on domestic bond market deregulation. Effective April 1, 1986, further relaxation of Euroyen restrictions allowed Japanese corporations to issue currency conversion and floating rate Euroyen bonds, in addition to the fixed-rate bonds already permitted. The holding time before repatriating funds to Japan from abroad was reduced from 180 to 90 days. And nonresident firms with credit ratings of A or better were permitted to issue

---

[89]Tomomitsu Ōba (MOF vice-minister of International Affairs), "En no Kokusaika o Megutte," speech at the annual meeting of the Federation of Bankers Associations (December 1985); Hiroshi Takeuchi, "Internationalization of Financial Market in Japan," *Asian Wall Street Journal*, September 7, 1986.

[90]Gaikoku Kawase Nado Shingikai, Senmon Bukai (Foreign Exchange Advisory Commission subcommittee), "Kinyū no Jiyūka Oyobi En no Kokusaika ni Tsuite no Genjō to Tenbō," May 30, 1984; partial translation in *Money and Finance*, August–September 1984, pp. 1–12.

[91]Whereas Euroyen transactions had already been deregulated to a considerable extent, medium- and long-term Euroyen loans were snagged on the domestic division between long-term and short-term banks. Subcommittee on Foreign Exchange and Other Transactions, "Internationalization of the Yen," March 5, 1985.

Euroyen bonds, increasing the number of authorized foreign firms from 150 to 200.[92]

The Reemergence of the Offshore Market

The subcommittee's endorsement of the Tokyo offshore market came unsolicited from the Americans this time. As long as foreign banks would be prevented from raising funds on the offshore market for use in domestic operations, it would be of little use to them. And to the extent that section 65 applied to IBF activities, even Japanese banks would still conduct most of their international financial business overseas, where they were free to engage in securities activities. But there was a new coalition of enthusiasts joining the bureaucrats in the International Finance Bureau: politicians and regional banks. Politicians were always looking for uncontroversial causes to sponsor, and smaller banks lacking foreign branches hoped to gain access to international finance without the expense of establishing foreign branches.[93]

On December 29, 1984, a group of fifty-three LDP politicians formed the Dietmember's League for the Promotion of an International Market (Kokusai Shijō Ikusei Giin Renmei). The politicians selected from among themselves Yoshitake Sasaki and Seiichi Ohta to lead and coordinate.[94] Both Sasaki and Ohta were respected for their grasp of economic policy matters; Sasaki was a former bureaucrat in the Economic Planning Agency, Ohta had

[92] Atsushi Arichi (MOF International Finance Bureau, Foreign Capital Division), "Yuroensai Jiyūka no Shinten to Hakkō Jōkyō," *Kinyū Zaisei Jijō*, October 28, 1985, pp. 34–35; "Ōkurashō, Yuroensai nado no Kisei o Ōhaba Kanwa," *Kinyū Zaisei Jijō*, April 7, 1986, p. 53; Nobuyoshi Araki, "Kinyū Jiyūka Unagasu En no Kokusaika," *Ekonomisuto*, April 14, 1986, p. 84; Shōji Mori (MOF International Finance Bureau, Foreign Capital Division), "Yuroensai Jiyūka e Kisei Ōhaba Kanwa," *Kinyū Zaisei Jijō*, April 21, 1986, pp. 20–21.

[93] "Ofushoa Shijō o," *Mainichi*, October 10, 1984; "Tokyo Ofushoa Shijō Sōsetsu ni Iyoku," *Nikkan Kōgyō*, January 22, 1985; Richard Hanson, "MOF Putting the IBF on Positive Study," *Japan Financial Report*, February 25, 1985, p. 2; "Tokyo Ofushoa Shijō 61 Nendo nimo Sōsetsu," *Nikkei*, March 6, 1985; "Nichigin mo Kekkyoku Kentō," *Nikkei*, March 7, 1985.

[94] "Tokyo o Kokusai Kinyū Shijō," *Nikkei*, December 30, 1984; "Ginkō, Seijika Tōshin Sakidori," *Nikkei*, March 28, 1985.

been a professor of economics, and both were from outlying districts where small banks are particularly strong.[95]

Many of the politicians in the league were unclear as to exactly what an offshore market was, and some initially were allured by the presumed possibility of a massive landfill and construction project somewhere out in Tokyo Bay.[96] Others perhaps were hoping to parlay the popular notion of "internationalization" into flattering news coverage. But all were drawn to the idea of promoting Tokyo as a center of international finance, particularly a center that would benefit even the local banks back in the district. The league convened monthly, reviewing materials prepared by the International Finance Bureau and by various financial institutions that were asked to prepare statements.[97]

The league grew in popularity within the LDP and eventually nearly doubled in size.[98] But not all went smoothly for the Diet members. In a survey of 108 financial institutions conducted in March 1985 by the Japan Center for International Finance, less than 43 percent of the respondents declared unqualified interest in an offshore market; 48.15 percent favored its establishment only under certain conditions.[99] The deregulation of the Euromarket had already swept aside the concern of the long-term credit banks and trust banks that their monopoly in long-term banking be further eroded. Now the dispute was between banks and securities firms over section 65.[100]

---

[95]*Seikan Yōran* (Tokyo: Seisaku Jihosha, 1985), pp. 62, 258.

[96]Bureaucrats in the International Finance Bureau delight in recounting the politicians' misinterpretation of "offshore."

[97]"Tokyo o Kokusai Kinyū Shijō," *Nikkei*, December 30, 1984; "Liberalization Makes Tokyo Grow into a World Finance Center," *Japan Economic Journal*, July 26, 1985.

[98]Though this group attracted many ex-MOF bureaucrats, including Kiichi Miyazawa, Ganri Yamashita, Tatsuo Murayama, Takujirō Hamada, and Jun Shiozaki, there were also "nonfinancial types" such as Susumu Nikaido and Mutsuki Katō. "Kokusai Shijō Ikusei Giin Renmei," International Finance Bureau documents.

[99]Ken Matsui, "Saifujōshita Tokyo Ofushoa Shijō Kōsō," *Kokusai Kinyū*, July 1, 1985, p. 44.

[100]"Jitsugen ni Mukau Tokyo IBF Kōsō," *Kinyū Zaisei Jijō*, March 18, 1985, pp. 26–27; Hideo Kiuchi, "Tokyo IBF Sōsetsu ni Atsui Kitai Yoseru Gaitame Burōkā,"

The securities industry wanted securities transactions included in the offshore market; that is, they wanted interest payments to nonresidents from samurai bonds and other foreign securities exempted from withholding tax and trading exempted from stamp tax and transactions tax. Their argument was twofold: (1) in an age of "securitization" in international finance (the substitution of papers sold or traded on the market for bank loans), to limit Japan's offshore market to a commercial banking center would ignore the global trend and cut Japanese institutions (securities firms) out of the profits to be made; (2) granting tax relief to commercial banking activities without doing the same for securities firms was unfair.[101]

Banks did not object to securitization per se, but cared a great deal about who would be able to benefit from it. Their greatest fear was that securities firms would use an offshore securities market to underwrite and trade commercial paper, thereby seizing much of the banks' short-term loan business. Banks would agree to an offshore securities market only if they could join in this business. To this counterproposal, the securities firms objected vociferously. Rather than allow such an egregious encroachment into their territory, the securities industry would prefer not to get involved in the offshore market at all.[102]

This turf battle continued to roil for some time, surfacing only occasionally into public news. On September 2, 1985, a preliminary report of the Advisory Council's subcommittee stated it was considering ways of preventing tax leakage through the trading of offshore securities. But on the following day the same subcommittee stated that there would be no participation of securities firms in the offshore market.[103] The Dietmen's League, nevertheless still interested in the possibility of including securities activities, dispatched a

Zaisei Shōhō, April 22, 1985, pp. 13–15; Andreas Prindl, "Japan Steps Out Gingerly," *Banking World,* April 1985, pp. 26–18.

[101]"Ofushoa Shijō to Shōken Gyōmu," statement prepared by one of the Big Four securities firms (June 17, 1985), pp. 4–5.

[102]Fuji Bank Research Division, "Kentō Dankai ni Haitta Tokyo Ofushoa Shijō Sōsetsu," *Fuji Times,* June 1985, pp. 9–10; Takehiko Isaka, "Ginki, Shōken no Kaigai Shinsutsu to Ofushoa Shijō Sōsetsu," *Kinyū Jānaru,* March 1986, pp. 35–38.

[103]"Ofushoa Shijō Kokkaku Katamaru," *Nikkei,* September 2 and 3, 1985.

group of their members on a fact-finding mission to New York, Washington, and London from September 8 through 15.[104]

While the politicians were still away, Takashi Hosomi, the author of the original IBF idea, issued his "Offshore Market, Plan II," which included offshore securities activities. Because the traditional deposit and loan business is a declining part of international finance, Hosomi asserted, Tokyo would have to provide securities services if it wanted to be a world-class market.[105] On September 21, the *Nikkei Shimbun* editorial staff supported Hosomi, arguing that an international financial market without securities transactions did not make sense in this day.[106] The Advisory Council's subcommittee, however, stayed with its earlier conclusion in its final recommendation to the MOF on September 18, 1985. Beset by irreconcilable differences between the banks and securities firms within its ranks, it called for the minimalist solution of allowing only commercial banking operations offshore.[107]

The debate was still not over. As the MOF proceeded to package the offshore market in legal text for passage through the Diet, both the banking and securities industries continued to press their interests. It was now the banking community that sought permission to engage in securities activities in the offshore market and securities firms that fought to protect section 65 even at the cost of blocking themselves from the IBF. The securities industry wanted to ensure that the overseas securities subsidiaries of Japanese banks not gain

[104]"Jimin no Ikusei Giren ga Eibei Shijō ni Shisatsudan," *Nikkei,* September 6, 1985; "Hakusha Kakaru Tokyo IBF Sōsetsu no Ugoki," *Kinyū Zaisei Jijō,* September 16, 1985, pp. 6–7.

[105]Takashi Hosomi, "Tokyo Ofushoa Shijō Sōsetsu ni tsuite no Hosomi Dainiji Shian," *Kinyū Zaisei Jijō,* September 9, 1985, pp. 18–25; "Hosomishi ga Dainiji Shian," *Mainichi Shimbun,* September 7, 1985.

[106]*Nikkei* editorial, September 21, 1985.

[107]Tokyo Shijō no Kokusaika ni Kansuru Senmon Bukai (Special Committee on the Internationalization of the Tokyo Market), "Tokyo Ofushoa Shijō no Sōsetsu ni tsuite," September 18, 1985; "Gaitameshin Senmon Bukai ga Hokoku," *Nikkei,* September 19, 1985; Hiroshi Tomizawa (chief of International Finance Bureau, Research Division), "Gaitameshin Senmon Bukai Tokyo Ofushoa Shijō de Hōkokusho," *Kinyū Zaisei Jijō,* September 30, 1985, pp. 16–17; Tomo Miyamura, "Soto-soto Gentei ni Nyūyōkugata o Tenbō," *Kinyū Zaisei Jijō,* October 14, 1985, pp. 20–23.

entry into the underwriting business in the offshore market.[108] At one point in December a leak to the newspapers seemed to indicate that a compromise had been reached, allowing limited tax-free investment in samurai bonds from IBF accounts.[109] But securities firms ultimately rejected this step on the grounds that, through it, banks would attempt to gain a foothold in the securities business.[110]

The LDP accepted the earlier compromise for a commercial banking center, with the single addition that small financial institutions also be allowed to participate. This overruled the MOF's concern that small banks were not prepared to launch themselves into international lending.[111] Necessary amendments to the Foreign Exchange and Trade Control Law were deliberated on the floor of the Diet and passed in May 1986, with the only reservations coming from Japanese Socialist party finance expert Masao Hori, who asked how the Tokyo IBF was ever going to compete with other offshore centers unless there were more tax and other incentives. Toyoo Gyohten, director general of the International Finance Bureau, answered, "We will start with something small, but will enlarge the scope of the market as circumstances permit." They all knew what he meant: if and when the section 65 barrier between banking and securities activities was lowered or reinterpreted for the Japanese market, the revision would apply to the offshore market as well. Until the banking and securities sectors could agree on a compromise, however, the offshore market would remain a strictly commercial banking facility.[112]

By the time the Japan Offshore Market was instituted in December 1986, it was a far cry either from the original hope of foreign

[108]"Ofushoa to 65 Jō," *Kinyū Zaisei Jijō*, September 23, 1985, p. 34; Mutsuhisa Fujii (IBJ International Management Division), "Ofushoa Shōken Gyōmu e no Kakudai ga Kentō Kadai," *Kinyū Zaisei Jijō*, October 14, 1985, pp. 24–29; "Zenginkyō Yōbōsho," *KZJ*, October 14, 1985, p. 8; Shigeru Aoyama, "Tokyo Ofushoa Shijō Sōsetsu ni tsuite," *Zaikei Shōhō*, October 7, 1985, pp. 2–6; "Saimoku no Gutaika ga Susumu," *KZJ*, December 9, 1985, p. 10.

[109]"Tokyo Ofushoa Shijō Shōken ni mo Sannyū no Michi," *Nikkei*, December 31, 1985.

[110]"Ofushoa Shijō no Shikumi," *Kinyū Jānaru*, March 1986, p. 38.

[111]"Ofushoa Shijō no Sōsetsu ni Tsuite," MOF blueprint for the IBF (March 1986); interviews with MOF bureaucrats, politicians, and small bank officials, 1985–1986, Tokyo.

[112]Proceedings, Lower House Finance Committee, May 16, 1986.

88

banks for an alternative source of funds for their domestic operations or from the subsequent ambitions of the U.S. government for dramatic internationalization of the yen. Foreign bankers expressed their disappointment with the restrictions remaining on Tokyo BIF transactions, and four of them—Deutsche Bank, Credit Suisse, Security Pacific, and Hong Kong & Shanghai—declined to set up IBF accounts.[113] John Loughran, director of Morgan Guaranty's North Asia operations, had testified before the Advisory Council's subcommittee in May 1985: "Theoretically, it is no longer valid for the Japanese regulatory authorities to engage in an intermediate step towards full liberalization by establishing in Japan an IBF structure."[114] But as Loughran was aware, the MOF was bound more by domestic constraints than by theory.

By the end of January 1987, the size of the Japan Offshore Market stood at $115 billion in assets, above the original estimates of the market participants. This figure compares respectably with the New York IBF at $260 billion, Singapore at $140 billion, and Hong Kong at $130 billion, at the end of 1985. But its relatively large size belies its importance, for a large part of the offshore activity consists of fund movements between parent banks' offshore accounts in the Japan Offshore Market and their overseas branches, as well as between banks operating in various offshore markets around the world. As long as the holding and issuance of securities are prohibited in the Japan Offshore Market, Tokyo will be no substitute for the Euromarket.[115]

Shifting Cost-Benefit Calculations and Bank-Driven Deregulation

Despite the Ministry of Finance's years of practice in dealing with foreign pressure of various sorts, its job has not become any easier.

[113] Yūsuke Kashiwagi, "JOM no Hassoku to En Kokusaika no Zentō," *Kinyū Zaisei Jijō*, February 2, 1987, pp. 18–22; "Gaigin ni Ofushoa e no Fuman," *Kinyū Bijinesu*, August 1986, p. 13; "Kitaisho to Kakehanareta Tokyo Ofushoa Shijō," *Kinyū Zaisei Jijō*, November 24, 1986, p. 17.

[114] John F. Loughran, "The IBF's Experience in the U.S.: Relevance for Japan," presented before the Special Subcommittee on the Internationalization of the Tokyo Market (May 14, 1985), pp. 15–16.

[115] Akira Arai, "Bank Domination Dulls Offshore Market Glitter," *Japan Economic Journal*, February 21, 1987, p. 10.

89

Nor would it appear that the United States has become more skilled in wielding its arsenal of sticks and carrots. For in fact it is Japan's domestic circumstances that make the MOF willing to change some things, but tenaciously resistant to tampering with other matters that appear on foreign agendas.

This is not to say that Japan is impervious to involuntary change; there are several avenues through which foreign desires press hard on Japan. This first is at the summit, between Japanese and foreign political leaders. The ruling Liberal Democratic party, and the prime minister in particular, zealously guards at least the public appearance of foreign relations. And since the United States is the country most important to Japan's health and well-being, ties with Washington are treated with utmost care. Although Prime Minister Nakasone capitalized politically on diplomatic finesse more than most Japanese leaders in the recent past, he simply excelled at doing what all Japanese prime ministers must do: keep U.S.-Japan relations on even keel without excessive costs to key domestic interests.[116]

Prime Minister Nakasone personally endorsed the Yen-Dollar Committee negotiations in 1983, urged the MOF to grant licenses to foreign trust banks in 1984, included financial liberalization in his market-opening "Action Program" of July 1985, and commissioned a group headed by former Bank of Japan governor Haruo Maekawa to draw up an impressive list of reforms in time for the Tokyo Summit in May 1986. Nevertheless, many of these "strides" were either in the realm of rhetoric, as in the case of the Maekawa report, or imparted a formal blessing to developments that were occurring for other reasons. The deregulation schedule for large-denomination bank deposits announced in the Action Program, for example, went no further than the small banks would tolerate.[117] And as in the Banking Law controversy between the banking and securities industries, politicians backed off from the dispute over the

[116]More recently, the "strong yen recession" has smudged his record because it smacks of accommodation without sufficient compensation.
[117]Junichi Takagi, "Ōguchi Yokin Kinri Jiyūka no Akushion Puroguramu," *Kinyū Bijinesu*, August 1985, pp. 14–17; Kiyoshi Hosoguchi, "Akushion Puroguramu de Shimesareta Kinri Jiyūka no Tenbō," *Zaikei Shōhō*, August 19, 1985, pp. 27–29; Kazumoto Suzuki, "Kokusai Kinyū Mondai o Meguru Mūdo no Henka," *Zaikei Shōhō*, November 4, 1985, pp. 2–5; "Maekawa Ken Hokoku," *Kinyū Zaisei Jijō*, March 10, 1986, pp. 12–13.

application of section 65 to the IBF. Politicians are themselves, after all, beholden to domestic interest groups and must factor election performance into their policy choices.

The Ministry of Finance may at times be bolder, riding the momentum from foreign pressure to further its own aspiration of consolidation of the financial sector. The Foreign Exchange Advisory Council's subcommittee, as we noted, used the commotion surrounding Yen-Dollar discussions to reopen the sensitive issues of bank disclosure and deposit insurance. The December 1987 agreement in principle of twelve Bank for International Settlements (BIS) member countries to adopt a bank capital-asset ratio of 8 percent by 1992 also buttressed the MOF's drive for stability of the financial system.[118] The MOF's efforts have been only partially successful, as the banks vetoed tougher disclosure provisions and the MOF itself ended up underwriting much of the costs of an upgraded deposit insurance scheme. The BIS capital asset ratio of 8 percent, moreover, will apply only to Japanese banks that operate in foreign markets. The MOF will permit banks with solely domestic operations to reach a 4 percent capital-asset ratio by 1990. For Japanese banks abroad, it is the fear of retaliatory exclusion which serves as the real incentive to match the standards of foreign banks.[119]

[118]Although the MOF had prescribed a 10 percent capital-asset standard for Japanese banks until 1985, when the MOF set a more realistic 4 percent ratio, in practice the top five city banks have capital-asset ratios ranging from 3 to 5 percent, including unrealized capital gains on equity holdings. Japanese banks actually began boosting their domestic capital in the early 1980s to avoid exclusion from foreign markets. In 1983, for example, the city banks began issuing their equity at market instead of at par, as they had traditionally done. On the BIS standard, however, which will allow banks to include only 45 percent of their unrealized capital gains, the banks' capital-asset ratios still range from 2.5 to 3 percent. See S. Matthews, T. Nakagawa, and K. Inoue, "Capital Adequacy and the Big Five City Banks," *Barclays de Zoete Wedd Research*, April 14, 1988. The countries that adopted the recommendations of the Supervisory Committee of the Bank of International Settlements (more commonly known as the Cooke Committee) are the United States, Japan, Germany, Great Britain, France, Italy, Canada, Switzerland, Sweden, the Netherlands, Belgium, and Luxembourg. "BIS Kijun Tassei e Baibaidata Itchō Doru Toppa," *Nikkei*, April 11, 1988; "Jiko Shihon no Sokutei to Kijun ni kansuru Kokusaiteki Tōitsuka e no Teigen," *Kinyū Bijinesu*, May 1988, pp. 68–81.

[119]Hideki Uchida, "Kinyū Seido Chōsakai Seido Mondai de Shingi Saikai," *Kinyū Zaisei Jijō*, October 14, 1985, pp. 14–15; "Jiyūka Taio e Keiei Puroguramu no Kakuritsu o Isoge," *Kinyū Zaisei Jijō*, November 18, 1985, pp. 18–30; Kazuo

Financial Politics in Contemporary Japan

Threats of retaliation are a second and more direct route by which foreign governments effect change in Japan. It is the conspicuous success of Japanese financial institutions abroad that makes them especially vulnerable to foreign demands for at least reciprocal treatment in Japan, a sort of reverse osmosis. From the MOF's point of view, these threats, even though annoying, are the easiest to deal with because little additional maneuvering or cajoling is necessary to persuade the targeted party to accept change. The German government banned lead underwriting of Deutschmark bonds by Japanese financial institutions until the Japanese agreed in 1985 to allow foreign securities firms to act as lead underwriters for Euroyen bonds.[120] Similarly, reciprocity threats by Germany and the United Kingdom forced Japan to allow European universal banks to operate in the Japanese securities market.[121] Indeed, the MOF has granted foreign institutions freedoms that their Japanese counterparts are still denied, thus containing foreign pique without disrupting the domestic equilibrium.

Until recently the U.S. government has resorted to direct threats less frequently than the Europeans, at least partly because of ambiguous domestic interests at home.[122] The U.S. securities industry, for example, is waging its own battle against a reform of the Glass-Steagall wall. American demands have been perceived in Tokyo as threats, albeit somewhat diffused ones.[123] The difficulty for the

---

Fujiwara, "Tempo Tsūtatsu Minaoshi," *Kinyū Zaisei Jijō*, May 19, 1986, pp. 18–19. In April 1988 the Federal Reserve Board, citing the BIS standards, ordered a leasing subsidiary of the Nōrin Chūkin Bank to increase its capital-asset ratio before granting a license. Norin Chukin gave up its plans to operate in the United States rather than attempt to meet the higher capital-asset ratio. "Bei, Shinshutsu ni Bureki," *Nikkei*, April 11, 1988, p. 1.

[120]"Gaigin no Kinyūsai Hakkō," *Kinyū Bijinesu*, August 1985, pp. 64–65.

[121]"Gaigin ni Shiten Ninka," *Nikkei*, June 8, 1985; "Ichiren no Kokusi Kaigi," *Kinyū Bijinesu*, July 1985, pp. 12–13; "Freeing the Euroyen and Samurai Markets," *Euromoney*, June 1986, p. 27.

[122]Stephen Krasner suggests that the United States has only recently begun considering retaliation, or what he calls "specific reciprocity," as a serious trade policy alternative to multilateralism, or "diffuse reciprocity." Krasner, "A Trade Strategy for the United States," *Ethics and International Affairs* 2 (1988), 17–35.

[123]In June 1987 the MOF granted permission to subsidiaries of four American banks to underwrite and trade in Japan securities in Tokyo, for fear of retaliation against Japanese financial institutions possessing or seeking a securities license in the United States. "Hōginkei Shōken no Bei Shinshutsu Yokusei," *Nikkei*, May 31, 1987; Eric Berg, "Japan Lets 4 U.S. Banks Underwrite Securities," *New York Times*, June 4, 1987.

MOF is that the "Japan, Inc." image that seems to inform American views leaves the burden of coercion to the MOF. U.S. insistence that the MOF expand the membership of the Tokyo Stock Exchange, for example, overlooked the extreme care with which the MOF deals with the securities community. The United States got its way, but not before depleting the MOF's limited store of goodwill with the financial community, its regulatory lubricant. Of course, to minimize its own loss, the MOF construed the American demands in the strongest possible terms. The same was true in the trust banking incident.

America's first explicitly retaliatory threat against Japan in the financial arena was a provision in the Omnibus Trade Bill of 1988 that warned of possible curtailment of Japanese participation as primary dealers in the U.S. government securities market if American financial institutions were not granted more substantial involvement in the Japanese government bond syndicate. The Japanese government lost no time in expanding the share of foreign institutions in the government bond syndicate from 2.5 percent to nearly 8 percent and increased the portion of ten-year bonds auctioned from 20 percent to 40 percent.[124] Japanese financial institutions were eager not to trigger the American threat of retaliation because as of September 1988, eight Japanese financial institutions were among the forty-six licensed primary dealers in the United States, a privileged status in underwriting and brokering U.S. Treasury securities. The auction system for U.S. government securities is an open process in which technically any bidder can participate, with no minimum for the bid as long as the offer is competitive. In practice, however, about one-half of the purchasing on the primary market and trading on the secondary market is conducted through primary dealers.

The United States may continue to threaten retaliation against Japanese and other foreign banks that are taking advantage of the loose regulatory environment in the U.S. market without affording similar opportunities to American financial institutions in their domestic markets. But as long as the United States adheres to its more traditional demands for "national treatment" rather than the

[124]"Ginkōkan Yokin no Jiyūka Meguru Ōkurashō, Nichigin no Kakusui," *Kinyū Bijinesu*, August 1985, pp. 62–63; "Tokushū: Henmōsuru Kokusai Hakkō Shijō," *Kinyū Zaisei Jijō*, September 26, 1988, pp. 18–27.

more far-reaching "reciprocity" standard, retaliation will likely play a relatively small role in Japan's financial deregulation.

A third type of outside influence on Japan's financial system is the availability of foreign alternatives to domestic services. More lenient regulations in the Euromarket have led to substantial relaxation of Japan's bond market rules and lending practices. Indeed, the Euromarket's competition for wholesale financial services was far more instrumental in spurring the deregulation of large-denomination deposits and loans in Japan than were American demands for change, however vituperative they may have been.

The barrage of foreign pressures notwithstanding, some aspects of Japan's financial system remain more or less intact. For even when the Japanese feel some concessions are unavoidable, precisely what concessions those should be and which groups domestically will bear the costs are often matters of considerable discretion. This surviving configuration is a topological map, as it were, of the ever changing landscape of power and interest in Japan's financial sector. Much as in domestic regulatory legislative change, the forging of new international accords forces the parties involved to match strength with strength, leaving behind a clearer delineation of what each is desirous and capable of preserving. As the theory of regulation would predict, the financial industry agreed to forgo protective regulation only when changed international circumstances rendered that regulation no longer beneficial.

That the U.S. government's diplomatic onslaught in the 1980s left much unchanged in Japan's financial system was not simply because the MOF was able to capitalize on various inconsistencies in the long American wish list. Potentially contradictory requests, such as to increase the value of the yen and to remove capital controls, did afford the MOF an added measure of maneuverability, at least in the realm of rhetoric. More fundamentally, the pockets of institutional survival reflect the domestic powers to which the MOF itself is accountable.

Though not unscathed, the walls that have divided various types of financial institutions since World War II still stand, because of the tenacity of entrenched interests and vigilant monitoring from the MOF's watchtower. City banks, for example, will be barred from making long-term loans in the Euroyen market until the long-term credit banks and trust banks receive suitable compensation, such as expanded securities powers. Foreign bank entry into the trust banking business probably set back the timetable for a bargain since that episode raised the trust banks' price of an additional compromise. It is the political power of these various groups rather than economic rationale that protects them, but the MOF is capable of forging and enforcing compromises among them as circumstances, such as a changed pattern of profit-making opportunities, require.

The MOF has also managed to fend off foreign demands for a short-term government bills market. For two decades the MOF has benefited from the predictability and low cost of placing its bonds with the Government Bond Syndicate. Although the price of government bonds has increasingly followed the dictates of supply and demand, the predictability of placing medium- and long-term bonds still makes the Finance Bureau officials' lives somewhat easier than they would be otherwise. The strongest resistance to a full-fledged short-term government bond market, however, comes from the banks, which realize that Treasury Bills would make inroads into their deposit bases.[125]

Third, the entire array of retail financial services remains little affected by the wave of financial deregulation. Given that small depositors and borrowers have few good substitutes for traditional postal deposits, bank accounts, and loans, financial institutions have not been forced to compete more fervidly for their customers.[126] International finance is an inherently wholesale business. Lacking international alternatives, consumers of retail financial services will have to await the outcome of the slower domestic competitive process between domestic banks and the postal savings system.

[125] "Ginkōkan Yokin no Jiyūka Meguru Ōkurashō, Nichigin no Kakusui," *Kinyū Bijinesu*, August 1985, pp. 62–63.

[126] The Ministry of Finance and the Ministry of Posts and Telecommunications have agreed that small-denomination deposits will be deregulated. A compromise between the two groups fixes short-term small deposits (3 million yen) to large-denomination CD rates and longer-term small deposits to government bond coupons. See Yō Makino, "Banks Brace for Free Market as Rate-Decontrol Era Dawns," *Japan Economic Journal*, October 29, 1988, p. 1.

4

The Banking Act
of 1982

The Banking Act of 1982 was the first comprehensive revision of banking legislation since 1927. In spite of the years, indeed decades, of debate that preceded the new law, only two provisions stand out. First, banks would be permitted to retail and deal in government bonds. Second, in an affirmation of the status quo, banks would not face substantially stricter disclosure requirements.

These two provisions in the new law are remarkable, if not in substance then certainly for what they tell us about financial policy making in Japan. Most factors are held constant, since the stage is set within the same political and economic environment and the same configuration of interest groups. But the processes leading to the inclusion of the two provisions were strikingly different: the disposition of the government bond issue was a model of bureaucratic leadership, whereas legislators played an active role in drafting, or at least redrafting, the disclosure clause.

I examine these two provisions in the Banking Act as separate case studies, tracing their respective historical roots before focusing on the legislative process. In examining variations in the policy-making process, I delineate the conditions under which active involvement of politicians is likely to take place in financial policy making in Japan. We shall see that the Ministry of Finance is institutionally capable of equilibrating among clashing interests under its jurisdiction in consonance with the theory of regulation, but that its willingness to provide protection is a function of the costs. Because of changes in Japan's domestic and international economic environment, the Ministry of Finance is charting an increasingly narrow course between the Charybdis of small bank failure, on the one side, and the Scylla of political instrusion into financial administration, on the other.

Section 65 and a New Banking Act

The Shifting Profit Structure and Government Debt

Although banks had dominated the financial landscape in prewar and postwar Japan, banks became less popular in the mid-1970s, not because of waning political influence but because section 65 of the Securities Exchange Act of 1948 guaranteed securities firms a monopoly of certain lines of business that in time proved highly profitable. Banks, by contrast, began to face new limits to the growth of their traditional banking operations. With slower economic growth after the oil shock, firms pared down bank debt and began to opt instead for increasing their financial flexibility. Loss to banks was exacerbated by the increasing burden of government debt.[1]

In 1965, to combat a tenacious recession, the Diet passed a special one-year law permitting deficit financing to supplement the general account budget. It is ironic that Takeo Fukuda, an ex-MOF bureaucrat known as a fiscal conservative, was the finance minister who presided over this historic departure from a balanced budget.[2] By contrast, Kakuei Tanaka, the finance minister before Fukuda, had kept a tight rein on the budget. The difference in their economic environments goes far in explaining their respective choices. Unlike Tanaka, Fukuda was responding to a serious budget shortfall due to a business downswing.[3]

A Government Bond Syndicate was formed in the fall of 1965 to

[1]C. Dosse, "The Position of Banks and Securities Companies in the Japanese Financial Market and Its Effect on International Capital Flows," Working Paper, Direction des Etudes, Banque de France (Paris, Fall 1985).

[2]A decade later, when he was prime minister, Fukuda was once again the big spender as he tried to respond to Carter's request to pump-prime the Japanese economy so that Japan's domestic economic expansion could serve as a "locomotive" for the world economy.

[3]Yasuji Abe, *Ginkō—Shōken Kakine Ronsō Oboegaki* (Tokyo: Nihon Keizai Shimbunsha, 1980).

function as an alternative to an open market for the new issuance of government bonds. Every December, when the outline of the government budget received the LDP's stamp of approval, leaders of the banking community would negotiate with the manager of the Debt Division of the Finance Bureau. Once they decided on a mutually acceptable size of the government bond issue for the entire year, the Buchō Sewanin Kondankai, a group of mid-management-level bankers, met once a month to discuss the schedule for the issuances over the year. Each month after this group reached agreement, officials from the BOJ and MOF met with representatives of the Government Bond Syndicate at the BOJ to make the schedule official. This way the MOF was able to place bonds with the syndicate at below market cost, keeping its debt service burden at a minimum. The cost to financial institutions was also relatively low, since the BOJ reabsorbed about 90 percent of the bonds at par one year after issuance. In any case, the amount of bonds placed with the syndicate each year was small. The greater cost was to investors, who could have been earning higher rates of return.[4]

In the United States, by contrast, over 60 percent of the government debt is financed in the short-term market in the form of Treasury Bills. The TB market is highly liquid and reflects the market supply and demand for short-term funds. Consequently, the Federal Reserve's open-market operations in TBs is an important tool of monetary policy in the United States. In Japan, by contrast, banks have opposed short-term government instruments that would compete with their deposits. The MOF, moreover, prefers the stability and predictability of long-term debt. Until the mid-1970s the original syndicate arrangement had proved workable, and long-term bonds had accounted for roughly 60 percent of the annual government issuance.

Soon after the Government Bond Syndicate was formed, banks signed a memo with the securities firms ceding, for the time being, banks' right to deal in government bonds.[5] Although banks were

[4]Ryūji Akane, *Toshi Ginkō Konwakai* (Tokyo: Kanki Shuppan, 1984), pp. 64–94; interviews with MOF officials and bankers, June–October 1986.
[5]Masaaki Tsuchida (then director of the Banking Bureau Research Division), "Shōken Sangensoku wa Kinyūkai no Zenshin e no Buseki," *Kinyū Zaisei Jijō*, February 23, 1981, pp. 14–19; Kizan Muramatsu, "Ginkōhō Kaisei Sōdō no Haikei ni Aru Mono," *Ekonomisuto*, April 14, 1981, pp. 28–34.

allotted 51.5 percent of the issuance (this dropped to 42.2 percent in 1968), the Bank of Japan had agreed to absorb 90 percent of the bonds after a one-year maturation period; banks were not, therefore, intent on engaging in bond retailing. Selling bonds over the counter would merely shift funds out of deposits into government debt, the majority of banks thought.[6]

Only the largest banks were eager to deal in government securities. Hisashi Kurokawa, chairman of Mitsubishi Bank, argued strongly in 1965 for banks' freedom to sell government bonds to the general public. Mitsubishi, one of a handful of banks large enough to handle the securities business, had been advocating bank *sōgōka*, or the offering of comprehensive services. But the smaller banks sided with the securities firms against bank involvement in government bond retailing.[7]

Scholars had been calling for small denominated bonds to be sold on an open market, where consumers could take advantage of market rates. Hiroshi Kawaguchi, for example, an economist from Chūō University, pointed out that small savers should have access to viable and attractive alternatives to both low-yield bank deposits, on the one hand, and the volatile stock market, on the other.[8] But these rhetorical stones could bring down the regulatory edifice only if joined by a mass movement. If aroused, the public could have pressured their representatives in the Diet with their voting power. For as the economists said, losses to the public from low-yielding bank deposits were indeed substantial. But at the individual level, losses to each saver were insufficient to feed a time-consuming, costly, and cumbersome grass-roots campaign for reform.

The first oil shock of 1973 gave even the smaller banks reason to reconsider. On the one hand, the issuance of government bonds took a quantum leap to battle the recession that ensued, giving the banks large portions to hold. In 1975 banks held 4.5 trillion yen in

[6]Nor did the MOF want banks to sell government bonds over the counter because that would have encouraged a secondary market in government bonds, with market-determined interest rates higher than the artificially low rates for new issues.

[7]Takuji Matsuzawa, *Watakushi no Ginkō Shōwashi* (Tokyo: Tōyō Keizai Shimpōsha, 1985), pp. 108–9; Abe, *Ginkō—Shōken Kakine Ronsō Oboegaki*, p. 107.

[8]Hiroshi Kawaguchi, "Kokusai no Kinri Jiyūka to Kinyū Baibai ni Fumikire," *Kinyū Zaisei Jijō*, May 1, 1978.

99

government bonds. The amount kept rising, to 11 trillion yen in 1977 and 18.4 trillion yen in 1978. On the other hand, the Bank of Japan was no longer willing to buy back such large quantities for fear of fueling inflation. The BOJ's absorption of government bonds, heretofore, had been carried out as part of its routine money supply operations because the amounts were so small. Once Japan's economic growth slowed, there was less need to provide "growth currency."[9]

Banks, left holding growing quantities of government bonds, became concerned about the profitability of their portfolios. A debate quickly ensued as to the legal basis for banks retailing government bonds to get them out of their portfolio quickly and at minimum loss, and for trading government bonds in the secondary market to earn additional income. In defense of their monopoly, the securities industry cited section 65 of the Securities Exchange Act; banks countered that the law was unclear on the disposition of government bonds. Because the law's complexity and ambiguity left the issue open to various interpretations, the two sectors remained in deadlock for some time.

It was not until banks began to show significant losses from government bond holding that they began to push seriously for new rules. In a historic turnabout, in 1978 Nomura Securities reported higher earnings than the top banks, Fuji and Sumitomo. The others of the "Big Four" securities houses—Nikko, Daiwa, and Yamaichi—also were gaining rapidly on the banks. The banks would not wait passively to be swept into obsolescence by the global wave of "secularization" which was driving the profits of the securities firms.[10]

Securitization, or the substitution of papers sold and traded on the market for bank loans, was precisely what the banks in the Bond Arrangement Committee had worked to fend off for many decades. But in the 1970s it was the government bond market and not the corporate one that began to eat into bank profits. While securities firms were profiting from their buying and selling of government bonds on the secondary market, banks were holding large chunks of

[9]Michihiko Matsuno (director of the Debt Division, Finance Bureau), *Kokusai* (Ōkurashō Zaimu Kyōkai, 1983), p. 28.

[10]"Honban ni Totsunyūsuru Ginkō-Shōken Sensō," special supplement to *Daiyamondo*, December 1, 1981, pp. 16–18.

Table 2. Profitability of top Japanese banks and securities
firms, 1965–1985 (average percentages and billions of yen)

Year	Return on equity		Operating profits	
	City banks[a]	Big Four[b]	City banks[a]	Big Four[b]
1965	18.4%	5.4%	25.9	7.0
1975	16.1	14.2	51.1	15.8
1985	20.4	33.6	142.0	137.3

[a]"City banks" in this case refers only to the top six city
banks.
[b]The "Big Four" securities houses.
Source: Atsushi Satō, "Gyōmu Kisei no Kanwa wa Naze
Hitsuyō Ka?" Kinyū Zaisei Jijō, December 8, 1986, p. 22.

each issue, only to book a loss when selling them after the mandatory one-year holding period.[11]

On December 12, 1977, the City Bankers' Club (Toginkon) petitioned not only for over-the-counter sale of bonds but also for the opportunity to trade bonds in the secondary market. The banks argued that the projections of government bond issuance in the following year exceeded by 10 trillion yen banks' ability to absorb without booking losses. Therefore (1) the Finance Bureau's Investment Funds Account (Shikin Unyōbu) should undertake more of the debt burden than its current 15 or so percent, and (2) individuals should have a right to buy government bonds. Banks were now requesting a change in regulation that they originally opposed: their losses from the status quo were judged to exceed the losses they might suffer from the shift of some depositors into government bonds. Banks were faced with a dilemma: their accounts were hurting precisely because government bonds were issued at rates below the market level. But if government bond yields were *too* attractive, depositors would shift en masse. So their second point was a smokescreen for what they really wanted, namely, the freedom to sell not-too-attractive bonds to individuals, so as not to seriously undermine their deposit base. Because bonds would be paid for out of deposits anyway, the banks wanted at least to earn the retail commission in the process.[12]

[11]Toshiro Kusano (president of Mitsui Bank), "Shoken to no Nyūkai Bubun no Chōsei," Kinyū Zaisei Jijō, May 2, 1983, pp. 18–22.
[12]Muramoto Shūzō (representative of the Government Bond Syndicate and managing director of Daichi Kangyō Bank), testimony before the House of Representatives Budget Committee, February 9, 1978, as recorded by Kinyū Zaisei Jijō, February 20, 1978.

This set of concerns was restated by the General Committee of the Federation of Bankers' Associations on December 15, 1977. As changes in Japan's economy have wrought an unlevel playing field among different types of financial institutions, the federation has had difficulty presenting a unified position to the MOF and the politicians. Most initiatives for regulatory revision came from the big banks, which are more prepared to diversify their activities, whereas small, specialized banks appealed for a slower pace of change. But by 1977 there was general agreement among the banks on the desirability of their selling newly issued government bonds over the counter.[13]

The Ministry of Finance was not opposed to the banks' suggestion. More precisely, if the MOF did not do something about the banks' losses, the banks would likely take their cause to the politicians.[14] But the securities industry met these developments with dismay and argued that a better solution than increasing the retail network of bonds would be to issue the bonds at a market price— through the securities companies. In the fall of 1977 the Securities Business Council petitioned the MOF for an auction system for the new issue of government bonds.[15]

The MOF's Finance Bureau, which is responsible for managing the government bond issuances, staunchly opposed an auction for the long-term bonds because it enjoyed the stability, predictability, and below-market interest rates of the syndicate system. This left the Banking Bureau and the Securities Bureau with a narrower margin for maneuver. If long-term bond issuance had been set on an auction system, the rancorous government bond problem might have been resolved short of legislative change.

Though the Finance Bureau preferred the syndicate system as

[13]"Kokusai no Ōryō Hakkō ni Kansuru Iken," *Kinyū*, January 1978, pp. 22–23; "Zenkingyō no Shin Taisei," *Kinyū to Ginkō*, special supplement to *Tōyō Keizai*, June 8, 1981, pp. 8–9.

[14]Interviews with Ministry of Finance officials, 1985–1986, Tokyo.

[15]Abe, *Ginkō—Shōken Kakine Ronsō Oboegaki*, pp. 110–13; "Kokusai Hakkōkon de Zengaku Shichū Shōka o Yōsei," *Kinyū Zaisei Jijō*, January 2, 1978, p. 10; Yasuji Abe, "Madohan Mondai to Hōritsu Yōgō no Futōitsu," *Kinyū Zaisei Jijō*, January 16, 1978, p. 5; "Kinmonken de Shōken ga Kokusai Madohan ni Surudoi Hanron," *Kinyū Zaisei Jijō*, February 27, 1978, p. 6; Takashi Fujiyama, "Kokusai Shōka no Genjitsuteki Kaiketsu," *Kinyū to Ginkō*, special supplement to *Tōyō Keizai*, February 17, 1983, p. 84.

long as the BOJ was reabsorbing the bonds, the large issues of government bonds after 1975 outpaced the syndicate's absorption capacity. A secondary market matured spontaneously, which in turn set parameters for the price of new issues. So for the Finance Bureau, the benefits of the syndicate diminished rapidly. Even stability was threatened as the banks continued to balk at the subscriptions. The Finance Bureau, therefore, began leaning toward the idea of bank participation in the retail and secondary markets of government bonds as a way of smoothing issuance. This is a clear example of the changing costs of regulation to the *bureaucracy*. But the solution was not that simple; the MOF still had to deal with the stir over section 65 of the Securities Exchange Act.

Faced with a fierce deadlock between the banking and securities industries, and dissension within its own ranks, the MOF took a conservative step. It adopted in 1978 a quasi-auction system that offered the syndicate a range of terms for medium-term bonds. The securities firms were permitted to offer "Medium-term Bond Funds" (Chūki Kokusai Fund) to the general public to help retail this new type of government bonds. In the first year Nomura alone had sold 562 billion yen in these funds; in the second year the figure doubled, despite the MOF's limit on the yields at 5.5–5.6 percent, just between banks' six months deposit at 5.25 percent and one year deposit at 6 percent. Unlike U.S. financial authorities, the MOF continued to limit assiduously the competition between banks and securities houses.[16]

The banks were still dissatisfied, worried that medium-term bonds, with a maturity of three years, would compete with bank deposits rather than ease their debt burden. Banks would have much preferred government bonds with longer maturities, since these would compete with the postal savings ten-year deposit and not with bank deposits. The MOF had suggested two-, three-, and four-year bonds. The two-year bonds were vetoed by the banks as too competitive with deposits, and the four-year bonds were vetoed

[16]"Kokusai no Shichū Baikyaku Kaku Kimaru," *Kinyū Zaisei Jijō*, January 23, 1978, p. 7; "Kokusai no Tentō Kakaku Nehaba Seigen Teppai e," *Kinyū Zaisei Jijō*, March 6, 1978; "Ginkō vs. Shōken," *Kinyū to Ginkō*, special supplement to *Tōyō Keizai*, February 15, 1980, pp. 20–23; "Honban ni Totsunyū suru Ginkō-Shōken Sensō," *Daiyamondo*, December 1, 1981, p. 17.

by the Industrial Bank of Japan and the Long Term Credit Banks, which issue four-year debentures.[17]

Banks also made their displeasure known on the matter of low yields and losses. In July 1978, for the first time in the history of the syndicate, banks boycotted the entire issue of long-term government bonds. Meanwhile, the Federation of Bankers Associations held its thirty-fifth annual meeting on July 4, 1978, at which banks restated their desire to sell government bonds to the public. Prime Minister Suzuki, Finance Minister Watanabe, Economic Planning Agency director Komoto, and all of the MOF officials present prudently avoided mention of the problem.[18] The syndicate continued to bid for the new medium-term bonds, but the amount absorbed was far short of the MOF goal. At this pace, the MOF would face a sizable funds shortage at the end of the fiscal year.[19]

The MOF wasted no time. On July 30, it announced that banks would be allowed to set aside a reserve fund with tax advantages for use in smoothing out fluctuations in the bond price, effective September 1978. But this was not enough; bank losses persisted, as did their demand for change.[20] Banks were particularly vexed in 1978 when the new ten-year government bonds issued at 6.1 percent fell to a lower price on the secondary market because of the market expectation of higher interest rates in the near future. City banks alone reported losses of 400 billion yen from government bonds, or twice the amount of the previous year.

In December 1979 the MOF announced an additional measure. Banks would be permitted to choose an alternative accounting method in order to hide some of their book losses from their shareholders and depositors. Given the choice in accounting methods,

---

[17]"Atarashii Chūki Kokusai, Rokugatsu kara Hakkō e," *Kinyū Zaisei Jijō*, May 29, 1978; "Shin Chūki Kokusai o Keiki ni Chōkisai mo Nyūsatsusei ni seyo," *Kinyū Zaisei Jijō*, May 22, 1978.

[18]"Shichi Gatsu Kokusai, Hajime no Kyūsai," *Kinyū Zaisei Jijō*, July 20, 1978, p. 9; "Hachigatsu Kokusai no Jōken Mondai mo Shinkokuka," *Kinyū Zaisei Jijō*, July 20, 1978, p. 4.

[19]"Shinkokusa Fuyasu Kokusai no Shōkanan," *Kinyū Zaisei Jijō*, October 9, 1978, p. 5.

[20]"Okurashō, Kokusai Kakaku Hendō Hikiatekin o Shinsetsu," *Kinyū Zaisei Jijō*, August 7, 1978, p. 7.

Table 3. Amount of Japanese government bonds outstanding and
FILP's underwriting share, 1973–1983 (billions of yen and
percentages)

Year	Government bonds (A)	FILP-underwritten share (B)	B/A
1973	1,766.2	294.0	9.6%
1974	2,160.0	420.0	19.4
1975	5,280.5	840.0	15.9
1976	7,198.2	1,013.8	14.1
1977	9,561.2	1,000.0	10.5
1978	10,674.0	300.0	2.8
1979	13,472.0	2,664.1	19.8
1980	14,170.2	3,968.4	28.0
1981	12,899.9	4,424.0	34.3
1982	14,044.7	3,400.0	26.3
1983	13,345.0	3,700.0	27.0

Source: Michihiko Matsuno (director of the Debt Division, Finance Bureau), Kokusai (Tokyo: Ōkurashō Zaimu Kyōkai, 1983),
p. 133.

then, most banks chose to report government bonds at the original
purchase price (genkahō) instead of the lowest price, whether book
or market (teikahō), so their financial statements would not look so
bad to shareholders and depositors. Although an editorial in Tōyō
Keizai decried this measure as a sleight of hand meant to fool the
public, there was no general outcry.[21] In another policy change, the
MOF began using its Fiscal and Investment Fund in 1979 to absorb
a much greater portion of the government debt.[22] The Fiscal Investment and Loan Program's (FILP) share of new bond issues was 10.5
percent in 1977, 2.8 percent in 1978, 19.8 percent in 1979, and 28
percent in 1980.

[21] Hideo Ōkubo (assistant director of the Banking Division of the Banking Bureau), "Kokusai Kakaku Hendō Hikiatekin no Sōsetsu ni Tsuite," Kinyū Zaisei Jijō,
August 21, 1978, pp. 12–14. Nearly 90 percent of the local banks and seven city
banks opted for the purchased price method; six stayed with the lowest-price
method. Matsuno, Kokusai, pp. 30–33; Tōyō Keizai, March 22, 1980, pp. 50–51.
[22] The process of compiling the FILP is in many ways similar to that of the General
Account Budget. Projects requested by ministries and various institutions are examined by the MOF Financial Bureau and by the LDP Finance Committee; the total
package must be voted on in the Diet along with the General Account Budget.
Materials from "Workship on Control of Off-Budget Expenditure/Credit Practices," Ministry of Finance (1985); Fujiyama, "Kokusai Shōka no Genjitsuteki
Kaiketsu," pp. 82–85.

105

Section 65 Reevaluated

In 1976 the MOF had commissioned a special subcommittee of the Public Finance Advisory Council (Zaisei Seido Shingikai) to examine the government's debt financing problem. The MOF's proposed solution as voiced through this group in the fall of 1978 was to reduce the budget deficit by raising taxes and cutting spending. The MOF's problems with the syndicate would be over. The final word on public finance, however, belongs to the LDP rather than to the MOF. And Prime Minister Fukuda had just promised domestic constituents and the Western world at the Bonn Summit in June that Japan would prod its economy into 7 percent growth even though the MOF was keen to reduce the deficit. Rather than cut the budget, the LDP increased the Fiscal Year 1979 budget by 17 percent over the previous year.[23]

The MOF was thus not free, given the political constraints, to pursue its preferred policy of slashing deficit spending, and banks were still dissatisfied with the MOF's various palliative measures. All things being equal, the MOF, and the Finance Bureau in particular, gladly would have allowed banks to retail government bonds. Since the buyers would be small savers who had few alternatives to low-yield bank deposits, the Finance Bureau would not have to worry about the cost of government bonds climbing much higher. The larger the market, the better. But it was, of course, the securities industry that objected that new entrants into its corner of the market. The securities industry's position spelled trouble for banks: securities firms would have no difficulty selling government bonds, provided the rates were based on market conditions and a secondary market could provide ready liquidity.

The Banking Bureau's own advisory board, the Finance Research Group (Kinyū Mondai Kenkyū Kai), had already reached a conclusion in support of new legislation permitting banks to retail government bonds. Like it or not, the group argued, bank income would have to rely increasingly on international business and securities transactions. By contrast, the Securities Exchange Advisory Council, a group of scholars and private-sector leaders attached to the

[23] "Zaizeishin de Kokusai Hakkō no Hadomesaku Kentō," *Kinyū Zaisei Jijō*, October 23, 1978.

Securities Bureau, continued to argue that bank entry into the government bond retail business could and should be avoided.[24]

Deadlock between the two industries held the MOF motionless, searching quietly for a compromise. Ignoring the bank-securities snarl was never an option for the MOF. But because it was a matter that would have to be addressed in the new banking law that the MOF was in the process of drafting, the matter was all the more pressing. The MOF was eager to defuse the conflict before politicians became involved in making promises to one side or the other. In May 1980, in another small concession to the banks, the MOF shortened the mandatory holding period of government bonds before resale from one year to six months.[25]

Later in 1980 the debate resurfaced. On October 15, 1980, the Securities Industry Association issued a statement opposing banks' retailing of and dealing in government bonds. Already, by way of the securities firms' sales network, individuals bought an average of 20 percent of the government bonds issued annually. Moreover, it declared, the secondary market was flourishing with no help from the banks. In short, there was no reason for bank entrance into the market save the banks' greed.[26] The statement's rhetoric thinly disguised the securities industry's key concern: banks had no advantage in the retail business because they had more branches and customers.

On October 22, the City Bankers Club fired back a response. Banks, they charged, suffered a capital loss in 1979 from government bond holdings in spite of the new accounting system. In a veiled threat to the MOF, the banks warned that from the standpoint of sound bank management, they simply might not be able to absorb many government bonds in the future.[27]

Meanwhile, in late October, the LDP was reviewing the matter in its party committees, the Public Finance Committee (Zaisei Bukai),

[24]"Madohan wa Benign Neglect ka, Jukushi ka," *Kinyū Zaisei Jijō*, November 13, 1978, pp. 10–11.

[25]City Banks' Club, "Kokusai no Banyaku Seigan Teppai ni Kansuru Yōbōsho," October 22, 1980, in *Kinyū Zaisei Jijō*, November 3, 1980, p. 69.

[26]Japan Securities Industry Association (*Nihon Shōkengyō Kyōkai*), "Ginkō ni yoru Kokusai nado no Madohanbai oyobi Dealing ni Tsuite," October 15, 1980, in *Kinyū Zaisei Jijō*, October 27, 1980, pp. 62–64.

[27]City Banks' Club, "Kokusai no Banyaku Seigan Teppai ni Kansuru Yōbōsho."

the Financial Issues Research Commission (Kinyū Mondai Chōsa-kai), and the Securities Market Study Group (Shōken Shijō Kon-dankai). It was these party committees' deliberations, rather than those of the House Finance Committee, which gripped the attention of the financial sector and the MOF. But the LDP ultimately tossed the thorny issue back to the MOF without making any pronouncements on the dispute between banks and securities firms. Even Michio Watanabe, the minister of finance and a rising figure in the Nakasone faction, kept his silence, leaving the details of the solution to his bureaucratic subordinates. "If we [the LDP] play this one badly," said Watanabe, "we're likely to get burned."[28]

In late November the Banking Bureau and Securities Bureau finally hammered out a proposal they thought might reasonably satisfy both the banking and securities industries. The Securities Bureau approached the securities industry first before making any commitments within the MOF because they were essentially agreeing to allow banks into retailing and trading government bonds. The concessions to the securities industry, however, were four-fold:(1) banks' securities activities would be limited to government bonds and would be legally considered among banks' "other activities" rather than as a normal part of their business; (2) under the Securities Exchange Act, banks would have to individually apply for a securities license from the Securities Bureau; (3) banks would be required to wait an unspecified length of time before being granted licenses; (4) securities firms would be allowed to trade the short-term securities issued in the Euromarket, including certificates of deposit and commercial paper, once the MOF gave the go-ahead for them to be transacted onshore.[29]

Under the existing laws, certificates of deposit (CDs) and commercial paper (CPs) were not defined as securities and therefore were off limits to securities houses. The Securities Exchange Act would be revised to categorize CDs and CPs as "quasisecurities" so that, conceivably, either banks or securities houses could handle them. This concession was an important victory for the securities

[28]"Ginkō-Shōken Hyakunen Sensō," *Kinyū Zaisei Jijō*, October 27, 1980, pp. 10–11.
[29]"Kinpaku suru 'Ginkō no Shōken Gyōmu Kitei' no Kōbō," *Kinyū Zaisei Jijō*, January 12, 1981, pp. 16–17.

industry. (When CDs were finally introduced in October 1987, the conditions of issuance and underwriting reflected a carefully balanced consideration of the interests of both the securities and banking industries.)[30]

When banks learned what the conditions were, and that the Securities Bureau had already been in consultation with the securities industry, they were livid. Hajime Yamada, chairman of both the National Federation of Banks and Mitsubishi Bank, said that the director of the Banking Bureau had assured him back in July that he would look out for the banks' best interest. But this, said Yamada, was a betrayal. Under the existing banking law, banks argued, they were already authorized to engage in securities activities as part of their "attendant business."

This new wording would represent a step backward, particularly if banks were blocked from trading in the commercial paper market once it was allowed onshore. Banks insisted on strict limits on the nature of CDs and CPs to be traded, lest they lose both depositors and borrowers to these more attractive alternatives. CPs would have to be denominated in 200 million yen or more, and only CPs issued by the strongest firms could be traded in Japan. CDs would have to be denominated in 500 million yen increments or more, and only those issued by the top 150 banks in the world could be traded in Japan.[31] Banks also argued it would be decidedly unfair to be licensed by the Securities Bureau since that Bureau would surely be influenced by the securities industry's urging to stall. Banks wanted to get into the business *immediately*.[32]

On December 30, 1980, the General Committee of the Federation of Bankers Associations decided by majority vote to reject MOF's draft of the new banking law, with its proposed settlement of the

[30]Hiroshi Yoshimoto (then director of the Securities Bureau), "Madohan ni Taisuru Ginkōkai no Shisei," *Kinyū Zaisei Jijō*, June 22, 1981, pp. 26–30; "Ministry Outlines CP Rules," *Japan Economic Journal*, May 23, 1987, p. 10; "Shī-pī Rūru Sakusei Ōzume," *Nikkei*, April 7, 1987, p. 5.

[31]Hajime Yamada, "Ginkōhō Kaiseian ni Igi ari," *Ekonomisuto*, February 17, 1981, pp. 36–39; "Ginkō vs. Shōken: Koko ga Senba," *Kinyū Zaisei Jijō*, February 17, 1981, pp. 36–39.

[32]"Ginkō no Kaotate," *Kinyū Zaisei Jijō*, May 26, 1980, pp. 10–11; "Ginkōhō Kaisei ni Kansuru Ōkurashō Ginkōkyoku no Kangaekata oyobi Zenginkyō Iken," *Kinyū Zaisei Jijō*, January 19, 1981, pp. 14–20.

government bond issue.[33] The securities industry had accepted the deal, but the banking community had not. On January 8, 1981, the Securities Activities Committee of the Federation of Bankers Associations restated a resounding no. The syndicate met on January 12 and hinted that the government might have trouble issuing any bonds in February. From the beginning there was some disagreement among banks as to how stubbornly to resist. The only "court of appeal" was the LDP, and that party had made it clear that it did not want to become involved in that dispute.[34] Other avenues of bank resistance were closed off: neither the MOF nor the LDP would hear more. The MOF did, however, voluntarily use the Fiscal Investment and Loan Program to absorb 34.3 percent of the government issue for 1981, the highest percentage in history.[35] On the other hand, the MOF knew the syndicate would not boycott bonds indefinitely lest banks undercut their own desire to retail and trade government bonds.[36]

On March 2, 1981, Finance Minister Michio Watanabe called in five leaders of the banking community: Hajime Yamada, chairman of the Federation of Bankers Associations; Ichirō Yoshikuni, chairman of the Association of Regional Banks; Kisaburō Ikeura, president of the Industrial Bank of Japan; Takeshi Tashiro, chairman of the Association of Trust Banks; and Takuji Matsuzawa, managing director of Fuji Bank. Of these men, Matsuzawa of Fuji Bank was the only one who did not represent an association of banks. But it was not a mistake that he was invited. Matsuzawa was known to be basically in favor of the new law, even though the terms for entry into the government bond market were not all that banks had hoped. The MOF hoped Matsuzawa would quell any attempt to gut the law altogether. "The matter has been decided," Watanabe declared. "We cannot entertain any further revisions on the banking-

---

[33] Ibid. The banks were also unhappy about the MOF's proposed disclosure rules, as will be discussed in the "Bank Regulation" section of this chapter.

[34] "Yodan Yurusanai 'Shōken Gyōmu' no Chaku Jiten," *Kinyū Zaisei Jijō*, January 19, 1981, pp. 10–11; "Ginkō no Kokusai Madohan Mondai," *Daiyamondo*, June 1, 1981, pp. 92–94.

[35] "Ginkōkyoku vs. Togin Rengō Kessen," *Kinyū Zaisei Jijō*, February 16, 1981, pp. 10–11.

[36] Kaiichi Shimura, "Ginkōhō Kaisei ni Sessoku wa Sakeyo," *Ekonomisuto*, November 18, 1980, pp. 34–39.

securities issue." When the meeting was over, Watanabe stated that he would not meet with bankers again until the law had been enacted.[37]

The banks' failure to induce political intervention on their behalf attested not to the banks' lack of political leverage on an absolute scale—because banks were and continue to be key supporters of the LDP—but rather to the securities industry's status as an important supporter of the LDP. The LDP would simply prefer to delegate to the bureaucracy decisions that are destined to invite more resentment than gratitude.

On March 5 the Securities Industry Association issued a statement warning that if any additional compromises were made with the banking industry, the securities industry would return to the original starting point of the disagreement and fight the entire battle over again. The securities houses had already made all the concessions they intended to make.[38] Although fierce rhetorical jabs between the banking and securities industries continued through April 1981, when the new banking law passed the Diet, the initial compromise proposed by the MOF stuck.[39] A neutral Committee of Three was appointed by the MOF and approved by the banking and securities industries to decide on the timing and other details of banks' commencement of government bond retailing and dealing. Members of the Committee of Three, all retired MOF officials, were Shōichirō Morinaga, once managing director of the Tokyo Stock Exchange and governor of the Bank of Japan; Naoru Sasaki, chairman of the MOF's Financial System Research Council and also former governor of the Bank of Japan; and Michikazu Kōno, chairman of the Securities Activities Advisory Council attached to the Securities Bureau.

The committee deliberated in guarded secrecy for two years,

[37]"Dohyōba de Motsureru Ginkōhō Kaisei Geki," *Kinyū Zaisei Jijō*, March 9, 1981, pp. 14–15.

[38]Nihon Shōkengyō Kyōkai, "Ginkōhō oyobi Shōken Torihikiho no Kaisei ni Kansuru Shōkenkai no Iken," March 3, 1981, as reported in *Shōken Gyōhō*, May 1981, pp. 60–61.

[39]Nobuhiro Saijō (administrative director of the Council of Securities Associations), "Shinginkōhō to Ginkō no Shōken Gyōmu," *Inbestomento*, August 1981, pp. 18–30; Saijō urges that banks' dealing in government bonds will endanger the unwitting small investor.

assisted by the Research and Planning Division of the MOF's secretariat. But the basis for a compromise solution had already been established in the initial MOF proposal. Banks were permitted to sell government bonds over the counter from April 1983. In June of the following year banks were permitted to deal in government bonds in the secondary market to profit on the price fluctuations. In the interim, however, banks were unhappy about the delay and boycotted long-term government bonds for three consecutive months in the summer of 1981, and again in February 1982.[40] The securities industry, on the other hand, had been hoping for a more delayed bank entry and fewer participating banks. The MOF deemed a further barter necessary: early bank permission in exchange for allowing securities firms to lend money to customers using government bonds as collateral.[41]

Banks had succeeded in lobbying the LDP for concessions on other points of the law, but on the larger problem—bank involvement in the government bond market—the LDP would not budge.

Bank Regulation: The Battle over the Cost of Protection

The second noteworthy component of the new banking law is the treatment of bank disclosure. In fact, the disclosure requirements prescribed in the law are lenient—something akin to license for self-advertisement. Among the industrialized countries, disclosure of a bank's books is one of the most important resources the public has for evaluating a bank as an equity investment or as a reliable depository institution. In Japan, it could be argued, the MOF's implicit guarantee against bank failure is the functional equivalent of full disclosure. And that, for the MOF, is precisely the problem.

[40]"San Chōrō o Kujitsu no Enmaku ni Nitatsu Ginkō-Shōken," *Kinyū Zaisei Jijō,* November 23, 1981, pp. 10–11; "Nendonai Ketsuron e Kakyo no Michi o Saguru Sannin Iinkai," *Kinyū Zaisei Jijō,* January 18, 1982, pp. 12–13; "Sannin I no Sakaki o Mae ni Hyakkai Yakōsuru Shōken-Ginkō," *Kinyū Zaisei Jijō,* February 9, 1982, pp. 10–11.

[41]"Ginkō-Shōken Teikei no Tane," *Kinyū Zaisei Jijō,* April 18, 1983, pp. 14–15; "Senju Bōei kara Sekkyoku Tenkai," *Kinyū to Ginkō,* special supplement to *Tōyō Keizai,* August 12, 1983, pp. 12–15.

The MOF is the caretaker of a greenhouse that is becoming drafty and difficult to nurture. It would be hard to find clearer evidence of bank protection. Is the MOF indeed so assuredly captured? Is the MOF the mindless servant of banks?

Contrary to first appearances, the MOF has consistently sought an efficient, streamlined, internationally competitive banking sector. A financial system with a few powerful banks would be a regulator's dream: the MOF's job would be relatively easy, and the bureaucrats would look good. The story line to follow, however, is one of bank success in obtaining protective regulation despite the MOF's efforts to introduce market discipline. This greenhouse environment fostered the dozen or so powerful, world-class banks, while simultaneously nurturing the over one thousand small, local financial institutions.

The financial panic of 1927 led to greater consolidation of Japan's banking sector, strengthening the hand of the great zaibatsu (family-owned conglomerate) banks in particular.[42] The number of commercial banks, 1,697 in 1905, was down to 424 by 1936. Over 950 banks closed their doors and 1,333 were merged.[43] Looming in size over the new financial landscape were the big city banks, which had branches throughout the country. Of the seven big banks, all but Sanwa Bank were zaibatsu institutions. Four top zaibatsu held 48 percent of the capital in the financial sector just before the beginning of World War II.[44]

In the 1930s the military began mobilizing the economy for war, operating at first through the zaibatsu to gain greater control of economic activity. The zaibatsu banks, and Mitsubishi and Mitsui in particular, benefited from industrial concentration and from the boom in heavy industry. In 1941 the seven largest banks had 58

[42]Hiromi Arisawa, ed., *Shōwa Keizai Shi* (Tokyo: Nihon Keizai Shimbun Press, 1977), pp. 60–62. The Ministry of Commerce and Industry used the same market disruption to tighten up the small-business sector despite labor's oppositon to what it saw as an invitation to greater management control of labor. Labor cynically dubbed the MCI's "Temporary Bureau of Industry Rationalization" the "Bureau of Irrationalization."

[43]Hugh Patrick, "Japanese Financial Development in Historical Perspective, 1868–1980," in Gustav Ranis et al., *Comparative Development Perspectives* (Boulder, Colo.: Westview Press, 1983), pp. 312–13.

[44]Arisawa, *Shōwa Keizai Shi*, p. 297.

percent of the deposits, 66 percent of the loans, and 47 percent of the securities holding of the 245 ordinary banks. During the war the big banks became even more important because of the absorption of smaller institutions.[45]

In February 1942 the Bank of Japan law was abolished and replaced with a law that robbed the Central Bank of its autonomy from the MOF in monetary policy, while charging the BOJ to make unsecured loans to companies as demanded by the military, without limit.[46] At the same time, however, the new law gave the BOJ greater powers over private financial institutions. In May 1942 the Banking Control Association, the Local Finance Control Association, and the Short Term Market Control Association were established under BOJ and MOF auspices.[47]

By 1943 the military's need for money was so great that it enacted a law strengthening its authority to draw funds from private banks. At first 149 companies were on the military's list for acquiring loans upon demand; within a year more than 3,000 firms were similarly privileged. Banks, in turn, could not have kept the money flowing without steady loans from the BOJ. The money supply soared, unchecked; prices were restrained by price controls.

In 1945 regional banks were forced to merge, leaving one regional bank in each prefecture. Seventeen of these banks were then formed into a finance corporation for funneling their deposits to the cash-poor city banks. Under military rule the financial industry had become streamlined in a way the MOF could never have achieved on its own. The number of ordinary banks, 377 in 1937, had diminished to 61 by 1945.[48]

After the war, banks recovered more rapidly than other sectors of the economy, in part because of their exemption from strict anti-monopoly provisions. Moreover, the BOJ's disinflation policies placed a great deal of market power in the hands of banks. At first, the Occupation officials (known collectively as SCAP) had spoken of "democratizing finance," breaking the strong zaibatsu control of the financial sector by splintering the mammoth zaibatsu banks into

[45] Arisawa, *Shōwa Keizai Shi.*
[46] Ibid., p. 216.
[47] Ibid., p. 217.
[48] Patrick, "Japanese Financial Development," p. 315.

more numerous medium-sized institutions. The Corporation De-concentration Law was enacted in December 1947, forcing firms with monopoly power to divide into smaller segments. Banks were targeted along with other large firms; Mitsubishi, Yasuda, Teikoku, and Sumitomo were slated for dismemberment. But in July 1948, pursuant to a policy change at SCAP, banks were exempted from the law. Only Teikoku Bank was split, undoing the wartime merger of Mitsui and Daiichi Bank. The rest of the zaibatsu banks were ordered to change their names, but even this directive was revoked after two years.

In the fall of 1948, SCAP commissioned a Detroit banker, Joseph Dodge, to craft policies that would strengthen Japan's economy. Upon his arrival in Japan in February 1949, Dodge set about applying the principle of balancing revenues and expenditures for all parts of the government budget: the General Account Budget, special accounts, and public policy corporations. Dodge would not allow special accounts to be financed by government bonds or loans, nor would he permit their deficits to be covered by transfers from the General Account Budget. Dodge also ordered the Bank of Japan to tighten the money supply.[49]

Japanese industry would have preferred a stimulative path to recovery rather than the fiscally stringent one chosen by Dodge. In the summer of 1950, for example, the ruling Liberal party was eager to lower interest rates before the upcoming elections in order to win greater support from industry. The Occupation authorities would not allow a rate cut. Banks, on the other hand, had no qualms about SCAP's tight money policy, which increased their bargaining power over corporate borrowers.

Dodge also ordered the government's Reconstruction Finance Bank (Fukkō Kinyū Kinko) scaled back, blaming it for feeding inflation. The Reconstruction Bank, a brainchild of Finance Minister Tanzan Ishibashi, had been established in January 1947 to provide funds to basic industries that private banks would be reluctant to support. In 1947 the Reconstruction Bank's loans, 60 percent of which went to the coal and steel industries, overshot the total of all private banks. Even in 1948, when private banks had

[49]T. F. M. Adams and Iwao Hoshii, *A Financial History of the New Japan* (Tokyo: Kōdansha International, 1972), pp. 53–54.

more money to lend, Reconstruction Bank loans amounted to over a third of the private banks' total. All the while, the Bank of Japan cautioned against rampant inflation. Dodge's position was as much boon to the BOJ as it was bane to the mining and steel industries. But the private banks benefited from the scaling down of Reconstruction Bank lending as they took over the bulk of corporate finance.[50]

Of even greater import to banks was SCAP's intention, announced in August 1948, to revamp the Japanese banking system on the American model.[51] The plan was to establish a Banking Board much like the Board of Governors of the Federal Reserve. The board would be independent of the Ministry of Finance to ensure well-managed monetary policy beyond the reach of the cabinet.

The banking community was as delighted as the MOF was chagrined. Banks applauded the separation of fiscal and monetary policies, charging the cabinet with sacrificing monetary policy to its political need for fiscal stimulation or allocation of credit to small business. But representatives of industry, more concerned about the possibility of recession than about inflation, expressed concern about being controlled by a strong, independent monetary authority.[52]

The MOF responded equally fast in defense of its control of financial policy. "The American suggestion cannot be accepted in Japan without modification," Finance Minister Kitamura stated. "Monetary policy cannot and should not be separated from fiscal policy." A three-man committee was charged to study the problem: Finance Minister Kitamura, BOJ governor Ichimada, and Economic Stabilization Board director Kuritsuka.[53] After two weeks of deliberation, the committee agreed to the Banking Board—in name only. They would demote the board to an advisory body to the MOF. But two on the committee were politicians, and the third, Ichimada, was

[50] *Kinyū Zaisei Jijō,* July 3, 1950, pp. 7–8; August 28, 1950, p. 6.

[51] *Asahi Shimbun,* August 20 and 22, 1948; Chōtarō Sakairi, *Kinyū Seido Ron* (Tokyo: Kōbundo, 1977), pp. 186–87.

[52] *Nikkei Shimbun,* September 19, 1948; *Kinyū Zaisei Jijō,* July 11, 1950, p. 1. For an account of the heated dispute between the MOF and the BOJ over the control of monetary policy, see Mitsuo Takamoto et al., eds., *Jitsuroku: Sengo Kinyū Gyōseishi* (Tokyo: Kinyū Zaisei Jijō Kenkyūkai, 1985), pp. 265–74; Toshihiko Yoshino, *Chūō Ginkō Seido no Kaikaku* (Tokyo: Zenkoku Chihō Ginkō Kyōkai, 1959), pp. 236–39.

[53] *Asahi Shimbun,* August 22, 1948.

to become one years later. They and their colleagues in the Diet would not have passed a bill removing monetary policy from political grasp.[54]

In August 1950 the MOF announced plans to present a new banking law and new Bank of Japan law before the Diet. SCAP's scheme for a Banking Board was deftly avoided; instead, interest rates were to be determined by the MOF, upon the advice of the Monetary Policy Committee. Second, to ensure sound banking, bank deposits would be subject to a reserve requirement and a margin risk reserve. Third, the MOF would have the right to demand changes in commercial bank management if deemed necessary.[55]

Banks reacted strongly to the MOF's version of the laws. Employing the rhetoric of the day, banks decried the MOF's appropriation of monetary policy and other administrative powers as "undemocratic." Tatsu Amaya, director of operations of the Tokyo Bankers Club secretariat, declared: "We object to MOF's phrase 'As we deem fit.' This sort of bureaucratic arrogance is out of keeping with the times." Using another argument, the Federation of Bankers Associations stated that "because the Japanese economy has not yet recovered, adopting the American system is premature." Ichirō Machida, director of the Research Division of Chiyoda Bank (now Mitsubishi), insisted that the only condition for a control economy, save imminent national extinction, was that the government fully compensate the private sector for intrusion.[56] Though they employed a variety of arguments, banks were in agreement that the Banking Board should be strengthened and MOF's overweening control reduced. Banks, however, never asked for free competition instead in the financial markets. Their complaints were directed against those regulations that would transfer some of the costs of protection onto the banks themselves, such as the deposit and risk-reserve requirements.

The MOF knew its only chance for tightening up the banking sys-

[54]Ibid., September 4, 1948; *Sekai Keizai*, October 12, 1948.

[55]*Kinyū Zaisei Jijō*, August 28, 1950, p. 19; *Mainichi*, September 23, 1950; *Nikkei*, October 11, 1950; *Sankei*, October 30, 1950; *Jiji*, November 8, 1950.

[56]Tatsu Amaya, "Shin Kinyū Gyōhō ni taisuru Iken," *Kinyū Zaisei Jijō*, September 11, 1950, pp. 18–19; *Mainichi*, September 23, 1950; *Kinyū Zaisei Jijō*, November 13, 1950, p. 30; Machida Ichirō, "Keizai Tosei no Mitōshi," *Kinyū Zaisei Jijō*, February 26, 1951, p. 3.

tem was to borrow SCAP's weight—all in the name of reform.[57] But now, with the banks angered, the MOF had to abandon its schedule for submitting the draft to the Diet in November 1950. Dodge had stated his approval of the new law; but because the Occupation was soon to end, Dodge felt this was an issue the Japanese would work out themselves. Besides, his suggestions had already been "modified" beyond recognition. The MOF badly wanted Dodge's extra push for this piece of legislation, but he did not oblige. Dodge returned to the United States in December 1950 without giving any new orders, leaving the MOF to face the banks and the politicians alone.

Neither the ruling Liberal party (Jiyūtō) nor the Democratic party (Minshutō) was prepared to anger the entire banking community just before the April 1950 elections. The Minshutō, with its close ties to the banks, would not have moved against its supporters in any case; and the Jiyūtō could not afford to allow the Minshutō any preelection points gained from playing the white knight against the Jiyūtō administration. The MOF, then, was back where it had begun, reconsidering the disputed points.[58]

The politicians found another avenue of election support in the financial sector, though it was the Minshutō that was reluctant this time. *Mujin* were small, credit-union-like financial institutions that desired licensing from the MOF so they, too, could enjoy the MOF's protective umbrella. But the MOF was eager to streamline the banking industry, not expand it. Finding Jiyūtō and Socialist politicians more sympathetic, the Mujin successfully lobbied for a law, over the MOF's objections, which transformed them into mutual banks for small business.[59]

In September 1951 the MOF again tried to draft a new banking law. This time the MOF clarified its authority, as the banks had requested. Administrative guidance would be restricted, but the

[57]"Ginkōhō Daigo Shian o Dodge-shi ni Teishutsu," *Kinyū Zaisei Jijō*, October 23, 1950, pp. 8–9.

[58]"Ginkō Hōan no Isshōten," *Kinyū Zaisei Jijō*, November 27, 1950, p. 5; "Ginkō Hōan, Kokkai Teishutsu Konnan," *Kinyū Zaisei Jijō*, December 18, 1950, pp. 3–4; "Shin Ginkō Hōan no Yukue," *Kinyū Zaisei Jijō*, February 19, 1951, pp. 7–8; *Tokyo Shimbun*, July 20, 1951; *Nikkei*, August 18, 1951.

[59]*Kinyū Zaisei Jijō*, November 27, 1950, pp. 78–79; December 4, 1950, pp. 29–31; February 26, 1951, pp. 6, 39–44.

MOF would have legal authority to ban compensating balances, to establish ceilings for bank dividends and for bank employee salaries, to increase banks' mandatory capital ratio, and to prohibit bank lending to any one borrower in excess of 25 percent of the bank's net worth. Again, the banks fought back, taking their grievances to the politicians. And this time they had allies in industry. The 25 percent net-worth ratio on loans would have left steel, shipbuilding, textile companies, and their many subcontractors short on funds.[60]

On September 25, 1951, Finance Minister Ikeda invited leaders in the banking world to discuss the MOF's latest draft. But his conciliatory gesture was not enough, and it was too late. Already, a growing group of Ikeda's Jiyūtō party—including Kiichi Aichi, later to become finance minister himself[61]—was joining the side of the banks. Ikeda gave up.

Ikeda was replaced by Mukai as finance minister in 1952, but the MOF continued to study the new banking law and a new Bank of Japan law for a number of years through its newly established advisory organ, the Financial System Research Council (Kinyū Seido Chōsakai). Upon the merger of the two conservative parties into the Liberal Democratic party in 1955, however, the MOF began to have second thoughts about legislation that would place monetary policy more squarely in the hands of the cabinet. MOF officials said, "Neutrality of the BOJ is critical now that parties are making a row over government bond issuance and credit control." What they meant was, the MOF already has control of monetary policy through its influence over the BOJ; to bring the formal mechanism for monetary policy into the cabinet would rob the MOF of influence now that there is a dominant party in the Diet.

BOJ governor Naoto Ichimada wanted revisions in the Bank of Japan law for different reasons: (1) corporations were getting stronger relative to banks, making the Temporary Interest Rate Control Law unnecessary to prevent lending rates from skyrocket-

[60]Shūichi Suzuki, "Ginkō wa Sensen no Kenzensei o Torimodose," *Kinyū Zaisei Jijō,* September 2, 1951, p. 3; *Sankei,* September 17, 1951; *Mainichi,* September 26, 1951; "Daikigyō no Daiginkō Izon no Jōkyō," *Kinyū Zaisei Jijō,* October 8, 1951, pp. 20–21.

[61]"Tairitsu Gekika," *Kinyū Zaisei Jijō,* October 1, 1951, pp. 10–12; "Ikeda-Ichimada Kyōen," *Kinyū Zaisei Jijō,* October 8, 1951, pp. 8–9.

ing; (2) because bank borrowings from the Bank of Japan were decreasing, the BOJ was considering a change in emphasis from window guidance to open-market operations and reserve requirement manipulation in the direction of monetary policy. Ichimada was not to have his way.[62]

In 1956 the MOF presented yet another version of the banking law, this time dropping the Bank of Japan law revisions altogether. The MOF's focus was now on small problem banks; the MOF sought widened powers to change bank management in cases of (1) legal offense, (2) disobedience of the minister's directives, and (3) actions against the public interest. With many allies in the Diet, however, the small banks successfully blocked the bill from passage. Not for nearly another decade would the issue resurface.

This is not to say that all else was quiet in financial policy making. Two recurring debates on the floor of the Diet concerned, first, banks' "overloan" problem and, second, the compensating balances banks required of corporate borrowers. On the first point, Dodge had been critical of banks' excessive indebtedness to the Bank of Japan, upon which banks relied for making corporate loans. In the early postwar years city banks lent more than they had in deposits. But throughout the 1950s banks fought off legislation that would have limited the proportion of assets they could lend to any one customer. On a second point of controversy, corporations were angry about compensating balances, but they acquiesced as long as they received access to a steady stream of loans. The MOF's Banking Bureau promised the Diet that it was limiting the extent of these forced deposits, but when it was discovered that banks were vastly underreporting the balances, the Democratic Socialists suggested legislation to compel stricter compliance. Nothing came of the DSP proposal.[63]

The 1960s brought a new wave of attempts at financial reform. At a New Year's party of the National Federation of Banks in 1964, Finance Minister Kakuei Tanaka stated, "We welcome bank mergers in a consolidation effort to make the financial system more compatible with an open economy." In 1964 the MOF planned accession to article 8 of the IMF and to join the OECD, pledged

[62]*Nikkei*, September 11, 1955.

[63]See, for example, *Nikkei*, May 2, 1956; Kasuga's Diet speech, *Kinyū Zaisei Jijō*, October 19, 1964, pp. 46–47.

allegiance to the industrialized world's principles of free trade and capital flows. The MOF skillfully employed this foreign pressure, as it would again, in its domestic struggle to streamline the banking sector. The real problem was a domestic recession that was putting pressure on the financial system, starting with the weakest links.

Finance Minister Tanaka was willing to float the MOF's balloon, but he had his own political reasons. The LDP was also wooing small businesses, which happened to be the group hardest hit by banks' compensating balances. "If there are banks that cannot survive without demanding compensating balances," Tanaka stated on the floor of the Diet, "they will have to be absorbed by stronger banks."[64] Tanaka was also attempting to woo large banks from his rival faction leader, Takeo Fukuda. Indeed, Tanaka succeeded in drawing several banks closer to his camp, including Sanwa, Saitama, and even Mitsubishi.[65]

Not a great deal actually happened. There was little incentive for small banks to give up their independence as long as the MOF was behind them with an implicit guarantee of solvency. Nor could the MOF revoke its guarantee; small banks were well organized and politically influential. It was this power that had prevented the MOF from passing the costs of protection onto the banks themselves by way of a more robust deposit insurance system paid for by the banks. In August 1964 Daiichi Bank did absorb an affiliated institution, Asahi Bank. And in the following year Sumitomo acquired Kawauchi Bank, of which it already had partial ownership. But this was far from being the massive spate of mergers and acquisitions that the MOF would have liked to see.[66]

The MOF's Efficiency Campaigns

In 1967 the MOF's Banking Bureau launched its first "efficiency campaign." By "efficiency," the MOF was referring not to the

[64]Tanaka's statement, intentionally or unintentionally, misconstrues the nature of compensating balances. The balances were a way to equilibrate demand and supply of credit by raising its effective cost, despite regulations on ceiling loan rates—that is, a market response to regulation.
[65]Matsuzawa, *Watakushi no Ginkō Shōwashi*, pp. 116–17; "Ginkō Gappei no Taitō to Saihen no Hōkō," *Kinyū Zaisei Jijō*, January 4, 1965, pp. 56–57; Toshihiro Nakajima, *Aru Ginkō Gappei no Zasetsu* (Tokyo: Tōyō Keizai Shimpōsha, 1979), pp. 143–44; "Kakuei Kinyū Kōsō," *Zaikai*, October 1, 1972, pp. 34–37.
[66]Matsuzawa, *Watakushi no Ginkō Shōwashi*.

121

economic notion of Pareto-optimal credit allocation, but to stability of the financial system, which the MOF bureaucrats needed for their work to proceed smoothly. In the aftermath of the 1965 recession, corporate bankruptcies put pressure on a large number of small banks. But in the absence of a strong deposit insurance system and strict bank disclosure requirements, allowing a bank to go under was unthinkable. The alternative was to get rid of the weakest banks through mergers.

Arguing that greater market discipline was needed in the financial system, Banking Bureau Director General Satoshi Sumita guided two laws through the Diet which facilitated bank mergers—that is, provided material incentives for consolidation. Plums included tax breaks, exceptions to the Antimonopoly Law, and the prospect for small institutions of moving up the ladder to become full-fledged banks. Although small financial institutions receive some preferential treatment such as tax exemption on their real estate holdings, there are ceilings on the size of corporations to which they can lend. Some of the stronger credit institutions were therefore eager to become full-fledged banks. Banks, on the other hand, opposed small institutions being called banks.[67]

Small financial institutions have been remarkably successful in using the political process—specifically, LDP politicians—to thwart MOF "efficiency" measures against their interests. Over the next five years, between 1968 and 1973, there were 121 mergers, and in a number of them smaller institutions "graduated" to higher asset categories to become bona fide banks.[68] But that is about as far as the "efficiency campaign" went. In February 1968 Tetsugorō Obara, chairman of the Credit Institutions Association (*Zenshinren*), warned that small institutions would not sit back idly and watch themselves become prey to the big banks. They would use

[67]"Chūshō Kigyō Kinyū Seido no Seibi Kaizen no tame no Sōgō Ginkōhō, Shinyō Kinkohō nado no Ichibu o Kaiseisuru Hōritsu" and "Kinyūkikan no Gappei oyobi Tenkan ni Kansuru Hōritsu," in Matsuzawa, *Watakushi no Ginkō Shōwashi*, p. 118; Okura Mondo, *Ōkurashō Ginkōkyoku* (Tokyo: Pāru Books, 1985), pp. 34–42; Nakajima, *Aru Ginkō Gappei no Zasetsu*, pp. 138–39.

[68]Matsuzawa, *Watakushi no Ginkō Shōwashi*, p. 118; Nakajima, *Aru Ginkō Gappei no Zasetsu*, pp. 226–27; *Asahi*, February 8, 1968; "Kinyū Kikan ni Miru Gappei Tenkan Mūdo," *Kinyū Zaisei Jijō*, February 19, 1968, pp. 33–38; "Ishu Kinyū Kikan no Gappei Tenkan," *Kinyū Zaisei Jijō*, March 11, 1968, pp. 25–27; *Kinyū to Ginkō*, April 18, 1980, p. 32.

their political clout to the extent necessary. Indeed, most of the mergers that occurred were between small credit institutions willing to forego autonomy in exchange for full bank status. Two mergers between large financial institutions also took place. In 1971 Taiyō Mutual Bank merged with Kōbe Bank, a city bank, to become Taiyō Kōbe, one of the twelve city banks. In 1973 two city banks, Daiichi and Kangyo, merged to become Daiichi Kangyō, the largest of the city banks.

Rigid entry barriers, branch restrictions, separation of types of financial institutions, and the fixed interest rate structure still protected the weakest banks. Granted, all banks, weak and strong, benefited from these constraints on competition, and particularly on low deposit rates. But this would remain true only insofar as depositors had no preferable alternatives to bank accounts. For the time being, the MOF was able to maintain equilibrium among the financial institutions under its umbrella.[69]

If change was slow in coming, the MOF did not give up its deliberations. In July 1968 the MOF's Financial System Research Council issued a report, Interest Rates and the Scope of Activities of Financial Institutions, in which the council proposed upgrading the deposit insurance scheme. It specified no timetable.[70]

The MOF's next attempt to tighten up the banking industry did not come until nearly a decade later, when the post-oil-shock recession rippled through the banking community. In 1977 the new director general of the Banking Bureau, Hiroshi Tokuda, promptly chose as his goal the "new efficiency campaign." Tokuda had served as the chief of the MOF's Financial System Research Council secretariat and in that capacity was largely responsible for the report calling for efficiency, more mergers, and a stronger deposit insurance system. Tokuda's zeal earned him nicknames in the banking community as "Mr. Consolidation," "His Unsmiling Highness," and "Mr. Loss" (Sonda), this last being a pun on his name which indicated how banks viewed his financial policies. Now, in 1977, Tokuda stated without apology: "There are too many financial

[69]Akiyoshi Horiuchi and Kikuo Iwata, "Nihon ni okeru Ginkō Kesei," Keizaigaku Ronshū, April 1984, pp. 2–33; Yoshi Suzuki, "Nihonno Kinyū Jiyūkan—sono Seiji Keizaigaku," Kinyū to Ginkō, December 12, 1984, pp. 22–29.
[70]Matsuzawa, Watakushi no Ginkō Shōwashi, p. 121.

institutions. Even thirteen city banks is too many. Small institutions in particular should consider market conditions more seriously."[71] To assist him in his work, Tokuda hand-picked members for a private brain trust for the Banking Bureau—the Finance Study Group. In June 1978 this group issued a report giving Tokuda's consolidation plan total backing with arguments for economic efficiency and the public good; but these were small arrows with which to fight a battle with the banks.[72]

Not surprisingly, the small banks fought Tokuda the hardest. They accused him of favoring the strong and of advocating the survival of the fittest, which of course was true. When the chairman of Sumitomo Bank approached Tokuda about possible absorption of the smaller Kansai Mutual Bank, which was not interested in merger, Tokuda promised his full support. Others in the MOF were less enthusiastic. The former directors general of the Banking Bureau, who met two to three times annually, cautioned Tokuda about acting too rashly. "Don't ignore the political clout of the mutual banks and the credit institutions," they warned. Choosing not to heed their advice, Tokuda proceeded with the merger plans; but his predecessors were right. The merger scheme fell through and Tokuda's campaign more or less ground to a halt along with it.[73]

The chain of events began when the National Mutual Bank Association rallied to the aid of Kansai Mutual Bank. The association maintained a united front against big bank encroachment, which was without exception aimed at the biggest, healthiest mutual banks. Allowing the strongest mutuals to get bought up increased the threat to the rest of them.

Small banks, in most cases, are managed by fiercely independent entrepreneurs who have a particular aversion to being bought out by bigger institutions. Moreover, they have political clout by virtue of their importance in localities, close ties with local businesses, and

[71]Nakajima, *Aru Ginkō Gappei no Zasetsu,* pp. 139, 147. See also Tokuda's statement before the Upper House Budget Committee on April 4, 1978, advocating bank mergers; in *Kinyū Zaisei Jijō,* April 17, 1978, p. 27.

[72]Nakajima, *Aru Ginkō Gappei no Zasetsu,* pp. 146–47; interviews with Tokuda, June 1985 and June 1986; "Ōkura Jinmyaki no Kyōi," *Shūkan Gendai,* September 24, 1981, pp. 52–56.

[73]Nakajima, *Aru Ginkō Gappei no Zasetsu,* pp. 148–50; interviews with Tokuda.

relationships with politicians from their district. Unlike big banks, which give campaign contributions to the LDP as a whole, the small banks give to individual Diet members and to faction leaders, thus enhancing their influence over key policy makers. They also have more vote-gathering power than big banks by virtue of their community role and the importance of personal ties at that level of financial transactions.

In September 1978 the association held a two-day series of meetings (*Sōgin Kondankai*) to plan its line of defense. Of the seventy mutual banks present, sixty-nine opposed and only one favored the merger. The mutual banks also enlisted the support of the other small financial institutions in opposing the merger. Tetsugorō Obara, chairman of the Credit Institutions Association (Zenshonren), stated to the press on September 21 that the merger posed a threat to the entire financial (that is, small financial institution) community. The MOF was attempting to bulldoze them into making more room for the big banks, he said.

Later, on November 16, Prime Minister Fukuda gave the keynote address at the annual Mutual Banks convention, indicating his support of their cause. Once it was clear how strongly opposed small financial institutions were to the merger, it did not take long for the talks between Sumitomo and Kansai Mutual to fizzle out. On November 25, 1978, Tokuda told Sumitomo's chairman that further discussion would be fruitless.[74]

Despite this serious setback, Tokuda did achieve some of his goals during his tenure as director general. Under his directorship, in 1978, banks were permitted to issue certificates of deposit at market rates. Of course there was opposition from weaker banks, since this would raise the cost of capital and attract large deposits away from them, putting pressure on their already fragile balance sheets. The large banks welcomed the measure, because securities firms were soaking up corporate funds through their short-term repurchase securities (*gensaki*). The compromise solution was to permit CDs, while keeping the denominations very high in order to minimize the damage to weak banks.[75]

[74]Nakajima, *Aru Ginkō Gappei no Zasetsu*, pp. 153–212.
[75]James Horne, *Japan's Financial Markets* (London: Allen & Unwin, 1985), chapter on MOF.

Financial Politics in Contemporary Japan

Three decades, a foiled banking law, and two efficiency campaigns later, the MOF was not appreciably closer to a consolidated,
easily managed banking sector. Granted, Japan's top banks had
become world-class banks in the 1970s; eighteen were in the top
hundred and sixty-two in the top five hundred by 1986.[76] But it was
the many more weak ones the MOF was concerned about, because
the MOF had to function as guarantor for all. Operating a convoy
was difficult enough when Japan was a more or less closed economy. Now there were numerous leaks in the system, the largest
being Japanese corporations' fund-raising ability abroad. Domestic
banks no longer had the market for money cornered, which meant
that banks had to compete on a global scale even at home. The
MOF, then, was more eager than ever to introduce some market
winds into the greenhouse. The MOF would not let the small
financial institutions disappear, but it could at least have an easier
time consolidating the industry.

The MOF had been considering, since 1975, another banking
law. In March 1979, after four years of deliberations, the Financial
System Research Council (FSRC) produced a report stating that
a sound banking system required further consolidation, stronger
MOF oversight powers with sanctions, higher net-worth ratios, and
stricter disclosure rules. Moreover, the FSRC recommended that
interest rates should eventually be market determined, following a
gradual transition period.[77] True to form, the banking community
reacted promptly. Takuji Matsuzawa, speaking as chairman of the
National Federation of Banks, stated that the only thing really
needed was legal authority for banks to engage in government bond
retailing and dealing. Expanded MOF powers were not welcome;
financial soundness should be based on banks' self-responsibility.
Nor were more disclosure rules needed; banks, he said, should be
free to present its books to investors and depositors as each bank
sees fit.

There were also those who were critical of the FSRC report for
the opposite reason. Bunkichirō Horiga, a finance professor at
Waseda University, argued that even with the new law as proposed,

[76]Quek Peck Lim, "The World's Top Banks," *Euromoney*, June 1986, p. 105.
[77]Takujirō Hirata, *Dare no Tame no Ginkō* (Tokyo: Otsuki Shoten, 1981),
p. 226; *Nikkei*, March 20, 1979.

126

there still would not be enough competition in the system. The MOF, said Horiga, should take more decisive measures to introduce market discipline into the financial system. In an editorial, *Nikkei* also criticized the council for being too timid. The FSRC, *Nikkei* suggested, should have urged the development of a short-term government bill market to speed the deregulation of interest rates. But these voices of opposition did not resonate sufficiently among the public at large to launch a grass-roots campaign for change.[78]

Despite the chilly reception by the banking community, Finance Minister Kaneko announced that the MOF hoped to submit a draft of the new banking law to the Diet, based on the council's recommendations, within the year. In the general elections of September 1979, however, the LDP suffered a serious setback in both houses of the Diet. From the MOF's vantage point, the LDP, with its ties to various interest groups, was difficult enough to maneuver past; a stronger opposition, however, would make matters worse. The opposition, also tied to small business, was even more opposed to the MOF's efficiency campaign than was the LDP. The MOF feared the opposition would attempt to attach riders knocking big business and big finance, and otherwise obstruct the MOF's efficiency goals.

In August 1979 the MOF did submit one bill, the Small Financial Institution Law (Chūshō Kigyō Kinyū Hō), to replace the Mutual Bank Law of 1950. As long desired by the mutual banks, the law would allow mutual banks to drop the "mutual" from their title, thus giving them greater credibility with the depositing and investing public. Second, the restrictions on lending to large firms would be relaxed, allowing this class of banks to compete more directly with the larger local banks or even city banks. The MOF's purposes would also be served, since lowering the walls between the different categories of financial institutions would introduce a greater degree of competition and, thereby, a natural selection process. Mergers would be inevitable, the MOF reasoned. But the local banks fought a successful campaign with the LDP against the law, and the cabinet's Legislation Committee (Naikaku Hōseikyoku) quashed the bill before it even reached the floor of the Diet for deliberation. The bill the Diet eventually passed in April 1981 allowed the mutuals

[78] *Nikkei,* April 28 and June 21, 1979; *Asahi,* June 8 and 21, 1979.

and other small financial institutions to engage in foreign exchange operations, but the mutuals had to keep their title.[79]

Disclosure Provisions

In the June 1980 elections the LDP won by a large margin, in part a show of the public's condolences for Prime Minister Ōhira, who died in mid-campaign. Banking was not a campaign issue. Nonetheless, the stage was now set for the MOF to resubmit a banking law to the Diet, since there would be less effective interference from the opposition parties in legislating it.

As always, the MOF was striving for a workable mix of carrots and sticks, knowing further steps toward greater competition would be impossible without positive incentives. The sticks: (1) banks would be required to meet stricter disclosure rules, which would expose shaky banks and force them to merge with stronger banks; (2) banks would have to reduce their loans to any single borrower to 25 percent of their assets, with the goal of foisting some of the costs of maintaining a stable banking system onto the banks themselves. In exchange, the sweetener would be to allow banks entry into the government bond business.[80] A brilliant plan, it would appear.

Banks reacted with less than gratitude. They wanted the carrot without the sticks. Disclosure, lending considerations, and bank management, the banks argued, should be matters of each bank's judgment. And as discussed earlier in this chapter, banks argued that the sweetener was not sweet enough: they wanted to retail and deal in government bonds now, and with no hitches.[81] Banks took their case to the LDP. The LDP would do nothing to invite a sharp backlash from the securities industry, but it could do something about the MOF's "sound banking" provisions. On February 17, at a meeting sponsored by the securities industry (*Nikkō Seminar*), the chairman of the LDP Policy Affairs Research Council, Shintarō

[79] *Nikkei*, February 22, 1980, and April 17, 1981; "Yonesato Ginkō Gyōsei o Hihansuru," *Kinyū to Ginkō*, April 18, 1980, pp. 30–31.

[80] *Nikkei*, December 18 and 25, 1980; "Kinkyū Kaisetsu," *Kinyū Zaisei Jijō*, January 12, 1981, pp. 16–17.

[81] *Nikkei*, December 31, 1980, January 11, 14, 15, 22, and 30, 1981, February 3, 5, and 11, 1981; "Ginkōhō Kaisei," *Kinyū Zaisei Jijō*, January 19, 1981, pp. 14–20; "Shin Ginkōhō," *Tōyō Keizai*, January 31, 1981, pp. 102–6; "Ginkōhō Kaisei, Part II," *Kinyū Zaisei Jijō*, February 16, 1981, pp. 14–17. For an annotated version of the banking law, see *Kinyū Zaisei Jijō*, February 23, 1981, pp. 22–34.

Abe, stated, "The proposed disclosure requirement and loan restriction are remnants of the post–oil shock anger at banks and big business."[82]

Through much of the 1960s and 1970s the banking industry was the object of public criticism. Bank profits were little affected by the recessions that wracked other sectors of the economy, and in good times banks did better than any other institution. In the aftermath of the 1971 oil shock, when Japan suffered severe inflation, banks lent huge sums of money to trading companies, which in turn purchased large tracts of real estate before land prices peaked, thus contributing to the inflation. The MOF, responding to pressure from the Diet in the early 1970s to "do something about banks' irresponsible loans," but also acting with system stability in mind, had restricted the amount lent to a single customer to a proportion of the bank's total net worth up to 20 percent. The targets were to be reached by 1979. For the MOF, this had been a welcome opportunity to reintroduce the provision that had fallen to political opposition back in 1950.[83]

Most banks complied easily by 1979 to the net-worth-loan rule, less because of their sacrifice than because firms were increasingly diversifying their sources of funds. But Mitsui Bank was still over-lent to Mitsui Bussan, which was struggling with a beleaguered petrochemical complex in Iran. Lacking legal sanctions, the MOF could do little more about Mitsui's defiance of administrative guidance than slap the bank's wrists: licenses for three new branches to open in 1980 were revoked. This time the MOF wanted stronger deterrence capability, namely, legal authority to impose more serious penalties.[84]

The economic and political environments had changed. Now, with lower profit rates and problems of their own, banks were

[82]Abe may or may not have known that there are public interest reasons for disclosure and lending ratios, such as to enhance prudential behavior of financial institutions. See, for example, Yoshio Suzuki, "Comparative Studies of Financial Innovation, Deregulation, and Reform in Japan and the United States," in Hugh Patrick and Ryūichiro Tachi, eds., *Japan and the United States Today* (Montpelier, Vt.: Capital City Press, 1987), pp. 156–67. In the United States the rule is a bank cannot lend more than 10 percent of its net worth to a single customer.

[83]*Tōyō Keizai*, April 4, 1980, pp. 38–41.

[84]Toshiaki Kaminogo and Kinosuke Kubota, eds., *Ginkō: Shoaku no Kongen* (Tokyo: Seiji Kōhō Center, 1978), pp. 95–115; "Ōguchi Shinyō Kisei" (Mitsui Bank mimeo, undated), p. 173.

perceived more as victims of MOF ambition than as villains work-ing against the public. "I doubt," said PARC chairman Abe, "that these kinds of provisions would get through the Diet in this day and time. Even if the MOF carts them out, the party won't go for them." Abe passed over the MOF's goal to foster competition. "In a time when private-sector vitality is essential, excess regulation is counter-productive. We'll only consider the bill after the MOF and banks have worked out their problems."[85] An MOF official, responding to the press's inquiry, declared: "We don't know why Abe said what he did, but we still intend to bring the bill to the floor. The LDP's Public Finance Committee [Zaisei Bukai] and Financial Is-sues Study Group [Kinyū Mondai Chōsakai] have approved the bill already, and party discipline should apply in this case as usual."[86]

Abe was right and the MOF was wrong, for banks had reached "an understanding" behind the MOF's back. The two LDP commit-tees examining the bill retracted their approval. Junichirō Koizumi, chairman of the LDP Public Finance Committee, and even Ichirō Satō, a former vice-minister of the MOF and chairman of the Financial Issues Study Group, turned against the bill. A few Diet members, such as former MOF bureaucrat and active member of the Public Finance Committee Takujirō Hamada, remained sympa-thetic to the MOF's aims, but they were in a small minority.

In joint sessions stretching from February to April, the Public Finance Committee and the Financial Issues Study Group redrafted much of the law. First, the disclosure requirements were all but removed. Banks were obliged to specify, in broad categories, who their borrowers were, and in what percentages. Second, no sanc-tions attending the lending limit provision, and the limit itself was raised from 20 percent to 25 percent of a bank's net worth, dis-counted bills excluded. Third, the MOF was foiled once again in its quest for legal authority to get rid of bad bank management (*kaizen kankoku*).[87] On May 25, 1981, the LDP's version of the banking law passed the Diet, to go into effect in April 1982.[88]

[85] *Nikkei*, February 17, 1981.
[86] Ibid.
[87] *Nikkei*, February 18, 21, 24, and 27, 1981, March 3, 5, 24, and 25, 1981, April 8, 14, 1981; "Shin Ginkō Hōan Ōhaba Shūsei," *Kinyū Zaisei Jijō*, April 27, 1981, pp. 14–16; "Ginkōhō Kaisei to wa Nandatta no ka," *Kinyū Zaisei Jijō*, May 4, 1981, pp. 98–101.
[88] *Nikkei*, May 25, 1981; *Yomiuri*, April 1, 1982.

What accounts for the LDP's about-face? Obviously, the LDP does not grant banks special favors automatically; banks had to pay for this one. It is not that banks and the LDP were not already friendly. Each of the thirty city banks, for example, reports contributions to the LDP on an order of 65–75 million yen annually.[89] But as long as banks' relations with the MOF were more or less on even keel, there was no incentive to spend larger sums on political campaigns. The banks wanted the politicians to be there when needed. For favorable revisions in the MOF's banking bill, however, banks allegedly paid to individual influential LDP politicians 500 million yen in unreported gifts over the usual contributions.[90] Fortunately for the banks, this time there was no countervailing group making contributions for the opposite cause.

When asked about the LDP's revision of the law, Finance Minister Watanabe responded, "That's politics."[91] The career bureaucrats were less sanguine. Banks had taken the carrot—namely, the government bond business—and escaped the sticks. Relations between banks and the Banking Bureau had never been worse. This situation was as bad for the MOF as for the banks, since smoothness of regulation depends on financial-sector cooperation to a considerable degree. The MOF set about mending the frayed relationship, replacing Banking Bureau Director General Hiroshi Yonesato in June 1981 with a new man, Yasutaka Miyamoto. Miyamoto felt that efficiency of the financial system was a medium-term goal rather than an immediate one. Nonetheless, he maintained that overt bank protection would have to go eventually, and the sooner the better.[92]

Although the MOF had intended to exchange bank entry into government bond activities for market discipline, the politicians relaxed the market discipline in exchange for political contributions. Apparently, the banks felt that escaping the MOF's stick was worth at least 500 million yen.

[89] In early September every year the Home Affairs Ministry reports sources of political contributions.

[90] This is allegedly a conservative estimate and is easily within the legally permissible sum for each participating bank. Fumio Ikeuchi (*Asahi* political reporter), "Zoku Giin to Riken," manuscript, p. 157; "Sankata Ichiryō Son," *Kinyū Zaisei Jijō*, April 20, 1981, pp. 10–11; Kenji Utsumi, "Atsuryoku Giin no Jittai," *Gendai*, August 1982, pp. 141–58.

[91] *Nikkei*, April 11, 1981.

[92] "Jiyūka Gyōsei o Sokushinsuru," *Kinyū Zaisei Jijō*, July 6, 1981, pp. 16–19.

131

Financial Policy Making and the Power of the MOF

As this legislative history demonstrates, there is no single form of financial policy making in Japan. When dealing with competing claims of the banking and securities industries, the Ministry of Finance presided over a compromise that both groups ultimately accepted. In the disclosure controversy, banks circumvented the MOF to obtain a political solution more to their liking.

The MOF, unlike financial authorities in the United States, is both capable and desirous of maintaining basic equilibrium among various types of financial institutions. Because the LDP is an alternative mediator for the groups the MOF regulates, the MOF's preemptive equilibration is effectively bound by the LDP's political calculus. The theory of regulation therefore describes Japanese financial policy making more accurately than it does the American counterpart. Although it is true that the MOF's administrative guidance circumvents the legislative process, banks comply only if they feel they are fairly compensated. What deceptively appears to be bureaucratic-led policy making, therefore, is high politics in disguise, little different in substance from the instances of direct political involvement.

The MOF's autonomy is greatest when dealing with competing interest groups of roughly equal political influence, but still the MOF must work with a narrow range of acceptable solutions. If either side were to deem the compromise too costly, it could pay the LDP to enforce the equilibrium point. There is no reason for the MOF to misstep, however, because it constantly avails itself of each group's reaction even while forging compromise solutions. In addition to meeting frequently, formally and informally, with leaders of the financial community, MOF bureaucrats also engineer "news leakages" to test reactions before committing themselves to a controversial policy position.[93]

[93] In October 1987 the *Nikkei* "leaked" news that the MOF was considering a "merchant bank" model as a preliminary step toward allowing commercial banks into the securities business. The adamant opposition of the securities industry suggested that the timing was premature. "Ōkurashō ga 'Tōshi Ginkō' Kōsō," *Nikkei*, October 14, 1987; Henny Sender, "The Shortcomings of Consensus," *Institutional Investor*, March 1988, pp. 76–78.

It is when working with a single well-organized group that the MOF has the least room to maneuver. A case in point is banks' success in keeping to a minimum the costs they bear for the stability of the financial system. In a world of increasingly effective international yield arbitrage, banks still enjoy a considerable degree of protection domestically.

The MOF has allies within the banking community, at least on some issues. As Japanese firms' increasing access to the virtually unregulated Euromarket provide large-scale investors and borrowers with attractive alternatives to staying at home, domestic banks must either lose business or make their own deposits and loans more competitive. This has driven a wedge between the large, strong banks that can and the weak banks that cannot.[94] Large banks, for example, began agitating some time ago for deregulation of certain interest rates, whereas the small banks continued to resist. The MOF's compromise solution was to deregulate large-denomination instruments, keeping the small deposits regulated.[95] Large banks have also been eager to begin new lines of business, such as trust banking and long-term banking, which have been traditionally off limits to regular banks in the interests of minimizing competition. Their efforts have been only partially successful in these areas because of the trenchant opposition from the financial institutions enjoying the protection.

The obvious solution for the MOF, were it primarily concerned with a stronger, more durable financial system, would be simply to allow small banks to go bankrupt. But there are still major obstacles: Japan lacks both the safety net of a sturdy deposit insurance system and strict bank disclosure requirements. Whereas depositors in the United States are insured up to $100,000 (12 million yen at 120 yen to the dollar), the Japanese depositor was insured only up to 3 million yen until recently, and since 1986 has been insured up

[94]Though a large bank is not necessarily strong, and a small bank not necessarily weak, there is a strong correlation because of economies of size and scope. Niche banks have to be very good at what they do to survive in an open market.

[95]In an example of big banks' breaking the ranks, in the fall of 1984 the country's top five banks announced their decision to issue equity at the market price. Traditionally, banks have parceled out shares to existing shareholders whenever they wanted to raise capital, fearing loss of control. But now higher capital ratios were becoming key to competing with foreign banks abroad. *Nikkei,* October 3, 1984.

to 10 million yen. To allow banks to fail in this environment would still be to risk monetary runs and panics.

In 1984, when the MOF proposed upgrading the deposit insurance system, along with a rider allowing the MOF to force mergers, the banks opposed and the bill got nowhere. By the time the bill finally passed the Diet in May 1986, the rider giving the MOF merger power had disappeared, and the cost increase to the banks was less than the increase in deposit protection.[96] Large, strong banks bore a disproportionate share of the cost, given that they are the least likely to make use of the pool of funds. Nonetheless, the increased payments were relatively small: from 8 yen per 100,000 yen of deposits to 12 yen per 100,000 yen for a threefold increase in coverage to 10 million yen. This was half the coverage in the United States. Presumably, the MOF/BOJ would still have to function as the lender of last resort on the occasion of a bankruptcy. Moreover, by way of compensation, the MOF further reduced the reserve requirements for bank deposits. On net, it was not clear whether or not the MOF was shifting any appreciable cost of stability onto the banks.[97]

In its attempt to introduce stricter disclosure requirements in the new banking law, the MOF failed even more miserably. Obviously, the MOF has been unsuccessful in forging a coalition, even with big banks, on issues on which market forces have not already acted. Although large banks could certainly withstand greater disclosure, they would rather not have to. Small-denomination bank deposits are another example of slower regulatory change. Because the Euromarket is primarily for large transactions, the small depositor does not have the alternatives that the large depositor has. As a result, no bank in Japan, large or small, is in a hurry for the MOF to remove the ceiling on small-deposit rates or to allow the creation of money market substitutes in small denominations. The only complication is competition from the postal savings system, which is the subject of Chapter 6.

[96] *Nikkei,* June 26 and October 12, 1984; "Jiyū Hōnin Shugi," *Zaikai,* September 18, 1984. Tsutomu Miyauchi, director of Research at the National Association of Mutual Banks, says the MOF is still not in a position to allow any bank to fail.

[97] Akio Nakamura (assistant director of the Research Division, Banking Bureau), "Yokin Hokenhō Oyobi Junbi Yokin Seido," *Zaikei Shōhō,* March 31, 1986, pp. 2–6; Proceedings, Finance Committee, House of Representatives, May 24, 1986.

As in other democracies, Japan's political system favors organized interests. That is not to say big business, as sometimes has been mistakenly concluded. Only recently have scholars noted the extent to which Japan's small- and medium-sized business sector influences policy making through their influence on politicians.[98] The same is true for small, locally rooted financial institutions, though not to the same degree. First, because banks are monitored by the MOF, they are not able to evade taxes in the same way enterprise owners do and thereby have smaller political slush funds.[99] Second, as long as the MOF has been willing and able to protect them, banks large and small have not needed the aid of politicians except in times of crisis.

At least the second factor has begun to change. As the costs of preventing bank failure become greater, the MOF is less willing to pick up the tab. Politicians' help, therefore, becomes more crucial. Moreover, since the Campaign Contribution Law placed a ceiling on contributions of big corporations, LDP politicians in particular have switched to a policy of "shallow and wide," becoming more solicitous of smaller donors, including small banks.[100]

None of this addresses the question of why the Japanese public should have tolerated bank protectionism, which was undertaken at their expense, for so long. The LDP's close relations with numerous interest groups notwithstanding, why have the opposition parties not seized initiative, exercised political entrepreneurship, and incited the slumbering public to vote for their own interests? One reason might be that the public's interest is not clearly in the deregulation camp. After all, the MOF has not allowed a single bank to fail since World War II, thereby protecting the depositor. On the other hand, small depositors have been paying a very high, and mandatory, premium for security, judging from bank profits.

Another, more plausible, answer is that the opposition parties are tied to their own special interests: labor, in the cases of the Socialist

[98] Gerald L. Curtis, *The Japanese Way of Politics* (New York: Columbia University Press, 1987); Horiuchi and Iwata, "Nihon ni okeru Ginkō Kisei," p. 18.

[99] Yasuyuki Kishiro, *Jimintō Zeisei Chōsakai* (Tokyo: Tōyō Keizai Shimpōsha, 1985), pp. 129–31. The Japanese phrase *ku-ro-yon* (nine-six-four) refers to the popular adage that salaried persons pay taxes on 90 percent of their income, enterprise owners on 60 percent, and farmers on 40 percent.

[100] Curtis, *The Japanese Way of Politics*; Ikeuchi, "Zoku Giin to Riken"; interviews with politicians, May–October 1986.

135

party and the Democratic Socialist party. Labor is no more eager for a consolidation of the banking industry than is weak management, if it would mean paring down the work force. Labor's concern has more to do with working conditions for bank employees than with deposit returns for the general public. Labor's strongest push in the Diet's banking law debates, in fact, was to reduce bank employees' work week from six to five days.[101]

Given the infrequency of public arousal, the primary avenue for greater competition in Japanese financial markets will be pressure from the Euromarket. In the next chapter, we will examine how leakages from the domestic market to the Euromarket have begun to change the motivations of domestic banks.

[101]"Ginkōhō Kaiseinado o meguru Shūgiin Ōkurai no Shitsugi," as recorded in *Kinyū Zaisei Jijō*, November 3, 1980; "Shin Ginkō Hoān ni Taisuru Kakutō no Kenkai," *Kinyū Zaisei Jijō*, May 4, 1981, pp. 90–96.

5

Coping with
the Euromarket

On November 28, 1986, the Ministry of Finance's Securities Exchange Advisory Council proposed a significant relaxation of restrictions on domestic corporate bond issuance. The number of corporations eligible to issue unsecured straight bonds would triple to 180, the issuing unit of privately placed bonds would quintuple to 10 billion yen, and firms would be permitted to issue at any time during the month instead of at month's end as formerly stipulated. Moreover, in a break with a long tradition, firms with a high enough corporate rating would be allowed to issue unsecured bonds even though they did not meet the conventional standards of eligibility.[1]

At first glance, this change would appear to be a serious blow to the interests of the banking community: the easier it is for corporations to issue bonds, the less they must depend on bank loans for their external financing. In fact, however, most banks did not fight the change.[2] This chapter explains why not. The story line unfolds as follows: banks succeed in squelching the domestic bond market, to the benefit of their loan business. Once firms become strong enough to raise funds in the Euromarket, however, they take their business overseas. Banks follow them abroad and recapture some of

[1] *Japan Economic Journal,* November 8, 1986, p. 2.
[2] This chapter primarily refers to large banks and their blue chip customers. Small banks are not directly affected by changes in bond market rules since small firms, their main clientele, do not have ready access to bond markets.

the business, but suffer nevertheless from the abandonment of the domestic market. In attempting to stem the trend toward securitization, banks cut their spreads on domestic loans. With the domestic loan market consequently less profitable and hence less worth fighting for, the banks finally agree to woo firms back home by making the domestic bond market more attractive, in exchange for a larger role for banks in the private placement market.

Deregulation of the bond market, however, is more than an interesting story. Changes in the bond market help to explain the trend toward direct finance in Japan. Second, an examination of the process helps to generate more general propositions as to the how and why of financial deregulation. Increasing corporate activity in the Eurobond market lowered Japanese banks' resistance to deregulation of the domestic bond market. Third, this case study affords a penetrating look at how the financial authorities and financial sector interact in Japan. For self-interested reasons the financial institutions, not the MOF, initiated the deregulatory process. This case is fully consonant with the theory of regulation.

The History of the Bond Market

The 1920s were the "golden age" of Japan's bond market. Buoyed by the demand for industrial and consumer goods from war-stricken Europe, Japanese manufacturers enjoyed an unprecedented production boom. And to finance capacity expansion, large corporations turned to the domestic bond market for one-third to one-half of their funding needs.[3] Firms were attracted to the convenience of the bond market because they were free to choose among maturities of one to thirty years, and among numerous denominations, large and small. Banks, moreover, did not mind that bank loans accounted for only 5 percent or so of the large corporate finance market; banks were free to underwrite corporate bonds and keep them in their own portfolios or pass them along to securities firms for distribution to the public.[4]

[3] Kamekishi Takahashi, ed., *Nihon no Kōshasai Shijō* (Tokyo: Diamond Press, 1963), p. 128; Yasuji Abe, *Ginkō—Shōken Kokine Ronsō Oboegaki* (Tokyo: Nihon Keizai Shimbunsha, 1980), p. 55.

[4] Yūichirō Nagatomi, *Antei Seichō Jidai no Kōshasai Shijō* (Tokyo: Ōkura Zaimu Kyōkai, 1978), pp. 20–21.

Coping with the Euromarket

Once Europe's economy recovered from the devastation of World War I, the floor dropped out from under Japan's expanded export sector. Many firms defaulted on their bonds, leaving bond holders, including banks, with nothing. Beginning with the collapse of the Bank of Taiwan and the subsequent bank panic in 1927, hundreds of banks folded in the following years. The total number of banks shrank from 1,283 in 1927 to 538 in 1932.[5] The Ministry of Finance was caught by surprise; there was no creditor protection mechanism in place, and the MOF was forced to subsidize numerous ailing banks from government coffers to contain the disruption in financial markets.

Politicians, meanwhile, were concerned about their small constituents, who claimed that they were bearing the brunt of the recession. In May 1929 the Giichi Tanaka cabinet responded to the small business sector's massive lobbying by drafting "An Outline for Restructuring Small Business Finance," which was a design for ensuring that the consolidation of the financial sector did not eliminate the flow of funds to small enterprises. In a policy measure that still applies today, the smallest tier of financial institutions was prohibited from lending to firms larger than a given size. In the following year the MOF's Finance Bureau (Yokinbu) was ordered to disburse 50 million yen gathered from postal savings to small business. At the same time, the Ministry of Commerce and Industry attempted to organize cartels and industry associations to help small business deal with "excess competition."[6]

To prevent such a financial debacle from recurring, the MOF took advantage of the widespread uncertainty to draft a new banking law in 1927. The new legislation gave MOF broad, vaguely specified powers of oversight. In exchange for tolerating more extensive government intervention, however, banks obtained the MOF's protection and assurance of no further entries into the banking business. For this, the banks would thank their friends in the Kenseikai, Seiyū Hontō, and the Seiyūkai.

The MOF was not able to reduce drastically the number of banks as it desired. The Seiyūkai spearheaded a movement in the Diet,

---

[5] Jūrō Teranishi, *Nihon no Keizai Hatten to Kinyū* (Tokyo: Iwanami Shoten, 1982), p. 333.

[6] Hiromi Arisawa, ed., *Shōwa Keizai Shi* (Tokyo: Nihon Keizai Shimbun Press, 1977), p. 62.

later joined by the Kenseikai and Seiyū Hontō, to lower the MOF's proposed minimum figure for banks' mandatory capital base. Thus a tier of small banks on the MOF's blacklist survived the postcrash consolidation. The alternative to protective legislation would have been the establishment of a robust depositor insurance scheme and the imposition of strict balance sheet rules that would limit bank risk taking to a certain proportion of their portfolios. Only a powerful, politically independent MOF could have obtained such a bill. Instead, banks received protectionist legislation.[7]

Now banks, though there are fewer of them, were on more solid ground with the MOF as their guarantor. Their next move was to strengthen their position against corporate borrowers. With the MOF's blessing, about thirty of the largest bond-underwriting banks formed the Kisaikai or Bond Issue Arrangement Committee (hereafter Bond Committee) soon after the bank panic in order to "clean up the bond market." The Bond Committee established the collateral principle, which persists in modified form to the present day: "Corporate bonds shall not be issued without sufficient collateral." In a successful power play, the banks then gained another source of income: according to the Bond Committee's rules, only "trustee banks" (*jutaku ginkō*) would be permitted to manage the collateral until the maturity of the bond, for a fee.

At the core of the Bond Committee were eight banks, with the Industrial Bank of Japan central among them. Security firms were given a cut of the market as underwriting members of the Bond Committee, but only banks could earn the collateral fee. When Yamaichi Securities attempted in the late 1920s to take over a trustee bank to capture some of the collateral-management business, the MOF blocked the move.[8]

One of the most enduring effects of the Bond Committee's rules

[7]Reizō Kanda, "Kinyū Seido Kaizen ni Kanshite," *Ginkō Ronsō*, February 1, 1927, pp. 1–6; "Shin Ginkō Hōan no Shihon Kinseigen Riyū," *Ginkō Tsūshinroku*, March 20, 1927, p. 95; "Shin Ginkō Hōan no Shūsei Kaketsu," *Ginkō Tsūshinroku*, April 20, 1927, pp. 106–7; "Zaikai Fuan ni Taisuru Zōshō no Seimei," *Ginkō Tsūshinroku*, April 20, 1927, pp. 123–24; "Ōkurashō no Sekkyokuteki Ginkō Gōdō Sokushin," *Ginkō Tsūshinroku*, August 20, 1927, pp. 55–65; "Ōkurashō no Ginkō Gappei Sokushin," *Ginkō Tsūshinroku*, October 20, 1927, pp. 63–64.

[8]Hanju Takeuchi, *Wagakuni Shihonshijō no Kōzō to Mondaiten* (Tokyo: Zenkoku Chihō Ginkō Kyōkai, 1963), pp. 20–21; Abe, *Ginkō—Shōken Kakine Ronsō Oboegaki*, p. 55.

was the shift it engendered in Japanese corporate finance to reliance on bank loans. Naturally, corporations responded to the new collateral requirement by reducing their reliance on bond issuance for financing. In 1931 bonds accounted for 29.9 percent of corporate external funding and bank loans for 13.6 percent. In 1934 bonds accounted for 6.3 percent of external funding; in 1936 corporations issued almost no bonds at all, depending instead on bank loans for 40.6 percent of their funding needs.[9] Firms continued, however, to rely on equity issues for a substantial part of their financing. In 1933 equity accounted for 31.1 percent of corporate funding, and in 1936, 33.5 percent. The figure only dropped dramatically during World War II, when savings were channeled into savings banks for the war effort, from 22.6 percent in 1943 to 9.1 percent in 1944 and 6.1 percent in 1945.[10]

In the decade between 1936 and 1945 banks lost any autonomy they may have had, and the question of bank power in the economy became a moot point. Beginning with the Temporary Law of Credit Allocation enacted in 1937, the military seized increasing control of the nation's financial mechanisms. Manufacturers of military hardware were ensured preferential access to money, whether through bank lending or through the bond market. In fact, the military found the Bond Committee a convenient apparatus through which to operate.

The Recovery and Years of Rapid Growth

In December 1945 the MOF's Financial System Research Council established a subcommittee to study the bond market. Representatives from the securities industry argued that banks should not be allowed to underwrite bonds as they had in the prewar years, because their aim would be to stifle the market in favor of bank loans. Bankers insisted otherwise. Because of the sharp disagreement, the deliberations sputtered to a near halt; the purge of 1946 of those "implicated in the war effort" delivered a final blow to the discussion when it removed most members of the council and its securities market subcommittee.[11]

[9]Nagatomi, *Antei Seichō Jidai no Kōshasai Shijō*, pp. 16–17.
[10]Ibid.
[11]Abe, *Ginkō Shōken Kakine Ronsō Oboegaki*, p. 52.

141

SCAP bypassed the dispute with its blueprint for the 1948 Securities Exchange Act. SCAP's purpose, drawn from the Glass-Steagall Act in the United States, was (1) to protect bank depositors from banks' risky portfolio management and potential conflicts of interest, and (2) to promote greater competition between indirect financing through bank loans and direct financing on the bond and equity markets. Although section 65 of the Securities Exchange Act precluded banks from underwriting public placement bonds, banks were allowed participation in the private placement market as in the United States, since the buyers would be knowledgeable institutional investors. But this was a minimal concession, because there were few incentives for corporations to seek private placement of their bonds. First, the volume for each issue was severely limited. Second, the "no return rule" prohibited corporations from ever resorting to private placement once they had placed bonds publicly. A more important concession to the banks was the admission of the collateral principle in the bond market. The Bond Committee survived not only the war but the Occupation as well.[12]

The government played a sizable role in allocating capital through the bond market in the earliest postwar years. But this should not be exaggerated, either in scope or in duration. Soon after the war ended, Prime Minister Yoshida appointed Hiromi Arisawa, an economics professor at the University of Tokyo, to head a group to examine strategies for resuscitating Japan's basic industries, such as coal and petroleum. Also in the group were young bureaucrats who would later make their mark in their respective ministries, including Yōichi Ōshima from MOF, Toshihiko Yoshino from the Bank of Japan, Saburō Ōkita from the Ministry of Foreign Affairs, and Hidezō Inaba from the National Economic Research Council.[13]

In May 1946 Tanzan Ishibashi, known for his preference for fiscal stimulation, became finance minister. Ishibashi lost no time in expanding the work and authority of the Coal Committee, and in June 1946 the cabinet approved his Provisional Financial Policy for Postwar Industrial Reconstruction (Sengo Sangyō Saiken no tame no Ōkyūteki Kinyū Taisaku). In July Ishibashi converted the Coal

---

[12]Takeuchi, Wagakuni Shihonshijō no Kōzō to Mondaiten, pp. 68–69.

[13]Toshihiko Yoshino, Sengo Kinyūshi no Omoide (Tokyo: Nihon Keizai Shimbunsha, 1975), pp. 119–27.

Committee into the Reconstruction Finance Committee, under his chairmanship. This group drafted the Reconstruction Bank Bill and the Temporary Law for Credit Allocation, which were passed into law in January 1947. The Credit Allocation Law placed the Bond Committee physically inside the Bank of Japan and added as committee members representatives from the Ministry of Finance, the Bank of Japan, and the Economic Stabilization Board. Once a month the Bond Committee met to set the terms of bond issuance, giving preference to fuel industries, steel, and utilities companies.

In November 1948 SCAP issued a nine-point memorandum calling for credit rationing measures even *stricter* than those the Bond Committee had been implementing. Citing inflation as an imminent danger, "only business contributing to Japan's recovery should be funded," the memorandum instructed.[14] In 1949 the Temporary Law for Credit Allocation was scrapped, but the Bank of Japan continued to exert influence on bond issuance until 1955 by granting the lowest interest loans possible to the banks that could put up "priority bonds" as collateral. The banks did not mind the government's hand in credit allocation, as long as the government guaranteed payment in full upon maturity of the bonds.[15]

The government, or at least parts of it, was not entirely content to leave credit allocation solely to the banks after 1955. In August 1962 a MITI advisory board, the Industrial Order Committee, advocated greater "public-private cooperation" in financing Japanese industry. By December MITI had drafted a Law of Special Measures for Strengthening the International Competitive Ability of Designated Industries (Tokutei Sangyō Kyōsōryoku Kyōka Tokubetsusochi Hōan). Shigeru Sahashi, director of MITI's Enterprise Bureau and architect of the plan, was seeking legal authority to tighten up Japan's industrial structure with government-facilitated mergers. Banks, under this law, would have no choice but to support financing plans for industries designated by MITI. Banks fought tenaciously for their autonomy and were joined in opposition to the law by weaker industries that would fall prey to MITI's consolidation plan. MITI nevertheless submitted the law to the Diet, diluting

[14]Ibid., pp. 195–99.
[15]Arisawa, *Shōwa Keizai Shi*, pp. 288–90; Yoshino, *Sengo Kinyūshi no Omoide*, pp. 127–31.

certain provisions as a compromise. But bank lobbying was success-ful, and MITI was forced to retreat. The Diet refused to pass the bill in three consecutive sessions.[16]

After the government had removed its hand from credit alloca-tion in 1955, the Bond Committee screened corporations on the basis of a matrix of capital ratios, granting eligibility to very few corporations. In the early postwar years, most bonds were floated by the electric utility companies and heavy industrial firms, since they met the demanding capital requirements, and by certain finan-cial institutions themselves.[17]

In 1946 SCAP had banned financial institutions from issuing bonds, on the grounds that banks would crowd other corporations out of the bond market. But this measure was overturned in 1950 at the insistence of the Industrial Bank of Japan, and a heated debate ensued within the financial sector as to which institutions should be allowed to issue debentures. The Bank of Tokyo, which specialized in international finance and also had few domestic branches, wished to raise money on the bond market as well. Most banks, however, preferred that they *not* be allowed to issue bonds because bond issuance by banks would spur competition among them and thus erode their profits. The MOF argued, on the other hand, that such competition was desirable.

Because the MOF and banks were unable to come to terms, the debate reached the halls of the Diet. In 1951, just before general elections in April, a young Minshutō politician named Yasuhiro Nakasone spearheaded an attack in the Diet against the Jiyūtō administration for allowing the Bank of Tokyo to issue debentures. This would lead to, in Nakasone's words, "excessive competition" among the banks.[18] Ultimately, a compromise allowed the three long-term credit banks, eight trust banks, the Bank of Tokyo, and

[16]Akiyoshi Horiuchi, "Economic Growth and Financial Allocation in Postwar Japan," discussion paper, Research Institute for the Japanese Economy, University of Tokyo (August 1984), pp. 57–58; Kazuhiko Hayashibara, *Makunouchi Tsūsan-shō* (Tokyo: Yell, 1979), pp. 479–83.

[17]Shōken Dantai Kyōgikai, "Shasai Hakkō Shijō no Genjō to Kongo no Kadai," May 6, 1986, pp. 19–21.

[18]*Kinyū Zaisei Jijō* recorded the spirited exchanges on the floor of the Diet: February 12, 1951, pp. 20–21; February 26, 1951, pp. 7–9; March 5, 1951, p. 7; March 12, 1951, pp. 10–11.

quasi-governmental institutions to issue debentures since all had few branches from which to collect deposits. So as not to compete with bank deposits, the maturity of the debentures was set at five and seven years for the long-term credit banks, and three years for the Bank of Tokyo.[19] It should be noted that the pattern of political involvement in financial policy making is not a recent development, as is often mistakenly assumed.

Banks reabsorbed over half of all corporate bonds and financial debentures themselves.[20] As investors, then, they had a decisive voice in determining the volume that could be issued each month. And they made sure the amount was not enough to cut into their lending business. The Commercial Code, moreover, prohibited a corporation from issuing bonds in excess of twice its capital base.[21]

Why was there not a revolt against the banks? Would not some group be better off without the Bond Committee? Certainly the small saver would benefit if market-yield bond instruments were to provide an alternative to below-market bank deposits. But predictably, the free rider problem prevailed. Because the payoffs of reform to any individual would amount to, say, a few hundred yen a year, mounting a costly campaign to overturn the status quo would simply not be worth the expense unless the costs could be distributed widely. No political entrepreneurship was forthcoming.

The other institutional investors, such as the life and casualty insurance companies and trust banks, also got higher yields on their long-term loans to the corporations under the regulated system. Even the representatives from the securities industry on the Bond Committee, which happened to be the "Big Four," did not protest vociferously. Although there were over 250 securities houses, these

[19]This compromise was enshrined in administrative guidance, not in statute. But it was challenged only decades later when city banks, limited to short-term deposits, wanted to raise long-term funds for loans in the Euromarket.

[20]Note that interest rates on bonds were low (lower than on long-term loans), so many corporations wanted to issue, but there were no takers. The MOF wanted low interest rates and did not want a secondary market to develop which would put upward pressure on the government bond issuance rate. Banks bought a disproportionate share of new corporate issues and agreed not to sell them on the secondary market. See Hugh Patrick, "Finance, Capital Markets and Economic Growth in Japan," in Arnold W. Sametz, ed., *Financial Development and Economic Growth* (New York: New York University Press, 1972).

[21]Takeuchi, *Wagakuni Shihonshijō no Kōzō to Mondaiten,* pp. 70–71.

145

four—Nomura, Nikkō, Daiwa, and Yamaichi—took turns lead-managing most issues and captured 75 percent of all underwriting commissions. These commissions, moreover, were fixed, precluding competition. Were they to rock the boat, they would certainly also get wet.[22]

Nor did the MOF have reason to object. First, the market was orderly and stable. There was little chance of another bond market disaster with the collateral principle in operation. Second, in the early postwar years, the committee agreed to undertake bond issuance for the basic industries targeted for rapid recovery. Third, after the government began issuing bonds in 1965, and in greater volume in 1975, the MOF had more reason to appreciate the committee. A constricted corporate bond market made it easier for the MOF to place its own bonds. By the early 1980s, 95 percent of all new bond issues in Japan were made either by governmental units or by one of the banks themselves.[23] This was an acceptable barter for both the banks and the MOF: banks would not lose their corporate loan business, and the MOF would have the bulk of the domestic bond market for its own issues. It is no mistake that the Bond Committee forms the core of the Government Bond Syndicate as well.[24]

Only industry had reason to object to the Bond Committee's deliberate suppression of the bond market's development. But even industry did not begin to voice strong objections until the 1970s. During the recovery and rapid growth years in the postwar economy, firms wanted access to a steady stream of credit more than anything else. Especially in the sectors in which investment was virtually synonymous with growth, leveraging with debt made a great deal of sense. Bank debt in particular could provide the stability for long-term planning. Second, firms wanted the availability of extra credit in bad times. For these assurances, firms were willing to pay a premium, as it were, to their main bank. But in any case, bank trustee fees for collateral reduced the cost differential for firms between the interest rates on bonds and on long-term loans. Third,

[22]Kikuo Iwata, "Kisai Chōsei ni Kansuru Somondai," *Sophia Economic Review* 29, no. 2 (1986), 12–13.
[23]David W. Wise, "Corporate Debentures and the Internationalization of the Japanese Bond Market," *Columbia Journal of World Business* 17, Fall 1982, p. 41.
[24]Interviews with bankers and Ministry of Finance officials, 1985–1986, Tokyo.

the alternative, which was a bond market based on a rating system, would require continuous disclosure for investor protection. And fourth, heavy industry was actually favored by the domestic bond market rules because of the importance accorded to plant and equipment. Steel corporations, for example, would have more difficulty placing bonds for a reasonable price in Europe than in Japan because the Euromarket rating system operates on the basis of corporate health rather than on volume of capital stock.[25]

Leakage to the Euromarket

The declaration of Japan's economic growth brought to an end industry's insatiable demand for bank loans. Japan emerged from the post-oil-shock recession of 1975, but with real GNP growth rates in the 3–6 percent range rather than the 10–12 percent range of an era gone by. Because slower growth meant lower profit rates and fewer lucrative investment opportunities for most corporations, an unwieldy portion of corporate earnings went toward interest payments on bank loans. The interest payments on large bank debt, which had been a reasonable insurance premium for steady credit, had become an unworkable burden.[26]

In what seemed to banks to be a stampede, firms began paring down their bank loans in the mid-1970s. Some firms managed to work within the limits of their retained earnings and depreciation allowances. Others that still needed outside financing turned to the equity market, to a limited extent to the domestic bond market, or

[25] Iwao Nakatani claims that the grouping of firms does not generally increase the rates of profit or growth of the firms, but that volatility of performance is significantly reduced. This is made possible, he asserts, by the implicit mutual insurance scheme among member firms and banks. Nakatani, "The Economic Role of Financial Corporate Grouping," in M. Aoki, ed., *The Economic Analysis of the Japanese Firm* (Amsterdam: North-Holland, 1984), pp. 227–58. Other scholars have stressed the protection provided by a main bank against bankruptcy; see Paul Sheard, "Main Banks and Structural Adjustment in Japan," manuscript for the Australia-Japan Research Centre (1986); S. Suzuki and R. Wright, "Financial Structure and Bankruptcy Risk in Japanese Companies," manuscript, July 15, 1983; Sadahiko Suzuki, "Kyūsai Yūshi ni okeru Main Bank Chikara, *Keiō Keiei Ronsō*, December 1980, pp. 18–39. Still others, such as economists Akiyoshi Horiuchi and Takaaki Wakasugi of the University of Tokyo, emphasize the economies of information that attend a main bank relationship.

[26] Nagatomi, *Antei Seichō Jidai no Kōshasai Shijō*, pp. 34–37.

147

increasingly to the Euromarket. The ratio of new direct financing from all sources to new indirect financing jumped from 11.49 percent in 1973 to 20.44 percent in 1975.[27] Only the small-business sector and the structurally depressed industries such as steel had no real alternative to bank borrowing, or in the case of heavy industry, to the domestic bond market.[28]

Even as Japan's economy was entering a phase of slower growth, at least the larger Japanese corporations were securing market share and name recognition abroad. And with that came access to foreign financial markets. The possibility of financing abroad spurred the trend toward smaller bank debt not only because it was an alternative but also because (1) in international markets the best corporate ratings, and hence the cheapest money, go to firms with a strong capital base or low debt-equity ratio; and (2) for a mature corporation in a slower-growth era, an assured stream of credit is not as urgent as considerations of cost and flexibility.

This is not to say that the typically high debt-equity structure of Japanese corporations has been transformed overnight. Some extraordinarily strong firms, such as Toyota Motors and Matsushita Electric, have managed to cut their bank loans down to zero on the strength of their retained earnings. Few firms, however, have resorted to large stock issues to retire debt. In Japan, where cross-shareholding is frequently a means of solidifying business ties and protecting management from takeover, equity capital is more costly than it might otherwise be. The stable shareholders are often compensated by a below-market purchase price of each new issuance of shares.[29]

Given the cost of domestic bond and equity issuance, the Euro-

[27]Stephen Bronte, "The Revolution in Japanese Corporate Finance," *Euromoney*, September 1978, p. 17; "Why Japanese Companies Prefer Equity Raising to Bank Loans," *World Business Weekly*, August 3, 1981, pp. 49–50; Atsuko Chiba, "Japan's Rising Stars in Corporate Finance," *Institutional Investor*, October 1982, pp. 157–64; Donal Curtin, "They're Queuing up to Issue Bonds," *Euromoney*, May 1983, pp. 77–79.

[28]Nagatomi, *Antei Seichō Jidai no Kōshasai Shijō*, p. 37.

[29]Colin McKensie, research scholar from Australian National University at the Bank of Japan Institute of Monetary Policy, private communication; interviews with bankers and securities dealers, 1985–1986, Tokyo. Others argue that stable shareholding is declining, though it is difficult to measure with precision. *Tōyō Keizai*, October 26, 1985, pp. 30–38.

bond market, where there are no collateral requirements, began to look attractive to Japanese corporations. The Ministry of Finance enforced a matrix of capital and asset requirements, mirroring the domestic rules, for Japanese corporations issuing bonds even in foreign currencies in the Euromarket. Not to do so would have been to render domestic restrictions meaningless. But even with similar asset requirements, funding abroad was cheaper because there was no collateral requirement, no mandatory prospectus, and because there was a panoply of flexible rate instruments and swaps that reduced interest rate and exchange rate risks to corporations. Beginning in the mid-1970s, the number of Japanese corporate bond issues in the Euromarket began to skyrocket.

A few firms had issued bonds abroad, beginning with Sumitomo Metals and Kawasaki Steel in 1961, but the total volume was small. In the early 1970s the Euromarket accounted for a total of 1.7 percent of Japanese corporate financing; the figure for the second half of the 1970s was 19.6 percent. By 1984 the figure was 36.2 percent of all corporate financing. As a percentage of all Japanese corporate bonds issued, the Euromarket accounted for 51.9 percent in 1984. Swiss Franc convertible bonds accounted for a large portion of Japanese Euromarket fund raising, because far more companies qualified for this category of issuance under the MOF's matrix.[30] In January 1986, for example, seven hundred Japanese companies were authorized to issue foreign currency convertible bonds in Europe, but only eighty were permitted to issue unsecured straight Eurocurrency bonds.

Whereas smaller corporations did not pass the minimum capital requirement, large trading companies passed on a portion of their foreign-raised funds in the form of trade credits to subcontractors. The flight from Japan's domestic loan market was serious.[31] Japanese banks responded not by relinquishing restrictions on the do-

[30]Nobuyuki Ichikawa (Research and Statistics Division, BOJ), "Kigyō Kinyū no Kōzō Henka wa Doko made Susundeiru no ka," *Kinyū Zaisei Jijō*, December 8, 1986, pp. 34–39.

[31]Honpō Kigyō no Naigai Hakkō ni Okeru Tekisai Kijun Hikaku, Ministry of Finance documents (January 1986); Morio Okazaki, "Nihon no Kigyō Kinyū— Sono Kokusaika no Genjō," *Kikan Keizai Kenkyū* 8, no. 1 (1986), 1–24; Kokumin Keizai Kenkyū Kyōkai, "Kinyū no Kokusaika to Jiyūka no Genjō," *Nira Output*, July 1985, pp. 135–45.

149

mestic bond market but by following the corporations abroad in hopes of recapturing some of the business. Unlike at home, the Euromarket had no equivalent to section 65, which barred banks from securities activities. Abroad, Japanese banks were free to ride the wave of securitization. In the early 1970s most of the large banks either established wholly owned investment bank subsidiaries or entered into joint ventures with British merchant banks. All was well, it seemed. Until the Japanese securities industry cried foul.

The Three Bureaus Agreement

In April 1969, in the early stages of Japanese entry into the Euromarket, a fully owned subsidiary of the Bank of Tokyo participated in an underwriting syndicate for a Eurodollar issuance by Honda Motors. Although Goldman Sachs and Nikko Securities were the lead underwriters, the securities industry argued that any Japanese bank participation in underwriting syndicates for Japanese corporate bonds ran counter to section 65 of the Securities Exchange Act. Banks would most certainly carry out most of their negotiations with the issuing firm on Japanese soil and simply book the transaction in Europe. Moreover, said the securities industry, banks would use their "main bank power" to ensure Japanese firms chose banks over securities firms.

What disturbed the securities industry was not the legal technicalities but the loss of their direct finance monopoly to the banking industry. Tough luck if indirect finance had fallen on hard times. Banks knew precisely what the securities firms meant to communicate, but countered with legal arguments. Because the Bank of Tokyo's subsidiary was incorporated under French corporate law, Japan's section 65 should not apply to its activities.

The MOF's response is revealing. It advised the Bank of Tokyo not to pursue Japanese clients "too actively" in the Eurobond market. Foreign clients would be fair game for either side.[32] For the MOF, as for the disputing sides, the underlying issue was not so much the letter of the law as it was market share. Maintaining a

[32]"Sankyoku Shidō no Keii to Pointo," Nomura Securities in-house material (March 5, 1985), p. 1.

balance between the banking and securities industries was critical to the smooth functioning of financial policy. Should either side force the matter into a full-blown political dispute, the MOF would lose credibility with the regulated parties and subsequently have difficulty mending the fissures.

During the transition between fixed and floating exchange rates from 1971 to 1973, the MOF exercised its emergency powers to prohibit Japanese firms from issuing any bonds overseas. No sooner had the ban been lifted than banks and securities became embroiled in another jurisdictional dispute. On April 24, 1974, Fuji-Kleinwort Benson became one of the managing underwriters for a convertible bond issuance for Cannon in the Euromarket. Once again, the securities industry objected. Banks joining underwriting syndicates was bad enough, but for them to become a managing underwriter was going too far, the securities firms contended. (Managing underwriters have more responsibility for the issue's success, for which they get substantially higher commissions.) Moreover, they said, Fuji was more likely to abuse its power as a lending institution than the Bank of Tokyo, since the latter specializes in international finance and has a weaker domestic client base.[33]

With tempers rising in both the banking and securities industries, in April 1974 the MOF's Banking Bureau, the Securities Bureau, and the International Finance Bureau issued a joint circular to "clarify" the government's position. Actually, the MOF was deliberately vague because it was still not sure where the line should be drawn to silence the dispute. The circular's two brief paragraphs advised: (1) when participating in the Eurobond market (especially as managing underwriters), foreign subsidiaries of Japanese banks should take care not to break the spirit of the Securities Exchange Act; and (2) banks in joint venture arrangements with foreign investment or merchant banks should be equipped to handle Eurobond placements without straining their own portfolios.[34]

Because the MOF was noncommittal, banks continued to test the waters. In 1974 the Industrial Bank of Japan (IBJ) submitted an

[33] *Nikkei*, April 27, 1974.
[34] The point here was that Japanese banks lacking placement power would likely hold too much of a given issue in their own investment portfolios. Ōkurashō Ginkō Kyoku, *Kinyū Nenkan* (Ministry of Finance Banking Bureau, Banking Annual), 1974.

151

application to the International Finance Bureau for a 100 percent subsidiary to engage exclusively in securities activities in the Euromarket. Permission would require agreement among the three overseeing bureaus, but the Securities Bureau opposed and the Banking Bureau supported IBJ's plan. The Securities Bureau, in agreement with the securities industry, argued that because this subsidiary would be located physically within the IBJ's London branch office, and because it would be capitalized only at 6 million yen, it was clearly intended as a paper company for the bank. Furthermore, if this subsidiary received a banking license in addition, it would have a great advantage over securities firms in raising capital.[35]

Permission for the establishment of IBJ International was granted in June 1975, but when it became the assistant lead underwriter for New Nippon Steel's Eurodollar bond issuance two months later, the Securities Bureau expressed reservations. On August 29, the three bureaus called in for consultation representatives from nine banks and eleven securities firms. The MOF gave the financial institutions two documents, one of which read:

> 1. Japanese banks participating in foreign corporate bond underwriting syndicates shall pay due respect to the experience gained by and the mandate given to the Japanese securities firms. Banks shall not act against the spirit of section 65 of the Securities Exchange Act.
> 2. In implementing the intent expressed herein, banks shall pay regard to the order of institutions listed on issuance announcements and tombstones.

The second document restated the concern that banks not rely on their lending power to drum up customers for their securities operations in the Euromarket, and that banks not carry out their negotiations with their issuing clients on Japanese soil. In closing, the statement urged banks and securities firms to cooperate rather than fight for the same business in the Euromarket.[36]

Rather than lay the bank-securities rivalry to rest, this meeting

[35] The memo written by the assistant director of the Coordination Division in the Securities Bureau is recorded in "Sankyō Shidō no Keii to Pointo," p. 5.

[36] "Hōgin no Kaigai Genchi Hōjin no Shōken Hikiuke Gyōmu ni tsuite," internal memorandum of the Banking Division, Banking Bureau, Ministry of Finance (August 29, 1980).

merely explained the game rules a little more clearly—or, more accurately, the MOF suggested a desirable goal but left the means to reach that goal to the institutions themselves. Banks could underwrite Eurobonds for Japanese corporations, as long as they did not upstage the Japanese securities houses. Securities firms later interpreted the MOF's mention of the tombstone and announcement listings as an injunction against banks becoming book runners or lead managers; but banks also had to be careful not to win a greater market share than the securities firms.[37]

For a while the Three Bureaus Agreement presided over peaceful coexistence in the Euromarket, incorporating minor clarifications as further disputes arose. Banks won free rein in the private placement market, for example, but securities firms established their supremacy in equity-linked instruments such as convertible bonds and warrant bonds.[38] Meanwhile, Japanese corporations' attraction to the Eurobond market continued unabated. On the other side of the coin, banks experienced more difficulty at home lending their available funds, which put pressure on their profit margins. The MOF could not ignore the changing profitability structure, which favored the securities firms over the banks, lest the banks circumvent the MOF in seeking a political solution. In 1981 the MOF sent signals to the private sector to the effect that the Three Bureaus Agreement perhaps had served its function. Corporations now had sufficient resources, MOF officials suggested, that banks would be unable to corner an undue share of the Eurobond market. In a break with precedent, bank subsidiaries were permitted to underwrite the parent bank's bonds in the Euromarket.[39]

The timing was premature. In exchange for banks' entry into government bond dealing, securities firms were given a second lease on the Three Bureaus Agreement.[40] In 1984 other events tipped the balance. In April the MOF loosened restrictions on corporate issu-

[37]"Gaikadate Kōbosai no Kanjidan Hensei ni Okeru Shōken Yūi ni Tsuite," memorandum of the Vice-Presidents' Club of the Big Four (June 24, 1983); Vickie Smiles, "Are Japan's Banks Losing Out?" *Euromoney*, September 1985, p. 105.

[38]"Sankyoku Shidō no Keii to Point," p. 10; Junichi Senda, *Henkakuki no Ginkō to Shōken* (Tokyo: Yūhikaku, 1986), pp. 172–73.

[39]Kazumoto Adachi (director of the Banking Bureau Coordination Division), "Jishusei no Hakkyaku o Tou," *Kinyū Zaisei Jijō*, July 6, 1981, pp. 20–24.

[40]Interviews with MOF officials and bankers, 1985–1986, Tokyo.

153

Table 4. Corporate fund raising in the domestic and foreign bond markets, 1975–1985 (yen in billions; fiscal year)

	Domestic		Overseas	
	Straight bonds	Convertible bonds[a]	Straight bonds	Convertible bonds[a]
1975	1,504.2	331.0	293.0	182.0
1976	1,166.6	55.5	213.5	153.3
1977	1,240.8	162.5	146.5	221.1
1978	1,313.3	277.0	127.1	428.1
1979	1,298.1	353.5	178.6	556.1
1980	993.5	96.5	168.0	514.9
1981	1,269.0	546.0	49.1	1,069.0
1982	1,047.5	464.5	681.2	693.3
1983	683.0	878.0	403.9	1,514.5
1984	720.0	1,614.5	1,134.5	1,660.6
1985	943.5	1,640.5	1,439.3	1,814.2

[a]The convertible bonds column includes warrants, that is, bonds with rights of subscription for new stocks.
Source: "Shihon Shijō o Meguru Shomondai," Securities Exchange Council (May 1986), p. 2.

ances of yen-denominated bonds in the Euromarket, and in June the MOF lifted the ceiling on the amount of foreign currency that corporations could exchange into yen. Both of these measures had the effect of spurring the trend toward Euromarket financing.[41] Also in 1984 the MOF announced that foreign securities houses would be permitted to act as the lead underwriter for Japanese corporate bond issues in the Euromarket.[42]

Banks were no match for a corporate world that wanted easier access to the Euromarket.[43] But banks latched onto the MOF's permission for foreign securities firms to lead-manage Japanese Eurobond issuances. This was reverse discrimination, protested the National Federation of Bank Associations in a memo to the MOF. If foreign financial institutions were allowed to compete with Japanese securities firms, Japanese banks should surely be allowed to as well. Moreover, the banks remonstrated, because it was the MOF's

[41]Yutaka Katō (director of research, Mitsui Bank), "Kinyū Jiyūka no Genjō to Tenbō" (November 18, 1985), p. 1.
[42]"Kinyū Kakumei Zenya ni Ōarare no Ōkura Kanryō," *Zaikai*, October 26, 1984, pp. 36–39. Chapter 6 examines foreign reciprocity threats, which were instrumental in wresting from Japan this concession for foreign underwriters.
[43]Banks did succeed, however, in reducing the number of corporations eligible for access to the Euroyen market by insisting on high capital ratios. *Nikkei*, March 5, 1985.

job to consider the international competitiveness of Japanese financial institutions, the MOF should remember that American and European banks were bound by no equivalent of the Three Bureaus Agreement.[44] The Banking Bureau was ready to meet the banks' demands, but the Securities Bureau was still under strong pressure from the securities industry to hold the line. The MOF would have to search for an acceptable barter.[45]

In March 1985 the MOF announced a "Comprehensive Settlement" of the bank-securities rivalry, lowering the dividing line between the two industries. The securities industry could keep the Three Bureaus Agreement for the time being; in addition, securities firms were granted permission to trade in the secondary market for CDs, broker in the new Bankers Acceptance (BA) market, and lend to customers who had government bonds as collateral. In exchange, banks were permitted to offer government bond accounts to their customers, participate in the new bond futures market, and become brokers' brokers. In addition, about thirty banks in the second tier of the banking industry were allowed to deal in government bonds.[46]

Anxious for the Three Bureaus Agreement to be lifted, banks were sorely disappointed. But securities firms contended that the only fair trade for the agreement would be freedom to engage in foreign exchange transactions without bank intermediation. Absolutely not, cried the banks.[47]

The Three Bureaus Agreement Assaulted

Despite the stalemate, Sumitomo Bank decided to test the limits of the Three Bureaus Agreement. In August 1984 Sumitomo had

[44]Although the U.S. banks were bound by the Glass-Steagall Act at home, there was no extraterritorial application of that statute. National Federation of Bank Associations, "Sankyoku Gōi Teppai ni Kansuru Yōbōsho" (July 16, 1984), pp. 1–2; "Sankyoku Gōi no Norikoe," *Kinyū Zaisei Jijō*, January 6, 1986, p. 110.

[45]"Kinyū Kakumei Zenya ni Ōarare no Ōkura Kanryō," *Zaikai*, October 16, 1984, pp. 36–39; Toshio Tsukada, "Junchō na Hikyojūsha no Yuroyensai Hakkō," *Kinyū Zaisei Jijō*, January 28, 1985, pp. 16–17.

[46]"Sankyoku Gōi no Teppai Sakiokuri," *Nikkei*, March 5, 1985; "Package Settlement Planned for Bank-Securities Firm Disputes," *Japanese Economic Journal*, March 19, 1985, p. 2; "Daini Raundo wa Jogai Rantō," *Kōshasai Jōhō*, April 1, 1985, p. 32.

[47]"Daini Round wa Jogai Rantō," *Kōshasai Jōhō*, April 1, 1985, p. 32; Hiroshi Saitō, *Nihon no Money Senshitachi* (Tokyo: Kanki Shuppan, 1985), pp. 183–200.

purchased a majority share in Gottardo, a Switzerland-based universal bank. On March 28, 1985, Gottardo announced it was to be the lead underwriter for a Swiss franc issuance for Itohman, an Osaka-based trading company with strong ties to Sumitomo Bank. The fact that Itohman and Sumitomo had a longstanding relationship actually worked against Sumitomo in this case, since Sumitomo would have difficulty establishing that it won the bid without exerting "main bank pressure." Indeed, it later became known that Sumitomo had attempted to recruit other trading companies without success: companies were afraid of alienating the securities firms that had been underwriting for them.[48]

On April 4, representatives from the Big Four securities firms met to join in declaring opposition to Sumitomo's circumvention of the Three Bureaus Agreement. Obviously a case of a main bank exercising its market power, said the securities firms. They demanded that at least the bond issue be changed into a private placement, since that would be within the game rules. Anything but an unfortunate precedent, the securities firms reasoned.[49]

The MOF, pressed by both industries, decided to let the Gottardo case pass as a "special exception" to the rule of no lead management of Japanese corporate bonds by Japanese banks. The MOF cited Gottardo's history as an underwriter before Sumitomo bought its shares; it had placement power on its own right. Although both industries accepted this solution, they interpreted the measure to suit their own purposes. "It was a clear indication that the Three Bureaus Agreement is on the wane. We will just have to give it time," said Hajime Yamada, chairman of the Federation of Bank Associations. Shōga Watanabe, chairman of the Securities Association, declared, "The Three Bureaus Agreement is as solid as ever."[50]

They were both right. The Three Bureaus Agreement was a provisional measure to prevent banks from taking an "undue" share of the bond business in the Euromarket. It will be revoked when either of two conditions are met: (1) banks' domestic profits fall so much

[48] Interviews with MOF officials and journalists, 1985–1986, Tokyo; "Sankyoku Gōi," *Nikkei Newsletter on Bond and Money*, April 8, 1985, pp. 2–5.

[49] "Sankyoku Gōi," p. 5; "Sankyoku Gōi no Nashikuzushi, Dankō Soshi," *Zaikei Shōhō*, April 15, 1985, p. 13; "Kakine Mondai Ketchaku," *Kinyū Bijinesu*, May 1985, pp. 12–13.

[50] "Gottardo Mondai ni Keri," *Kinyū Business*, June 1985, p. 62.

lower than those of the securities industry that the agreement no longer serves its intended equilibrating function; or (2) banks are willing to barter away another source of income, such as monopoly of the foreign exchange business.

Although the rancor between the two sectors reached several high points, neither side brought the problem to the politicians for a quick cure. As with the government bond dispute finally resolved in the Banking Act of 1982, the politicians are happy to defer delicate balancing of this sort to the MOF. And because the MOF could monitor the compliance to the compromise, there was little risk to either the banking industry or the securities industry of being cheated by the other.

Deregulating the Domestic Bond Market

Even as banks were struggling for market share in the Eurobond market, the domestic bond market was relatively stagnant. Japanese corporations had been raising money in foreign bond markets with increasing regularity since the mid-1970s. This was because banks, long after making their inroads abroad, continued to protect their domestic loan business by limiting access to and the attractiveness of the domestic bond market. By the end of 1984 the Japanese bond market was second in size only to that of the United States, with an annual transaction volume of over $12 trillion in the secondary market. Almost all of the transactions, however, were in government bonds. The outstanding amount of corporate bonds was a mere 13 percent of the corresponding U.S. figure, and corporations raised only 4 percent of their funds on the domestic bond market.[51]

Corporations' post-oil-shock shift toward direct finance instruments such as bonds and equity, as well as a greater diversity in the performance of Japanese industries and firms, were structural changes that attended economic maturity and slower growth. For firms no longer needing a bank's backing, bonds were a sensible alternative to bank debt because of the lower cost and flexibility in length of term they afforded. Banks began to fight for their corpo-

[51] Yoshihisa Tabuchi, "On the Deregulation of the Japanese Money and Capital Markets," Nomura Securities in-house document (November 2, 1985), p. 2.

157

rate customers. In the late 1970s, compensating balances began to shrink and loan spreads narrowed. To provide more attractive financial instruments, banks began issuing CDs in 1979, money market certificates (MMCs) in 1985, and longer-term CDs and MMCs in 1986. But banks did not loosen their grip on the domestic bond market until it no longer made sense for them not to.

In 1971 the Keidanren's Capital Policy Committee suggested that the rules for corporate bond issuance be relaxed, that bonds be offered in a greater variety of maturities, and that a corporate rating system replace the Bond Committee's set of self-styled rules.[52] Six years later, when an MOF advisory group made similar recommendations for bond market reform, the Bond Committee's rules were still much as they had been for over forty years.[53] These reports were little more than exercises in wishful thinking, because many firms still depended on bank debt for viability, and because the banking industry was still not feeling sufficient pressure from the Euromarket to reform the domestic rules.

By 1982, when MITI's Industrial Structure Council recommended that bond issuance rules be relaxed, bank resistance to change had begun to soften.[54] Trustee banks' revenues from managing collateral on domestic issuances had fallen off as firms went to the Euromarket, where issuing bonds was easier and cheaper. In 1981 domestically issued bonds increased 4.2 percent over the previous year, and Eurobonds increased 2.7 percent. By 1982 domestic bonds increased by 4.7 percent, and Eurobonds by 10.0 percent. By 1983 domestic bonds actually dropped by 1.0 percent, whereas external bonds increased by 22.9 percent.[55] Because Japanese firms were not trapped by the banks' domestic bond rules, they did not press for reform with urgency; rather, it was the banks that had cause for consternation.[56]

[52]Nagatomi, *Antei Seichō Jidai no Kōshasai Shijō*, pp. 206–7.

[53]Securities Exchange Council, Committee on the Working of the Bond and Stock Markets, "Report on the Desirable Bond Market for Japan" (October 18, 1977), pp. 1–62.

[54]Sangyō Kōzō Shingikai, Sōgō Bukai, Sangyō Kinyū Koiinkai, "Kongo no Nozomashii Sangyō Kinyū no Arikata ni Kansuru Hōkoku," September 29, 1982, pp. 61–67.

[55]Ministry of Finance, "Hōjin Kigyō Tōkei Kihō," and "Kokusai Kinyūkyoku Nenpō," 1981–84.

[56]Interviews with MITI officials in MITI's Industrial Finance Division and bankers, 1985–1986, Tokyo.

As changes in corporate funding patterns occurred, the U.S. government began pressing for freer Japanese financial markets. American motives and tactics were discussed in greater detail in Chapter 3, but here we should note that the MOF agreed to relax restrictions on the issuance of and investment in Euroyen bonds over the course of 1984 and 1985. Although this would not generate drastic changes in Japan's financial markets, since corporations had already been issuing bonds abroad in foreign currencies, the development of a mature Euroyen bond market at least incrementally increased the pressure on banks to ease the domestic system.[57] The ability to raise funds in yen was an automatic hedge against foreign exchange risk, and therefore an added attraction to Euromarket financing for Japanese firms.

Since 1983, banks had been negotiating with the MOF about how to deregulate the domestic bond market. If terms were to be made easier for corporate issues, securities firms would benefit so there would have to be some quid pro quo for the banks. The private placement market where banks had free rein, for example, should be enlarged. Moreover, the banks argued, a new rating system should not cut banks out of their traditional function of maintaining high standards for the domestic bond market.[58]

In January 1984 the MOF commissioned a Bond Study Group (Shasai Mondai Kenkyūkai), under the chairmanship of Nihachirō Hanamura, vice-chairman of the Keidanren, to examine the possibilities of reform in the domestic market. On the committee were representatives of the major groups with an interest in the problem: IBJ and the top six city banks, which were also the seven key members of the Bond Issuance Committee; the Big Four securities houses; the largest insurance companies and trust banks; and managers of Toyota, Hitachi, Mitsubishi Trading Company, Nippon Steel, Toray, and Tokyo Electric.[59]

After a year of monthly meetings, the group drafted what could variously be called a compromise, a stalemate, or an agglomeration

[57]"Yūtanpo Gensoku kara Kakuzuke Jidai e no Ikō," *Zaikei Shōhō*, January 28, 1985, pp. 14–15.

[58]Interviews with MOF officials, bankers, securities people, 1985–1986, Tokyo; "Henkakuki ni Chokumenshita Kokunai Kisai Shijō," *Zaikei Shōhō*, January 28, 1985, p. 15.

[59]Tatsuo Iida, "Aratana Saiken Kakuzuke Kikan no Setsuritsu ni Mukete" (February 11, 1985), pp. 10–15.

of conflicting views. Most in the group wanted to stress the importance of replacing the Bond Issuance Committee's rules with a system of independently conducted bond ratings. The banks, however, added their caveat to the report that bank management of collateral since 1933 was responsible for maintaining the safety and stability of the bond market, and that bond rating agencies were not necessary for the domestic market.[60]

The trustee banks were afraid of two things: (1) losing their loan business if bond issuance became too easy, and (2) losing their trustee commission income if the collateral principle was reconsidered. But their position was becoming less tenable. Firms were voting with their feet, as it were, in favor of the flexibility of the Eurobond market. And banks had already been forced to respond, albeit with great reluctance. In 1973, for example, Mitsubishi Trading, Komatsu, Marubeni, and Kawasaki Steel had requested the right to issue unsecured convertible bonds on the domestic market. Banks accommodated them to the extent of expanding their definition of collateral.[61] In 1979 Sears Roebuck successfully invoked reciprocity in obtaining permission to issue an unsecured straight bond in Tokyo.[62]

In 1983 and 1984 banks agreed to loosen the collateral restrictions on domestic straight bonds and convertible bonds. By the end of 1984, 20 companies were eligible to issue straight bonds, and 110 qualified for issues of convertible bonds. Of the latter, nearly half were permitted to issue convertible bonds without collateral. Because firms could issue without collateral on the Euromarket, the collateral principle also began to weaken at home.[63] Nonetheless, banks were not prepared to relinquish their control of the domestic bond market altogether. When, in the summer of 1984, the Securities Bureau suggested that Japanese bond rating agencies be

[60] Ibid.

[61] Ichirō Aoki (MOF Securities Bureau, Capital Markets Division), "Kokunai Kanzen Muytanpo Futsū Shasai no Hakkō ni Tsuite," *Zaikei Shōhō*, February 18, 1985, p. 10.

[62] James Horne, "The Yen Bond Market 1970–1982," in *Japan's Financial Markets* (London: Allen & Unwin, 1985), pp. 173–93; Wise, "Corporate Debentures," pp. 40–45.

[63] Aoki, "Kokunai Kangen Muytanpo Futsū Shasaino Hakkō ni Tsuite," p. 11; Trustee Banks Association, "Mutanpo shasai, Yuroensai ni Kansuru Kangaekata," *Kinyū Zaisei Jijō*, April 16, 1984, pp. 72–73.

established for the Euroyen market, banks objected. Banks feared bond rating would take root in the domestic market as well and render the Bond Committee obsolescent.

The Securities Bureau proposed a compromise: the IBJ and other trustee banks could join the Big Four securities firms to form a bond rating agency, the Japan Investment Service.[64] There was some disagreement within the MOF, not to mention industry, as to the appropriateness of a bond rating agency comprising underwriters and trustees. The Securities Bureau, however, sensing that this was necessary compensation for cooperation, wanted to give the group its imprimatur. Meanwhile, the International Finance Bureau favored another group of large institutional investors, including the Long Term Credit Bank of Japan, the trust banks, and the insurance companies.

The MOF was concerned that there would not be enough business to keep both prospective bond rating agencies in the black. In addition to these two, there were others already in existence. The Japan Bond Research Institute, a subsidiary of Nihon Keizai Shimbun, had been operating since the 1970s, though primarily as a publisher of bond-related information. Two American raters, Standard & Poor's and Moody's, also had offices in Tokyo since the 1980s, to gather information for Eurobond ratings. A fourth, Mikuni Investment Advisory Service, provided information to foreign investors on Japanese firms. Ultimately, however, the MOF granted licenses to the two newcomers as well. It would worry about a shake-out, or perhaps avoid one by establishing a division of labor, when the circumstances required. For the time being, the MOF bureaucrats reasoned, at least the machinery was in place for a gradual transition from the Bond Committee's rules to a bond-rating system.[65]

Despite some easing of collateral requirements since the 1970s, corporations were not returning to the domestic bond market from abroad. First, the number of corporations eligible to issue unsecured

[64]"Saiken Kakuzuke Kikan de Yureru Okurashō," *Ekonomisuto*, November 20, 1984, pp. 6–7; "Yūtanpo Gensoku kara Kakuzuke Jidai e no Ikō," *Zaikei Shōhō*, January 28, 1985, p. 14; "Ni Kakuzuke Kikan no Kokkaku Katamaru," *Zaikei Shōhō*, March 3, 1985, p. 12.
[65]"Togin-Shōken Irimidareru Shasai Kakuzuke Sensō," *Zaikai*, November 23, 1984, pp. 86–87.

bonds was still small. In January 1985 TDK became the first company to issue an unsecured straight bond in the domestic market since 1932; only twenty-three other firms were similarly eligible. For the others, issuance was more costly. Until the high capital requirements were lowered, even corporations such as Mitsubishi Shōji and Hitachi, with AAA ratings in foreign markets, would not qualify for unsecured straight bond issuance in Japan. The standard indeed was relaxed in October 1985, but still only fifty-seven corporations were now eligible to issue unsecured bonds.[66] Second, there were rigid issuing conditions, such as a single issue date each month. Third—and this was a legal provision rather than a customary rule established by the Bond Committee—firms could not issue in excess of twice their net worth.[67]

The MOF's Securities Exchange Council, which had issued the 1977 report proposing easier issuance terms, reconvened in May 1985 to have another look at the problem. And this time the situation was ripe for change. But as corporations and securities firms knew, an expansion of the domestic bond market would not come without some cost to themselves. Along with the council's proposal to "eventually abolish" the collateral rule, there was a call for tougher corporate disclosure rules to ensure market stability. The council also stated that the Big Four's monopoly on underwriting, with fixed commissions, should be corrected. The MOF still would have to work out the implementation of these pronouncements, but this was the basic compromise.[68]

Banks accepted, if reluctantly, the decision to double the number of corporations eligible for unsecured straight bonds and convertible bonds, to 180 and 330, respectively. In exchange, banks received an expanded private placement market. The "no return

[66]Toshio Nakajima (MOF Securities Bureau, Capital Markets Division), "Kokunai Mutanpo Futsūshasai no Tekisai Kijun no Kanwa ni Tsuite," *Zaikei Shōhō*, October 28, 1985, pp. 12–14; Toshinaga Koizumi, "Kanwasareta Mutanpo Futsū Shasai no Tekisai Kijun," *Kinyū Zaisei Jijō*, November 25, 1985, pp. 34–37.

[67]Toshimi Kanaya (MOF Securities Bureau, Capital Markets Division), "Shihon Shijō o Meguru Shomondai ni Tsuite," *Zaikei Shōhō*, June 17, 1985, pp. 2–6; Toshimi Kanaya, "Kisai ni Shikumi, Hakkō Gendo no Minaoshi o Kentō," *Kinyū Zaisei Jijō*, February 24, 1986, pp. 20–21.

[68]"Shōtorishin, Shasai Seido no Bappon Minaoshi de Bukai Hōkoku," *Kinyū Zaisei Jijō*, December 8, 1986, p. 8; "Jikkōsai no Kakuho e Akushyon Puroguramu ga Hitsuyō," *Kinyū Zaisei Jijō*, December 15, 1986, pp. 31–34.

rule," which prevented corporations from returning to the private placement market, was to be abolished, allowing banks to place issues for firms an unlimited number of times. Furthermore, the private placement concept itself had become more attractive to corporations since disclosure requirements, which were to be tightened for public placement, would be laxer where only institutional investors were involved.[69]

In March 1988 banks assented to further gradual relaxation of domestic bond issuance rules: a rating system would replace the traditional capitalization matrices as criteria for domestic corporate issuance; issuance of floating rate bonds and foreign currency bonds would be permitted in Japan; and the trustee bank's role would be limited to acting as a depository for the issued bond until maturity. In return for these concessions, the Ministry of Finance (and the securities industry) agreed to abolish the Three Bureaus Agreement by spring 1989. At last Japanese commercial banks would be free to act as lead underwriters for Japanese corporate issues in foreign markets.[70]

Why Deregulation?

Deregulation of the domestic bond market is not complete. By the beginning of 1988 only 180 corporations, a small fragment of Japan's corporate world, were eligible to issue unsecured straight bonds in Japan. Considering that no corporations could issue without collateral until 1983, however, the pace of change is rapid indeed.

The argument advanced here is that banks were forced by their own self-interest to relax domestic issuance rules because corporations had the alternative of the Euromarket. The changes, in other words, did not reflect either declining political influence of banks or independent MOF planning. This pattern of deregulation is precisely what the theory of regulation predicts. Once corporations began to value the flexibility of the bond market over the security of bank indebtedness, banks' second best option was to recapture

[69]*Nikkei*, November 7, 1986.
[70]"Ginkōkei ni mo Gaisai Shukanji," *Nikkei*, March 25, 1988, p. 1.

some of the bond business in the domestic private placement market. Banks were thus willing to trade away some control over domestic bond issuance.

Japan's international environment has effected significant changes in Japan's domestic market structure. This reverses the usual line of causality cited in foreign policy literature in which domestic politics is shown to generate changes in the international arena. Peter Gourevitch, who coined the phrase "second image reversed," posits that "the international system is not only a consequence of domestic politics and structures but a cause of them."[71] Gourevitch also concedes that, "however compelling external pressures may be, they are unlikely to be fully determining." Even market forces must filter through the domestic political system before they take on power to change institutions and structures. If banks possessed a monopoly of domestic political resources, for example, they would simply ensure that leakage to the Euromarket be cut off: no firms would be allowed to raise funds abroad. In fact, banks are one of a number of powerful domestic interest groups, and indeed, other groups were willing to tolerate a highly regulated financial market for reasons of their own. Japanese corporations appreciated the convenience of bank loans during their rapid growth period but also took increasing advantage of the Euromarket alternative. Nonbank institutional investors such as the insurance companies were satisfied with stable, predictable returns until recently.[72] And the securities firms were not eager to force change lest they forfeit their own protection, including fixed underwriting and brokering commissions.

Once banks found that corporations were not compelled to rely on bank borrowing merely because the domestic bond market was hard to access, the Bond Committee's control began to lose its perceived economic value. There is little point in holding the bottleneck if the bottle has a leak elsewhere.

Deregulation of the domestic bond market was a reaction to, rather than a cause of, changes in Japanese corporate finance. Ma-

[71] Peter A. Gourevitch, "The Second Image Reversed: The International Sources of Domestic Politics," *International Organization* 32 (Autumn 1978), p. 911.
[72] For evidence of change, see for example, "Trust Banks to Face Stiffer Pension Fund Yardstick," *Japan Economic Journal*, July 1986.

turing Japanese corporations had been moving away from bank dependence in favor of flexibility of direct financing since the early 1970s; the pressure on banks to accommodate the corporations increased as a growing number of firms began scaling down their bank debt and obtained access to the Euromarket.

The MOF–Financial Sector Nexus

Through most of this narrative, the MOF has orchestrated, facilitated, or equilibrated—rarely initiated. The MOF's role varies, naturally, with its stake in an issue. Given the MOF's overarching goal of smooth regulation, its subsidiary goals on the bond market are (1) market stability and (2) good relations with financial institutions. Only more recently, since the mid-1970s, did the MOF have its own interest in ensuring that corporate bonds did not crowd out government bonds in the issuing market. But because of the large pool of private-sector savings, this has never become a pressing concern.

The MOF was content to entrust the problem of bond market stability to the banks. Since the Bond Committee formed in 1933, the market had functioned well, and trustee banks ensured that investors received payment. The MOF permitted the banks to institutionalize their influence because this was a means of harnessing their commitment to the stability of the system. Thus the Bond Committee functioned as a sort of parapublic organization that simultaneously served a public and a private purpose. Without the MOF's sanction the Bond Committee could not have functioned.[73]

The MOF's second goal, of maintaining good relations with the financial institutions that it regulates, was perhaps more delicate than the first. Securities firms had a direct interest in an expansion of the bond market as surely as banks did not. Placating, or at least silencing, the securities industry did not prove to be an indomitable task, however. The bond market continued to grow steadily in the postwar decades, even though the Euromarket issuances of Japanese corporations overtook the domestic issuances in the early

[73]See Peter J. Katzenstein on parapublic institutions in Germany: *Policy and Politics in West Germany: A Semi-Sovereign State* (Philadelphia: Temple University Press, 1988), chap. 1.

1980s. At least securities firms could not complain of falling profits. Second, the Three Bureaus Agreement ensured that securities firms would not lose the Eurobond market to the Japanese banks. Third, the securities industry enjoyed its own protection in the form of fixed bond underwriting and brokering commissions. If the securities industry forced the banks' hand on the bond market, the banks doubtless would agitate for competitive commissions. Finally, the most powerful securities companies politically—unlike in the banking industry, where the small are strong in their own right—are the Big Four. These top four securities firms take three-quarters of all bond underwriting commissions, partly because of their membership in the Bond Committee.

The securities industry and would-be bond issuers demanded change in the domestic bond market, though both groups had reason for patience. Their demands were a constant; it was banks' acceptance of a barter that opened the way to bond market reform. Banks obtained a fivefold increase in the private placement market, in which they had free rein, in exchange for a doubling of the number of corporations that could issue unsecured domestic bonds. Securities firms accepted this as a step toward an increasingly free bond market in which the Bond Committee would be replaced by bond rating agencies. Corporations were pleased at the expansion of the private placement market since the disclosure requirements are more lenient; but they, too, took the agreement as transitional and moving toward greater freedom.

The trajectory of further changes in the domestic bond market is clear. As a growing number of Japanese firms secure access to Euromarket financing, banks will be forced to provide the funding needs and preferences of their clientele. The relaxation of bond market rules was but one in a succession of competitive accommodations, including the introduction of market-based deposit instruments and the slashing of compensating balance requirements. Furthermore, as Japan's financial system becomes increasingly open, a growing share of bank loans are to the small-business sector and to the declining industries.

6

Banks and the
Postal Savings System

In one of the most controversial tax bills ever enacted in Japan, the Diet voted in September 1987 to curtail drastically the tax-free status of interest income, effective April 1988. With an exception for savings held by individuals over age sixty-five, the physically handicapped, and single mothers, all interest income would be taxed a flat 20 percent.[1] Though the new taxation of interest payments on savings applied to bank deposits as well as to postal savings accounts, the banks quietly celebrated victory. Banks were pleased because the new tax spelled an end to tax evasion through the use of multiple tax-free postal savings accounts, and hence would mean a drop in the popularity of postal, as opposed to bank, accounts.[2]

The banks' troubles with the postal system were by no means over. The higher interest rates and more attractive terms of postal savings accounts continue to plague the banks, for the Ministry of Posts and Telecommunications (MPT) remains outside the interest rate structure that the Ministry of Finance maintains for private-sector financial institutions. Higher yields, as well as lax tax enforcement and the wide network of post offices reaching to Japan's smallest villages, were the reasons for the postal savings system's rapid expansion in the postwar years. By the end of 1985 the postal

[1] Of the 20 percent, 15 percent would go to the central government and 5 percent to local government. "Ginkōkan Yokin no Jiyūka Meguru Ōkurashō, Nichigin no Kakusui," *Kinyū Bijinesu*, August 1985, pp. 62–63.

[2] "Maruyū Haishi," *Kinyū Bijinesu*, March 1987, pp. 18–23; "Honkaku Genzei, Rokujūyonendo Ikō ni," *Nihon Keizai Shimbun*, July 11, 1987, p. 1.

savings system boasted a deposit base of over 100 trillion yen, making it by far the largest financial institution in the world, and in fact larger than the top five Japanese city banks combined.[3]

The "Hundred Years' War," as the bank–postal system controversy has become known, is unlike the ongoing rivalry between the banking and securities industries. Whereas the latter is tempered by the MOF's enforcement of compromises, the former is unbridled. The controversy between the banks and the postal system, for all its vitriolic rhetoric, attempts of both sides to woo the public through media, and frequent intervention of politicians, poorly fits the quieter, bureaucratically administered process predicted by the theory of regulation and exemplified by the instances of financial regulation and deregulation examined in earlier chapters.

In examining the history of battles and bargains in Japan's Hundred Years' War, we must first see how institutional structure delimits and constrains the policy-making process in ways the theory of regulation does not consider. Because the MOF has no authority to mediate between the banks and the postal system, the process perforce draws in political arbiters. The MOF must deal with the MPT as one ministry to another. If the MOF has some advantage because of its budgeting role, the MPT knows the MOF is dependent on postal funds for the MOF's Fiscal Investment and Loan Program. But when the two ministries cannot agree on what constitutes a fair bargain, the only place to turn for arbitration is the political arena.

The second, perhaps more challenging, task of this chapter is to peruse the historical record for information about the structure of power in this area of Japanese finance. However quiescent or cacophonous the policy-making process might be, policy outcomes depend to a large extent on how much political capital—money and/or votes—each side is willing and able to deliver.

Historical Background

Japan's postal savings system dates back to 1875, when the Postal Division of the Home Affairs Ministry (Naimushō Ekiteiryō) of-

---

[3]Eietsu Imamatsu, *Ginkō, Shōken wa Kinyū Saihen de dō Kawaruka* (Tokyo: Nihon Jitsugyō Shuppan, 1986), pp. 163–65.

fered interest on savings, first for its employees and then to the general public the following year.[4] The Postal Division began its postal and savings operations at post offices in twenty-one major urban areas around the country, but to expand more rapidly commissioned scores, soon hundreds, of landed gentry (*meibōka*), often village leaders (*shōya*), to undertake the postal business in exchange for exemption from land tax and a modest remuneration on the basis of transaction volume.[5]

Unaware of the difficulties the postal savings system would pose for control of the financial system in later years, the Ministry of Finance gave the system its blessing because at the time it hoped postal savings would help dampen inflation by drawing cash out of circulation. Second, the nascent banking industry was primarily engaged in the wholesale end of the market and thus not in competition with post offices for small-scale savings. Third, beginning in 1878 the postal system deposited all of its money in a special account in the MOF's Government Bond Bureau (Kokusai Kyoku), which the MOF welcomed. The Ministry of Finance reserved the right to establish the interest rate it would pay to the Home Ministry's Postal Division for these funds and would revert profits to or draw supplements from the general budget.[6] Discretion over use of these funds was less clearly specified, though the MOF had effective control over the money once it was turned over by the postal system and used most of the funds to buy government bonds.

In 1881 the Postal Bureau was transferred to the newly created Ministry of Agriculture and Commerce.[7] A major jurisdictional dispute erupted between the Ministry of Finance and the Postal Bureau's new oversight ministry in the mid-1880s when the two ministries began negotiations for the establishment of special government financial institutions to supplement the lending of private

[4]Kazuhisa Maeno, "Yūseihō Kenkyū," *Gendai*, August 1986, p. 112.
[5]Nobu Sadaka, *Nihon Kanryō Hakusho* (Tokyo: Kodansha, 1986), pp. 178–79.
[6]Jūrō Teranishi, *Nihon no Keizai Hatten to Kinyū* (Tokyo: Iwanami Shoten, 1984), pp. 45–46; Hugh Patrick and Jūrō Teranishi, "The Establishment and Early Development of Banking in Japan: Phases and Policies Prior to World War I," in Kazushi Ohkawa and Yūjirō Hayami, eds., *Papers and Proceedings of the Conference on Japan's Historical Development Experience and the Contemporary Developing Countries: Issues for Comparative Analysis* (Tokyo: International Development Center of Japan, 1978).
[7]Chalmers A. Johnson, *Japan's Public Policy Companies* (Washington, D.C.: American Enterprise Institute, 1978), p. 84.

banks and to be financed with money drawn from the postal savings. The MOF's conception was for the government banks to provide loans for local infrastructure development. The severe deflation of 1885–86 engineered by Minister of Finance Matsukata had put a serious strain on local economies, and politicians were calling for massive subsidies to localities. Rather than weaken national finances, the MOF sought to utilize postal savings and other special accounts in a government-sponsored loan program.

The Ministry of Agriculture and Commerce, on the other hand, wanted the special banks to extend lines of credit to specific firms and industries to facilitate the ministry's export promotion plan. The Home Affairs Ministry, though no longer in charge of postal savings, remained in charge of local government administration and also requested some say in how the funds were disbursed. The main point of contention, however, seemed to be a jurisdictional one: which ministry would have primary regulatory powers over the special financial institutions and their disbursements.

With the ministries unable to resolve their differences, they withdrew their conflicting plans. The Ministry of Finance continued to oversee the postal savings, but their use was limited by the government's Deposit Regulations (Yokin Kisoku) in 1886 to investment in government bonds.[8]

In 1885 the Postal Division became a ministry in its own right, the Ministry of Communications (Teishin Shō), paving the way for key politicians to forge a settlement that broke the jurisdictional stalemate. Between 1896 and 1900 three special government financial institutions funded by the postal savings were finally established: the Japan Hypothec Bank (Nihon Kangyō Ginkō) in 1896, the Agricultural and Industry Bank (Nōkō Ginkō) in 1896, and the Industrial Bank of Japan (Nihon Kōgyō Ginkō) in 1900. Under the compromise solution, the Ministry of Finance would have primary regulatory authority over the special banks, but the Ministry of Agriculture and Commerce and the Home Ministry would also have some voice in the use of the special banks' loans.[9] In the years following World War I, over a third of the investment account funds were allocated to these and other special government finan-

[8] Ibid.
[9] Teranishi, *Nihon no Keizai Hatten to Kinyū*, pp. 159–64.

170

cial institutions that had been established; these funds would, in turn, be used for loans to private-sector corporations and semi-private operations such as the South Manchurian Railway. In 1924, for example, another 17 percent went to purchase government bonds, 7.6 percent was invested in foreign bonds, 13.3 percent was allocated to the General Account Budget, and 12.7 percent went to local public corporations.[10]

In time, the Ministry of Communications learned the value of control over the funds it gathered and joined the jurisdictional fray. To the MOF's chagrin, when the Communications Ministry undertook the life insurance business in 1917 and the pension business in 1925 for its employees, it withheld these funds from the MOF and invested them at its own discretion until it had to relinquish them to the MOF for centralized disbursement during World War II.[11]

Not for several decades did the steady expansion of the postal savings system trouble the private banks. Because there was no interest rate ceiling on deposits, small deposits were not a particularly cheap source of funds. Banks raised their funds through security issues and lent to relatively large companies. Meanwhile, the post office was attracting the savings of small businesses that had little reason to deal with banks since most of their borrowing was from wholesalers in the form of interfirm credit.[12]

The post–World War I recession led to a succession of business failures, dragging numerous smaller banks to their demise. Because the MOF did not have a policy of guaranteeing banks, or for that matter bank deposits, investors and borrowers fled to safer large banks and small savers to the government-guaranteed post office.[13] By 1927, when the new banking law established a higher asset requirement for banks to keep their license, the banking community noted with some alarm that the pool of postal savings was growing more rapidly than were bank deposits. But there was still no ceiling

[10]Nobuyuki Teramura et al., *Zaisei Tōyūshi* (Tokyo: Tōyō Keizai Shimpōsha, 1985), pp. 233–36. See also Johnson, *Japan's Public Policy Companies*, pp. 85–86, for an account of the Terauchi administration's diversion of investment account funds (Yokinbu) via government financial institutions for the infamous "Nishihara loans" to Chinese warlords in 1917 and 1918.

[11]Kazuhisa Maeno, "Yūseishō Kenkyū," pt. 3, *Gendai*, October 1985, p. 132.

[12]Teranishi, *Nihon no Keizai Hatten to Kinyū*, pp. 405–7.

[13]Ibid., pp. 310–11, 327.

on deposit interest rates, and at least the larger banks did not care to compete for small savings.[14]

The military's wartime control changed the parameters of domestic turf battles. To encourage more private savings for the war effort, the postal savings launched a zealous savings campaign and began offering a more attractive savings instrument, a ten-year, fixed-interest deposit with no penalty for early withdrawal (known as the *teigaku chokin*), in 1941. In 1943 all postal funds, both savings deposits and postal insurance funds, were channeled through the MOF's "investment account funds" (*Yokinbu*). Nearly two-thirds of the investment account funds, in turn, were used to purchase government bonds.[15]

No sooner had World War II ended than the interministerial tug of war resumed. The MOF had enjoyed immensely having disposal of the postal savings because the investment account funds took some pressure off the general budget. When politicians—or during the war, the military—came with pet projects to be funded, low-interest-rate loans from one of the special government financial institutions (usually subsidized from budget expenditures to some degree) would sometimes be accepted in lieu of a larger piece of the budget. The funds from the postal system therefore aided the MOF in protecting the integrity of national finances. Second, the MOF could place a sizable number of its bureaucrats in government-related financial institutions as an added perquisite upon retirement.[16]

After the war, the renamed Ministry of Posts and Telecommunications sought to gain control over the disbursement of the postal savings funds. With larger coffers to work with, the MPT could help to fund Diet members' projects in exchange for political support for the MPT's other areas of jurisdiction. The availability of funds would represent valuable political capital.

Many politicians favored giving the MPT control over at least some of the postal funds because they expected the MPT to be less chary with politicians' requests. Second, the MPT's labor union,

[14]"Kinyū Daikōkyō to Yūbin Chokin," *Ginkō Tsūshin*, July 20, 1927, p. 98.

[15]Teranishi, *Nihon no Keizai Hatten to Kinyū*, p. 397; Maeno, "Yūseishō Kenkyū," p. 132.

[16]See, for example, Kōichi Katō, *Kanryō Desu, Yoroshiku* (Tokyo: TBS Brittanica, 1983), pp. 148–56; Mitsuo Takamoto, *Ōkurakanryō no Himitsu* (Tokyo: Chōbunsha, 1982), pp. 98–127.

Zentei, put pressure on the Socialists to ensure that the MPT received the right to manage postal funds.[17] Third, and most important, the MPT had the support of the four hundred or so commissioned postmasters from virtually every election district in the country.[18] On July 25, 1950, the Liberal party's administration decided that postal life insurance and pension funds should stay under the control of the MPT rather than be transferred along with postal deposits to the MOF. This postal life insurance and pension money was a fraction of the larger pool of postal deposits, but nevertheless represented about 10 percent of the MOF's investment account funds (*Yokinbu*) in 1950.[19]

The MOF had its own sets of allies. The first was the American Occupation officials, who felt it important that Japan streamline its economic reconstruction efforts through the MOF. SCAP insisted that the Investment Funds Account Act (Shikin Unyōbu Hō) explicitly give the MOF authority to manage and invest all postal funds as well as welfare pensions and national pensions gathered by the Ministry of Health and Welfare. Despite initial opposition from a sizable group of politicians, the law passed the Diet in March 1951.[20] A second and more permanent group of allies was local governments, which feared that the MPT would commit fewer funds to localities than the MOF was currently doing.[21] As soon as

[17]Maeno, "Yūseishō Kenkyū," pp. 132–33.

[18]Chalmers Johnson states that each of an average district's four hundred postmasters is said to be able to turn out two hundred votes, for a total of eighty thousand votes per district. Johnson concedes that this figure is probably somewhat overstated. "MITI, MPT, and the Telecom Wars: How Japan Makes Policy for High Technology," BRIE Working Paper no. 21 (September 1986), p. 22.

[19]"Kanpo, Nenkin No Ikan de Yokinbu Shikin Ichiwari Gen," *Kinyū Zaisei Jijō*, July 31, 1950, p. 11.

[20]The *Shikin Unyōbu Hō* replaced the *Yokinbu* accounts with a single new account called the "Investment Funds Account" (*Shikin Unyōbu*). The *Shikin Unyōbu* is sometimes referred to somewhat misleadingly in English as the Trust Fund Bureau, though a division in the MOF Finance Bureau oversees the account. Johnson, *Japan's Public Policy Companies*, p. 96; "Shikin Unyōbu Hōan wa Tsūjō Kokkai Teishutsu," *Kinyū Zaisei Jijō*, December 4, 1950, p. 7; "Shikin Unyōbu Hōan de Karamu," *Kinyū Zaisei Jijō*, March 26, 1951, pp. 13–15. As part of the *Shikin Unyōbu Hō*, an Investment Funds Account Operation Council (*Shikin Unyōbu Shingikai*) comprising MOF and MPT officials and private-sector individuals was established under the auspices of the prime minister's office to advise the MOF in overseeing the account. See Teramura et al., *Zaisei Tōyūshi*, p. 187.

[21]"Kanpo no Unyō de Ōkura, Yūsei Tairitsu," *Kinyū Zaisei Jijō*, August 14, 1950, p. 9; "Kanpo no Unyō Hōhō nado Chikaku Kettei ka," *Kinyū Zaisei Jijō*, September 25, 1950, p. 10.

the Occupation forces left in 1952 the Diet reconsidered the management of postal life insurance and pension funds; the final solution in October 1952 was to give joint jurisdiction over the funds to the two ministries.[22]

While this interministerial turf battle raged, banks looked on in dismay. From their standpoint, there need be no Investment Funds Account (Shikin Unyōbu) at all, or at the very most postal savings should be channeled into government bonds. Banks were apprehensive that government-affiliated financial institutions funded by the Investment Funds Account would cut into their loan business. Second, banks were concerned that the MOF's zeal to fill the Investment Funds Account would feed the growth of the postal savings system. For now that deposit rates were limited by the Temporary Interest Rate Control Law, banks were eager to capture all the private savings they could. At such low rates, a bank's profile would be directly proportional to the size of its deposit base. But instead of wanting to cut back the postal system in defense of banks, the MOF was in the compromised position of wishing the success of both the postal system and the banks.

Banks were at a disadvantage relative to the post office network in the drive to collect savings deposits, for two reasons. First, interest accrued from postal deposits was granted tax exemption, and although each individual saver was permitted only 150,000 yen in a postal account in the early postwar years, there were no serious attempts to expose tax evaders who carried multiple accounts spread across various post offices or by the use of pseudonyms. (There was no ceiling on the amount of savings in a bank deposit, nor was there a tax exemption for interest on bank savings accounts at that time.) The MPT guarded its turf jealously and refused to allow national tax authorities onto their premises to check for tax-evading depositors. Second, because the Ministry of Posts and Telecommunications and not the MOF established the interest rates and terms of postal savings, the postal system did not move in the slow lock step of the banking sector. Although the Ministry of Posts and the Ministry of

[22]"Kanpo Nenkin Dokuritsu Unyō," *Kinyū Zaisei Jijō*, November 3, 1952, pp. 8–9. For a brief description for how the MOF and the MPT share the use of the postal insurance and pension funds, see Teramura et al., *Zaisei Tōyūshi*, pp. 191–93.

Finance met regularly to coordinate postal and bank deposit rates with changes in the official discount rate, the two ministries frequently disagreed on what the postal rate should be, or at least on the timing of the interest rate increase or decrease. The postal system's most popular deposit, the *teigaku chokin* established during the war, still attracted savers with its combination of relatively high yield with liquidity. Many private banks could not have provided this kind of instrument even if the MOF had allowed them to try.

In July 1950 the Association of Regional Banks publicly protested the expansion of the postal system's business at their expense. The regional banks requested that (1) the Investment Funds Account (*Yokinbu*) be scaled back; (2) interest income from banks be given the same tax-exempt status; (3) tax authorities be allowed to check the post offices' books for duplication of accounts; (4) the MPT not be permitted to pay postmasters commissions on the basis of deposit volume; and (5) post offices not be allowed to expand in areas where banks were already established.[23] In November the Federation of Bankers Associations issued a similar statement, stressing that the postal system's 15–16 percent share of private savings deposits was intolerably high.[24]

Because the MOF was not capable of imposing a solution on the MPT, the dispute reached the floor of the Diet. But neither were the politicians in a position to abandon their commissioned postmaster friends. As part of the compromise, the Investment Funds Account was authorized to use up to one-third of its funds to underwrite long-term credit bank debentures. This was of no service to the vast majority of banks, which could not issue debentures anyway. In 1952 the Diet extended tax-exempt status to interest income from bank deposits of up to 150,000 yen, which also happened to be the maximum an individual could hold in a postal account. (This ceiling has been raised periodically over the years. Note that for banks, unlike for postal accounts, this amount was not a ceiling on how much a saver could deposit but only a ceiling for tax purposes.

[23]Shadan Hōjin Chihō Ginkō Kyōkai, "Yūbin Chokin Seido ni Kansuru Iken," *Kinyū Zaisei Jijō,* July 31, 1950, p. 39.
[24]Zenkoku Ginkō Kyōkai Rengōkai, "Ginkōhō Kaisei ni Kansuru Iken," *Kinyū Zaisei Jijō,* November 13, 1950, especially p. 33.

There has never been a ceiling on the amount a saver can place in a bank deposit.) Since the interest rates were so low, this income would not amount to a great deal, but at least bank accounts would be on equal tax footing with postal accounts.[25]

Despite their worries and complaints, banks were doing a very brisk business in the early postwar years. Miffed, in fact, that banks were sustaining high profit margins by refusing to pass on the low cost of deposits in the form of low-interest-rate loans to corporate borrowers, Prime Minister Yoshida ordered in July 1951 that interest rates on postal deposits be raised to chasten the banks. Though banks reluctantly raised their own deposit rates to keep pace, Yoshida did not attain his real goal of lowering bank lending spreads. As long as the corporate demand for funds was strong there were numerous, sometimes subtle, ways of maintaining a profitable lending business, such as through compensating balances.[26]

Rather than cutting back on postal funds for special government institutions, the government established many new special legal entities, including Japan National Railways (1949), the People's Finance Corporation (1949), the Housing Loan Corporation (1950), the Nippon Telegraph and Telephone Public Corporation (1952), the Electric Power Development Company (1952), Japan Air Lines (1953), the Smaller Business Finance Corporation (1953), and the Agriculture, Forestry, and Fishery Finance Corporation (1953). To meet the burgeoning funding needs of these institutions, the government added new accounts to the Investment Funds Account to create the Fiscal Investment and Loan Program (Zaisei Tōyūshi), or FILP, in 1953.[27] The Investment Funds Account, including the postal savings funds, welfare pensions, and national pensions,

[25]"Shikin Unyōbu Hōan Kakugi Kettei," *Kinyū Zaisei Jijō*, March 5, 1951, p. 9; Teranishi, *Nihon no Keizai Hatten to Kinyū*, p. 427. One way to view the tax exemption for interest income is a government subsidy in lieu of higher yields from the postal system or banks (which would have meant lower bank profits), a subsidy that might otherwise be necessary to lure savings to fuel economic growth.

[26]"Zōshō no Gōinsa no Ennetsusa no Araware," *Kinyū Zaisei Jijō*, August 27, 1951, pp. 8–9.

[27]The FILP, also known as Japan's "second budget" because of its size and importance as a source of government spending, was not formally reviewed by the Diet as part of the budget-making process until 1973, by which time the FILP had grown to about one-half the size of the General Account Budget and 5 percent of Japan's GNP. See Teramura et al., *Zaisei Tōyūshi*, pp. 204–7, 243–44.

amounted to over half of the FILP funds. These funds were supplemented by the Industrial Investment Special Account, which had its origin in Japanese counterpart funds from postwar U.S. government aid; Post Office Life Insurance; receipts from government-guaranteed bonds and loans; and in the early years some allocations from the General Account Budget.[28]

Banks and post offices continued their low-grade competition for savings deposits, and the MOF and the MPT negotiated as necessary to keep interest rates more or less in line. It was not until Kakuei Tanaka became the minister of posts and telecommunications in 1957 that the postal system was mobilized for political action. Tanaka's intention was not to make enemies of the banks but to equip the postal system to serve as a political machine at elections. With new allies in the Diet, however, the MPT was emboldened to tread farther into the banks' traditional preserve.

When thirty-nine-year-old Tanaka took office as minister of posts and telecommunications, there were about 1,150 post offices around the country operated by local notables on a commission basis. Because most of these postmasters were politically influential in their communities, Tanaka saw the potential of this group for building a nationwide election support system. If he could establish and cultivate enough of these post offices around the country, he would be able to place larger numbers of his own loyal coterie, his faction members, in the Diet.

The Socialists opposed the commissioned post office system altogether, not because they foresaw its transformation into a powerful vote-gathering machine by the LDP, but because the MPT's labor union, Zentei, preferred expansion of the MPT proper to the consignment of work to commissioned officers and other nonunion outsiders. In 1958 Tanaka not only ensured that the commissioned postmasters were spared, but he commissioned two thousand new postmasters over the course of one year. Tanaka's ambitious goal was to establish one post office for every six thousand citizens for a

[28]Since 1953, General Account allocations have disappeared, the Industrial Investment Special Account has remained small, and the *Shikin Unyōbu* has grown to be an increasingly large part of the Fiscal Investment and Loan Program. The postal savings alone amounted to 61.8 percent of the FILP's total of 179.8 trillion yen in 1985. For a description of how the FILP has evolved, see Teramura et al., *Zaisei Tōyūshi*, pp. 206–11, 238–46.

177

total of some twenty thousand in five to ten years. In classic Tanaka style, and to the astonishment of the MPT bureaucrats, the postal minister readily procured the necessary budgetary allotment for the first two thousand. Threatening the MOF with intransigence on postal interest rates unless the requested funds were forthcoming from the budget, Tanaka got what he wanted. Tanaka also encouraged more frequent meetings of the postmasters at their headquarters in the Ministry of Posts and Telecommunications.[29]

The commissioned postmasters were by no means Tanaka's only, or even main, source of organized support. A consummate politician, Tanaka excelled at using his cabinet positions to cultivate ever more bases of support, and he even won the confidence of much of the financial community during his tenure as Minister of Finance from 1962 to 1964.[30] Indeed, it is typical for cabinet ministers to represent the interests of their ministry not only because that is the path of least resistance but also as a means of building networks of funders and supporters. But Tanaka did not neglect the commissioned postmasters once he moved on to other posts; in fact he secured for his faction the postal minister position in twelve cabinets between 1957 and 1982 in order to keep the MPT's influence over sources of funding within his faction.[31]

Tanaka could not, however, keep the postmasters to himself. They offered campaign assistance to any LDP politician who expressly supported their interests in the party and in the Diet. Other factions became interested in gaining the postmasters' support in 1956 when Ei Tejima, an ex-MPT bureaucrat won handily a seat to the Upper House from the national constituency district (*zenkoku*) with the backing, primarily, of the postmasters. An even clearer measure of the postmasters' vote-gathering power was the 1981 victory of a heretofore unknown ex-MPT vice-minister, Yūji Osada, also from the Upper House's national constituency district.

In the unlikely scenario that the postmasters' network was responsible for all of Osada's one million votes, enough to give him

[29]Sadaka, *Nihon Kanryō Hakusho*, pp. 178–81.
[30]Ikkō Jin, *Ōkura Kanryō* (Tokyo: Kodansha, 1986), pp. 221–26.
[31]Prime Minister Nakasone has placed one of his own faction's members in the MPT post in every one of his cabinets. "Jimintō Yūsei Zoku," *Kinyū Bijinesu*, August 8, 1986, pp. 56–59; "Ōkura vs. Yūsei: Jingi naki Yūchō Sensō," *Gendai*, June 1981, p. 290.

fourth place nationally, the postmasters had garnered an average of about two thousand votes in each election district.[32] Clearly this would be an exaggeration, since Osada had other supporters. Furthermore, the fact that postmasters mobilized votes in the Upper House's national constituency district said less about their vote-getting ability at the local level, where other factors intervene. Nonetheless, Osada's victory was at the very least a magnificent public relations coup for the postmasters, a highly visible if somewhat overblown symbol of their clout. Even skeptical politicians would have to be brave indeed to test their doubts, given the high degree of uncertainty in most election campaigns.

In growing numbers from the 1960s on, LDP politicians joined the Diet's Communications Committee (Teishin Iinkai), the party's counterpart committee (Tsūshin Bukai) in the Policy Affairs Research Council, or the more informal Postal Operations Study Group (Yūsei Jigyō Konwakai). LDP politicians were attracted to the perceived vote-gathering power of the commissioned postmasters, as well as access to the fund-raising network represented by the MPT-related Nippon Telegraph and Telephone and its suppliers.[33] By 1980 the number of LDP politicians who counted themselves among the postal affairs caucus (Yūsei Zoku) exceeded three hundred, making it second in size only to the Construction Affairs Group (Kensetsu Zoku).[34] Although only forty to fifty politicians regularly attended the meetings of the Postal Operations Study Group, they showed up, two to three hundred strong, when an important issue was at stake. Moreover, the minister of posts and telecommunications, which had been considered a second-rung

---

[32]Nihon Keizai Shimbun, ed., *Jimintō Seichōkai* (Tokyo: Nihon Keizai Shimbunsha, 1983), pp. 116–19. Although the Osada episode overrepresents the postal network's campaign power, it provides something of an indication. Since then, a change in the election rules allows the parties to rank their candidates on a party ballot for proportional representation in the national constituency race, making it impossible to judge as effectively one individual's nationwide popularity.

[33]Interviews with LDP politicians, summer 1986, Tokyo.

[34]That the MPT regulates producers of telecommunications services and equipment is another reason for the popularity of the Postal Affairs Group in the LDP. The telecommunications industry is a dynamic segment of Japan's economy, and its campaign contributions to the LDP are increasing as it grows in prosperity and stature. See Takashi Inoguchi and Tomoaki Iwai, *Zoku Giin* (Tokyo: Nihon Keizai Shimbunsha, 1987), pp. 202–5.

179

cabinet position by LDP politicians twenty years earlier, was now regarded as a highly desirable appointment.[35]

The history of bank–postal system relations in Japan, at least in the postwar years, has been one of virtually continuous postal savings expansion and increasing bank resistance. But beginning in the 1970s, the rate at which the postal savings expanded considerably outpaced that of bank deposits. In 1965 postal deposits accounted for about 18.2 percent and deposits in city banks for about 28.6 percent of personal savings deposits in Japan; by 1975 the ordering was reversed, to 26.8 percent and 24.3 percent, respectively. Or in starker terms, deposits in all banks had grown by a factor of 13.6 and in city banks by a factor of 18.5 between 1960 and 1975, whereas postal savings increased by a factor of 22.[36]

The Embattled Savings Tax

Of the several reasons for the postal system's growing popularity with savers, the one banks were quickest to seize upon was the postal system's reputation for being lax with tax evaders. Because the postal authorities refused to allow national tax authorities to check their records, and because the postal system itself did not have all of its deposit transactions on a computer network, banks alleged that the postal savings system was an invitation to tax evasion. At the end of March 1979, for example, there were 235,950,000 tax-free postal accounts, which amounted to over two accounts for every man, woman, and child in Japan.[37] Though not all of these accounts were up to the allowable 3 million yen (up from 1.5 million yen in 1973), some were over the limit and many individuals carried multiple accounts in different post offices or in one post office through the use of pseudonyms.

The MPT claimed to reduce amounts to the allowable limit when-

[35]"Jimintō Yūsei Zoku," *Kinyū Bijinesu*, August 8, 1986, pp. 56–59; Yasuyuki Kishiro, *Jimintō Zeisei Chōsakai* (Tokyo: Tōyō Keizai Shimpōsha, 1985), pp. 25–26. The Postal Affairs Group (*Yūsei Zoku*), or the Communications Policy Group as it is otherwise known (*Teishin Zoku*), also dealt with the MPT's other regulatory areas, including telecommunications.

[36]"Kinyūkai no Fukōhei Zeisei Hihan," *Sengo Kinyū Zaisei Rimenshi* (Tokyo: Kinyū Zaisei Jijō Kenkyūkai, 1980), pp. 598–99.

[37]Takashi Inoue, *Gurīn Kādo* (Tokyo: Keiei Jitsumu Shuppan, 1980), p. 109.

Banks and the Postal Savings System

Table 5. Share of personal savings market by type of financial institution (percentage)

	1965	1970	1975	1980	1986
Postal savings system	15.9	18.9	22.8	28.7	30.9
City banks	21.5	20.7	18.5	16.2	17.9
Local banks	19.5	17.2	16.6	15.8	14.3
Mutual banks	9.9	8.5	8.4	8.0	6.9
Credit associations	13.0	13.2	12.8	12.1	11.6
Agricultural cooperatives	14.3	15.2	14.8	13.4	12.3
Other	5.9	6.3	6.1	5.8	6.1

Notes: "Savings" here refers only to savings *deposits* and does not include other personal savings instruments such as goverment bonds, trust accounts, and insurance. Furthermore, the table does not include deposits in credit cooperatives (*shinyō kumiai*). The share of postal savings is therefore somewhat exaggerated.

Sources: Cabinet secretariat, Cabinet Deliberations Office, *Kinyū no bunya ni Okeru Kangyō no Arikata: Kondankai Hōkoku Narabi ni Kanren Zen Shiryō* (Tokyo: Kinyū Zaisei Jijō Kenkyūkai, 1981), p. 57; and various issues of Bank of Japan's *Keizai Nenpō*.

ever it discovered cheating in postal accounts and put the excess in tax-exempt government bond accounts so their customers would not have to pay taxes. In 1979, for example, twenty-one thousand postal savers had their accounts pared down to 3 million, for a total of 22 billion yen over the limit placed in government bond accounts. Banks claimed that fully one-third of the postal deposits were attributable to tax evaders.[38]

Indeed, data showed that postal savers were no longer low income earners. Between 1965 and 1979 the postal system's most rapidly growing clientele was the highest of five income categories. Whereas postal savings by people with annual income of 5.6 million yen and above increased twenty times in that fourteen-year span, bank deposits by that income group increased 9.2 times over the same period. Broken down by occupation, the post offices' most rapidly growing customer base was made up of owners of small businesses. The banks therefore charged the postal system with harboring the growing pool of money that this group was failing to report as income.[39]

[38] Banks had no precise data on postal savings. "Kyojin na Ashikoshi: Seijiryoku, soshite Shomin Kankaku," *Tōyō Keizai,* March 28, 1981; "Ōkura vs. Yūsei," *Gendai,* June 1981, pp. 277–78.

[39] Cabinet Deliberations Office, cabinet secretariat, *Kinyū no Bunya ni Okeru Kangyō no Arikata* (August 1981), p. 58; "Gurīn Kādo, Keizai Onchi Seijika,"

181

What the banks did not mention was their own reluctance to check carefully for duplication of accounts lest they lose customers to the post office. The difference was that Tax Agency auditors had ready access to their books, of which savers were well aware. A much safer tax evasion strategy for an individual saver would be to place money in multiple postal accounts beyond the reach of the tax authorities. Some savers nevertheless had more tax-free savings than allowable in a given bank, and many banks simply paid the tax authorities out of their own profits in the event that savers govern-ment inspectors detected instances of attempted tax evasion.[40] Be-tween 1973 and 1978 banks were caught with 38 billion yen in accounts over the 3-million-yen tax-exemption ceiling.[41]

In the rapid-growth years when personal savings were increasing steadily with income, the banks' deposit base continued to grow de-spite the even faster growth of postal deposits. Banks could hardly make a good case for bridling the postal system when banks them-selves were doing so well. It was not until banks' profits suffered from slackened growth of the economy and the securitization trend after the oil shock of 1973 that they became alarmed enough to mobilize for political action.[42]

The opposition parties had long urged that tax exemption be limited to deposits of low-income earners, arguing that the across-the-board breaks on savings income weakened the impact of Japan's sharply progressive tax scale. Regardless of their income bracket, savers could deposit up to 3 million yen in a postal account, 3 million in a bank account, 3 million in government bonds, and 5 million (for salaried workers) in a retirement investment fund (*zai-kei hikazei chokin*), for a total of up to 14 million yen in tax-free accounts.[43]

Tōyō Keizai, March 28, 1981, pp. 20–23; Yasuyuki Kishiro, *Jimintō Zeisai Chōsakai* (Tokyo: Tōyō Keizai Shimpōsha, 1985), pp. 126–27.

[40]There were no limits on the size of bank accounts per se, but only on amounts on which interest was tax-free.

[41]"Ōkura vs. Yūsei," *Gendai*, June 1981.

[42]As discussed in Chapter 3, banks were also pressing at this time for entry into the government bond retail and trading markets. Banks used the postal system's increasing share of deposits as an argument for launching into new lines of business.

[43]Takuji Matsuzawa, *Watakushi no Ginkō Shōwashi* (Tokyo: Tōyō Keizai Shim-pōsha, 1985), pp. 202–3.

The MOF was also concerned about tax leakage through the postal system not only because banks demanded that something be done but now more intensely because the government deficit began to grow at an alarming rate after the first oil crisis. The MOF began to look for new sources of revenue and in 1975 commissioned the Government Tax Advisory Council (Seifu Zeisei Chōsakai) to study a comprehensive tax on interest and dividend income. The National Tax Agency estimated lost revenue from tax evasion through the postal system to be 200 to 300 billion yen.[44] When the Tax Advisory Council issued a report in December 1976 recommending the abolition or at least scaling back of the longstanding exemptions for savings, the LDP and the Postal Affairs Group in particular were not ready to countenance the idea.[45]

In 1979 a peculiar turn of events provided the MOF's Tax Bureau with an opportunity to broach the savings taxation matter to the LDP once again. A sordid scandal exploded in the press in October 1979 over the massive misuse of profits of the Kokusai Denshin Denwa (KDD), the quasi-government corporation that monopolizes Japan's international telephone and telegraph exchanges. Because KDD is regulated by the MPT, and many members of the LDP's Postal Affairs Group seemed to have been receiving political payoffs from the highest-ranking managers of KDD, the Postal Affairs Group was at a low point in internal LDP bargaining power. The news media continued to give splashy coverage of the incident, and the politicians involved, as additional evidence came to light through the spring of 1980.[46]

The Postal Affairs Group politicians were weakened but not destroyed. When the Government Tax Council proposed the abolition of all tax-free interest accounts, the LDP sent the plan back to

[44]Interview with MOF Tax Bureau officials, 1986, Tokyo; "G Kādo Zōshū 2000 oku en," *Asahi*, March 12, 1981.

[45]Takuji Matsuzawa, *Watakushi no Ginkō Shōwashi* (Tokyo: Tōyō Keizai Shimpōsha, 1985), pp. 202–3.

[46]Interview with an official who was in the MOF's Tax Bureau during this period, summer 1986, Tokyo; *Asahi*, October 13, 1979; *Nikkei*, October 22, 1979; *Nikkei*, October 24, 1979; "clear that MPT is involved," *Asahi*, October 29, 1979; "KDD received 100 million yen a year from suppliers as 'cooperation money,'" *Asahi*, November 16, 1979; "Takeshita and Kanemaru return 1 and 3 million, respectively, in party tickets earlier received from KDD," *Asahi*, December 17, 1979; "190 Dietmembers smudged by the KDD revelations," *Asahi*, April 6, 1980.

the drawing board.[47] In December 1979 the MOF presented the Diet with a seemingly more modest scheme that was designed to prevent tax evasion within the existing system rather than to overhaul the tax code itself. Each saver wishing to open, deposit into, or withdraw from a tax-exempt account would be required to show an identification card specially created for the purpose. The Green Card System, as it came to be known, was to come into effect on January 1, 1984, by which time the MPT would have a nationwide computer network to check for account duplication. The bill was passed into law in March 1980, without revisions either from the Finance Committee or from the floor.[48]

Although banks had been quietly supportive of the Green Card bill since they were at a disadvantage in the tax evasion battle, the banks began to feel uneasy about how effective the new law would actually be in eliminating the postal system's multiple accounts. The law left a number of important details unspecified, such as whether or not the Green Card would apply to accounts already in existence—for example, the postal system's ten-year deposits, which accounted for over 85 percent of postal funds. A liberal interpretation of the law would therefore continue to shield many tax evaders.

The banking industry's worst fears were realized. When the public learned of the Ministry of Posts and Telecommunications' avowed opposition to the retroactive application of the Green Card, depositors left banks for the post office in droves. The Green Card would eventually put a halt to abuse of the postal system, but only for deposits made after the time when the card would come into effect in 1984. In the meantime, savers could stash funds in the postal system's ten-year accounts. Reflecting, in part, savers' preference for the postal system's ten-year "tax grace period," the increase in deposits at city banks dropped 19 percent in 1980 from the previous year to

[47]"Maruyū Haishi no Ikō, Bunri Kazei mo Minaoshi," *Mainichi*, July 25, 1979; "Maruyū Tenaoshi wa Konnan," *Asahi*, August 9, 1979; "Maruyū Seido Sonzoku no Hōkō," *Asahi*, October 10, 1979; "Bangō Seido sara ni Kentō," *Asahi*, November 28, 1979.

[48]"Gojūkunen dara Ikō," *Asahi*, December 13, 1979; "Datsuzei Bōshi ni Shinheiki," *Asahi*, December 23, 1979; "Gurīn Kādo Jisshi Yōryō Katamaru," *Nikkei*, January 28, 1980; "Maruyū no Akuyō o Bōshi," *Asahi*, February 7, 1980; "Kokkai Hōkaiseian mo Kaketsu," *Asahi*, March 31, 1980; "Ōkura vs. Yūsei," *Gendai*, June 1981, p. 293.

an all-time low of 2.5 trillion yen, whereas postal accounts grew by 36 percent over the previous period, adding 9.4 trillion yen to the postal system's existing 50 trillion.[49]

The banks now realized that, given the postal system's continued reputation as a tax haven, the Green Card scheme had been a mistake. But the MOF could not be of much help. Although the Banking Bureau was sympathetic, the Tax Bureau was delighted by the prospect of increased tax revenue, though the taxation would be only on incremental duplicate accounts. And all the power of the MOF could not force the MPT to use the Green Card to apprehend the tax evaders who had already safely stashed away large sums in ten-year postal deposits.[50] In the summer of 1980, because the wave of discouraging statistics continued unabated, banks began to approach Diet members about either ensuring that postal accounts were as rigorously checked as bank accounts or reversing the Green Card altogether. Though it had been only months since the bill had been passed, the politicians were willing to reconsider.[51]

Banks having despaired of the Green Card, the MOF was the only remaining proponent. And for politicians concerned about the approaching general elections, the MOF's advocacy was not enough. On August 20, 1980, the LDP Financial Issues Study Group (Kinyū Mondai Chōsakai) began to conduct hearings to decide the fate of the Green Card.[52] Before long anti–Green Card sentiment had spread through the Diet like a brushfire. Tamisuke Watanuki, a known MPT sympathizer in the LDP, employed the rhetoric supplied by the banks, arguing that the Green Card would "disrupt the balance between the banks and the postal system." Watanuki and the others in the Postal Affairs Group had not switched sides

[49]"Gurīn Kādo wa Yūchō Yūgū," Asahi, August 13, 1980; "Kinyūkai, Yokin no Ryūshutsu Soshi," Asahi, August 14, 1980; Kazuo Tatewaki, Kinyū Daikakumei (Tokyo: Tōyō Keizai Shimpōsha, 1982), pp. 191–92; Matsuzawa, Watakushi no Ginkō Shōwashi, p. 202.

[50]The MOF assured the MPT of an adequate budget allotment for the installation of a computer system for keeping track of the nation's postal deposits, but the MPT retorted that it was checking deposits adequately already. Asahi, August 30, 1980.

[51]"Kinyūkai, Yokin no Ryūshutsu Soshi," Asahi, August 14, 1980.

[52]"Gurīn Kādo Kyōgi e," Asahi, August 15, 1980; "Rishi Haitō no Shūnyū Meihaku," Asahi, August 27, 1980; "Kōfu no Seireian Katamaru," Nikkei, September 14, 1980; "Kōhei e Hōteki Sochi," Asahi, September 17, 1980; "Nayose ni Nao Teiki," Asahi, September 27, 1980.

but were picking up support wherever it was to be had. The Ministry of Posts and Telecommunications and the commissioned postmasters were only too glad to have the banks on their side against the Green Card.[53] Socialist Masao Hori also echoed the banks' argument, stating that "the banks and postal system should be placed on equal footing" before such tax reforms could be introduced. But Hori added, lest his constituents wonder about his loyalties, that banks should "work harder to introduce attractive savings instruments."[54]

Perhaps even more critical than banks' dissatisfaction with the Green Card system as proposed was the staunch opposition of the small and medium-sized businesses that feared exposure of the large amounts of assets they had accumulated without paying full taxes.[55] The Democratic Socialist party, which had also gone along with the Green Card proposal at first, now reversed its position because of strong objections by large numbers of small and medium-sized businesses in its constituency.[56] Neither could the LDP afford to alienate the small and medium-sized business sector, which accounts for over a quarter of its electorate.

On March 14, 1981, Shintarō Abe, chairman of the LDP Policy Affairs Research Council, tolled the death knell for the Green Card system, declaring: "The [MOF] bureaucrats talked us into passing the Green Card bill before we had time to examine thoroughly the issues involved. Now we have had time to see that there are some serious problems with the scheme." On April 16 a group of about three hundred LDP politicians, centering around Shin Kanemaru and others in the Postal Affairs Group, banded together in a Diet

[53]"Yūcho: Waga Tō no Kangae," *Kinyū Jānaru*, November 1980, pp. 55–60.
[54]Ibid.
[55]Small businesses have found it relatively easy to stash away unreported income under existing tax laws and since the late 1970s have battled fiercely to block a value-added tax that would have provided the government with a more effective device for monitoring business income. See Hugh Patrick and Thomas Rohlen, "Small Family-owned Enterprises in Japan," in Kozo Yamamura and Yasukichi Yasuba, eds., *The Political Economy of Japan*, vol. 1: *The Domestic Transformation* (Stanford: Stanford University Press, 1987); Kishiro, *Jimintō Zeisei Chōsakai*, pp. 125–27, 169–87.
[56]"Yūchō: Waga Tō no Kangae," *Kinyū Jānaru*, November 1980; Arai Ryūichi, *Gurīn Kādo wa Gurīn da* (Tokyo: Seibun Dō, 1981), pp. 18–24.

members' League for the Reappraisal of the Green Card (Gurīn Kādo Saikentō Giin Renmei).[57]

In March 1983, a year before the Green Card system was to be introduced, the Diet voted to postpone its introduction for three years. Without waiting for the interim period to lapse, the Diet voted to reject the Green Card idea altogether in March 1985. For a number of reasons, but primarily because banks, the postal system, and the small and medium-sized business sector opposed the Green Card, this seemingly modest scheme to reduce tax evasion proved to be too hot for politicians to manage.[58]

The Interest Rate Controversy

In early 1981, when it was already clear that the Diet would not support the Green Card solution to the tax-evasion problem, the banks and postal system once again squared off, just as they had before the tax proposal was introduced. Banks were chagrined that the postal system had been steadily gaining in its share of the nation's savings, and tax evasion in the postal system was merely one issue the banks attempted to utilize in curbing the postal system's expansion.

On the banking community's list of grievances, in addition to the postal system's perceived advantage on taxation grounds, was the postal system's partial autonomy from the MOF/BOJ interest rate structure. Because neither ministry possessed legal authority to impose its own will over the other, the postal system managed to retain a savings instrument, the "fixed-amount deposit" (*teigaku chokin*), which posed a serious problem for the banks.

The postal system's fixed-amount deposit, introduced first in 1941 as part of the war effort, allowed savers to deposit money in an account for up to ten years, with semiannual compounded inter-

[57]"Jimin Giren Hatakakage," *Asahi*, April 16, 1981. Only the Japan Communist party had opposed the Green Card system from the beginning, on the grounds that the government would abuse a national identification system to intrude into the private lives of citizens. "G-Kādo Dōnyū ni Iron Sainen," *Asahi*, April 6, 1981.

[58]"Kakushi Yokinsō no Koe Daiben," *Asahi*, April 16, 1981. See also articles in all major newspapers betwen April 1981 and March 1985.

est at the initial deposit rate, and to withdraw funds from the account at any time after six months with no penalty except foregone interest income. Over four-fifths of all postal savings are in the form of these fixed-amount deposits.[59]

Although the interest rate attached to this postal savings instrument was kept in line with the rest of the small deposit interest rate structure, only trust banks and long-term credit banks were permitted to accept deposits or issue debentures with a maturity of over three years. And in any case, many of the smaller banks could not afford to pay compounded interest twice a year. In 1977 the director general of the Banking Bureau, Hiroshi Tokuda, had actually suggested the banks introduce an account with semiannual interest payments; but the resistance from weaker banks was overwhelming.[60]

Banks have leveled every conceivable criticism against the postal system, even if some of them may be mutually contradictory. Banks contended that the only reason the postal system could offer such an attractive deposit was the postal system's freedom from the "bottom line." Being a government institution, the postal system could pass off an operating deficit onto taxpayers by receiving subsidies from the general budget. Banks alleged that the postal savings system had been paying out more interest than it had been getting from the MOF's FILP, thus leading to large accumulated losses.[61]

Noting the shrinking Postal Savings Special Account deficit, banks then discounted the significance of these figures, charging that the postal system was shifting some of its losses from postal savings onto its mail operations.[62] Banks also have complained over the decades that the postal savings system has an unfair cost advantage because of its freedom from corporate and real estate tax, subsidized overhead from postal operations, and an unfair marketing advantage by

[59]Tsunezō Fuse, *Gurin Kādo no Subete* (Tokyo: Zeimu Kenkyūkai Shuppan Kyoku, 1980), p. 131.

[60]Yasuhiko Ōishi, "Ginkō yo, Ogoru Nakare," *Ekonomisuto*, June 2, 1981, p. 23.

[61]"Ginkō to Yūbinchokin no Keihi," *Kinyū*, April 1977, pp. 47–48; "Yūbinchokin ni Kansuru Kihonteki Kangae Kata," *Kinyū*, November 1980, pp. 9, 38–43; Kō Nishimura, "Gokai to Henken ni Motozuku Yūcho Kenkyūkai Hōkokusho," *Kinyū Zaisei Jijō*, October 20, 1980, pp. 14–20.

[62]The MPT denied the allegation, but cannot prove its case to the contrary since it does not disclose accounting details.

Table 6. Postal savings special
account, 1973–1979 (billions of
yen)

Year	Operating net profit	Accumulated net profit
1973	14.4	172.8
1974	−62.0	110.8
1975	−94.6	16.2
1976	−189.7	−173.5
1977	−109.0	−282.5
1978	−2.7	−285.2
1979	91.7	−193.5

Source: Kō Nishimura (chief of
Sumitomo Bank First Research Division), Kinyū Zaisei Jijō, October
20, 1980, p. 18.

virtue of its 22,810 post offices reaching into "every swamp and
marsh" in the entire country.[63]

With the failure of the Green Card as a means to eliminate the
postal system's presumed allure for tax-evading savers, the banking
community devised another plan to curb the postal system's expansion. They would lobby for a cabinet decision to bring postal interest rates under the MOF's jurisidiction, thereby ensuring parity of
terms with bank deposits.

The Ministry of Finance had been unable to wrest control of the
postal system's interest rates, despite its protests that a dual interest
rate structure impeded the effective implementation of monetary
policy. In July 1972, for example, when the Ministry of Finance
wanted to lower the interest rates on loans to help the economy out
of a slump, the Ministry of Posts and Telecommunications refused
to go along with the MOF's proposed deposit rate cut. And because
the postal system balked at a lower deposit interest rate, so did the
banks. Banks, in turn, did not want to cut their loan rate as long as
the deposit rate remained frozen, so no interest rates changed during the six months of negotiations between the MOF and MPT until

[63]Hajime Yamada (chairman, Federation of Bankers Associations), "Ginkōhō
Kaisean ni Igi ari," Ekonomisuto, February 17, 1981, p. 39. There are roughly
twenty thousand private bank branches in Japan, if one includes the credit associations (shinyō kinko); "Kyojin na Ashikoshi: Seijiryoku, soshite Shomin Kankaku,"
Tōyō Keizai, March 28, 1981.

they agreed on a coordinated drop in deposit interest rates. In exchange for its cooperation on interest rates, the MPT bargained for the right to lend a portion of the postal funds to postal customers rather than to the MOF's FILP. The resulting consumer loan (*Yūyū Rōn*) was the MPT's first step into the loan business. Although discussions between the two ministries were rarely this prolonged, the MPT continued to maintain that banks should be willing to make do on smaller spreads.[64]

On December 28, 1980, Minister of Finance Michio Watanabe, Minister of Posts and Telecommunications Ichirō Yamanouchi, and cabinet secretary Kiichi Miyazawa met at Prime Minister Suzuki's residence to discuss the possibility of a single interest rate structure. Although Yamanouchi disliked the idea, he suggested that the MPT might agree to further discussion if, in exchange, the MPT were permitted to offer individual pension plans (*kojin nenkin*) to its customers. This request for expansion into the pension business was not new, and in fact the Postal Affairs Group within the LDP had promised, before the 1980 general elections, to help the MPT push the plan through the Diet. This was expected to be a lucrative line of business for the MPT and the commissioned postmasters and would add money to the MPT coffers not earmarked for the Fiscal Investment and Loan Program. The MOF reluctantly agreed to the exchange.[65]

As decided, cabinet secretary Miyazawa proceeded to select a panel of five men of high repute from government and the private sector to conceive of a plan for a unitary structure of savings rates (*kinri ichigenka*). Chaired by professor emeritus of the University of Tokyo Hiromi Arisawa, the group's other members were Jirō Enjōji, former editor of the *Nihon Keizai Shimbun*; Saburō Ōkita, former minister of foreign affairs; Kiyoshi Tsuchiya, director of the prime minister's Comprehensive Policy Research Group (Sōgō Seisaku Kenkyūkai); and Ichirō Yoshikuni, a former official of the Bank of Japan. Called the Study Group on the Role of Government in Finance, the panel began holding hearings of the MOF, the MPT,

---

[64]Kunio Yamashita, *Kaisetsu: Yūchō—Ginkō Mondai* (Tokyo: Tōyō Keizai Shimpōsha), p. 77. See also Asahi Shimbun Keizaibu, *Itameru Zaisei* (Tokyo: Asahi Shimbunsha, 1980), pp. 202–6.

[65]Keiichi Hagiwara, *Yūbin Chokin no Shinkō* (Tokyo: OS Publications, 1981), p. 145.

190

the BOJ, the Economic Planning Agency, banking and insurance organizations, small business organizations, the Keidanren, labor organizations, and consumer groups in January 1981.[66]

The Ministry of Posts and Telecommunications was displeased with Miyazawa's choice of members from the start, charging that this group was predisposed to the banks' point of view. The MPT fought back, commissioning its own Postal Savings Research Group and providing support to a subcommittee in the LDP's Postal Affairs Committee (Tsūshin Bukai) to engage in parallel studies. The MPT also mobilized savers from around the country to lobby for "the only purveyor of financial services that really cares about the people."[67] The five members of the study group were inundated with postcards from housewives begging them not to cut back postal services in any way. Cities and townships also began to rally to the MPT cause, presumably because of promises from the MPT to absorb more local government bonds if given the freedom to do so. The MPT had something for everyone in its plan for expanded use of postal funds: housing and consumer loans, and purchase of local bonds. According to a survey carried out by the MPT at the end of July 1981, 55.9 percent of the 3,325 prefecture, ward, city, town, and village legislatures and councils supported the MPT's greater freedom in its use of postal funds. The smaller communities tended to show greater sympathy for the MPT, perhaps because postmasters have greater influence at that level, and because the MPT's offer to purchase their bonds or otherwise lend them money came with promises of greater local autonomy than the MOF offered.[68]

---

[66]"Ōkura vs Yūsei," *Gendai,* June 1981, p. 275. Hiromi Arisawa was appointed by Prime Minister Yoshida in 1946 to chair the Coal Committee, of which Ōkita was also a member. Chairman Tsuji Bihei of the Japan Chamber of Commerce, representing small business, spoke in favor of unifying control of interest rates under the MOF on grounds that high postal rates were preventing banks from lending at lower rates. Labor was divided, with the larger unions, Sōhyō and Dōmei, taking the postal position and the smaller Chūritsu Rōren taking the MOF/bank position. "Kinyū no Bunya ni Okeru Kangyō no Arikata: Kondankai Hōkoku Narabini Kanren Zen Shiryō," *Naikaku Kambō Naikaku Shingishitsu,* November 26, 1981, pp. 75–77, 283–84.

[67]A commissioned postmaster, quoted in "Seijiryoku ni Kōisareta Yūchokon no Ryōshiki," *Kinyū Zaisei Jijō,* June 22, 1981, pp. 10–11.

[68]"Seiji Kōsei ni Yurare Ugoku Yūchokon Tōshin," *Kinyū Zaisei Jijō,* August 17, 1981, pp. 6–7.

Banks countered with their own public relations campaign, though they kept a lower profile than they might have, partly because their main concern of the moment was battling the securities companies over the new banking law, and partly because they didn't want to advertise the postal system's advantages. The Structural Issues Study Group of the Federation of Bankers Associations invited a group of scholars to examine the postal savings problem, appealing to arguments for small government. Although most scholars agreed that the postal system should be curbed, the corroboration was mixed with unflattering observations such as "Banks don't lend enough to consumers," and "Banks have been relying on the MOF's protection for too long."[69]

The MOF and the MPT also engaged in a rhetorical slugging match over the postal savings issue while the Study Group on the Role of Government in Finance was still conducting hearings. The MPT, in a sixty-eight-page report issued on August 8, 1981, stressed its service to the small saver and decried the MOF's protection of banks at the expense of the average citizen. The banks simply wanted the postal system to drop down to their level of inefficiency and poor service. The MOF's strongest rebuttal in defense of banks was that the MPT was incapable of reflecting market forces because of its governmental status. The MOF also argued that monetary policy flexibility requires a single interest structure, but that, although the postal system is too aggressive in acquiring savings, the MOF's FILP still serves an important function and should be the sole administrator of postal funds. The subtle ambivalence of the MOF's position was not lost on the banking community, which would have been happier to see postal funds dry up all together, or at most be restricted to activities not competing with bank deposit gathering and lending such as the purchase of government bonds.[70]

The Study Group on the Role of Government in Finance pre-

[69]"Yūchō Mondai ni Kansuru San Kenkyū Dantai no Teigen," *Kinyū Zaisei Jijō*, August 3, 1981, pp. 129–31; "Yūchokon no Butai Ura ni Miru Kakehiki," *Ekonomisuto*, June 2, 1981, pp. 22–27.

[70]Yasuhiko Ōishi (chairman, MPT Postal Savings Research Group [*Yūbin Chokin ni Kansuru Chōsa Kenkyūkai*]), "Ginkō yo, Ogoru nakare," *Ekonomisuto*, June 2, 1981, pp. 10–15; "Yūchokon ni Taisuru Ōkura, Yūsei Ryōshō no Kenkai," *Kinyū Zaisei Jijō*, July 6, 1981, pp. 26–27; "Seiji Kōsei ni Yurare Ugoku Yūchokon Tōshin," *Kinyū Zaisei Jijō*, August 17, 1981.

sented its 16-page report with another 327 pages of attached materials to Prime Minister Suzuki on August 20, 1981. Much as the MPT had feared, the group's primary conclusions were: (1) the lack of a unified interest rate structure is a serious obstacle to effective monetary policy implementation, and legal amendment is probably necessary to address this problem; (2) the postal system's fixed-amount deposit should be "reconsidered," given the imbalance between the postal system and the banks; (3) the tax-free savings limit should not be raised to 5 million yen as the MPT had requested; (4) the commissions given to the postal system's workers for drawing in deposits should be at least scaled back; (5) there should be strict limits on the postal system's entry into new lines of financial business; and (6) the postal system should not have disposal of its own funds as the MPT desired, but these should continue to be turned over to the MOF's FILP. (The MPT, since 1952, had authority to invest part of the postal pension and postal insurance funds and was lobbying for control over more.) In short, the study group was suggesting that the postal system had accomplished its important historical role and should now phase back its operations.[71]

The MPT was as livid as the MOF and the banks were delighted. Even as cabinet secretary Miyazawa was reporting at a press conference that he expected full cabinet support for the group's recommendations, the Postal Affairs Group in the LDP was organizing a revolt. On the evening of August 20 Yoshihide Mori, chairman of the LDP Postal Affairs Committee (Tsūshin Bukai), gathered a group of about fifty colleagues to draft a statement castigating the study group's conclusions as "absurdly biased toward the MOF's point of view." Soon, 333 LDP Diet members, including eight members of the cabinet, had signed a petition against a unitary interest rate scheme. Cabinet secretary Miyazawa, Minister of Finance Watanabe, and Prime Minister Suzuki were in the minority.[72]

Some members of the LDP were more sympathetic to the banks, such as Noboru Takeshita, a "new leader" of the party and one-time

[71] "Kinyū no Bunya ni Okeru Kangyō no Arikata," *Naikaku Kanbō Naikaku Shingishitsu*, November 26, 1981, pp. 1–343; Kazumoto Adachi, "Yūchokon Tōshi o Hyōtei suru," *Kinyū Zaisei Jijō*, August 31, 1981, pp. 16–22.

[72] "Shimbun no Mōten: Yūchokon," *Kinyū Zaisei Jijō*, August 31, 1981, p. 10.

minister of finance; Junichirō Koizumi, chairman of the LDP Finance Committee; and Ichirō Satō, chairman of the LDP Committee on Financial Affairs (Kinyū Mondai Chosakai). In the summer of 1981, before the Group of Five had announced its recommendations, the banking community sponsored within the LDP, under the chairmanship of Noboru Takeshita, an informal organization called the Study Group on a Free Economy (Jiyū Keizai Konwakai). Recognizing the potential importance of bank support at election time, particularly since banks were advertising their intention to increase their support of particular sympathetic candidates, the Study Group on a Free Economy soon had over 200 members. Given a total LDP membership of 423 at that time, it was clear that there were over 100 LDP politicians who had placed their names on both rosters.[73]

Unlike the Green Card case, however, in which the Diet members ultimately could side comfortably with both the banks and the postmasters, interest rate issue pitted the banks against the postal system in fierce dissension. Though displeased that the MPT could wrench itself free of what the banks had thought was a prior commitment to the recommendations of the prime minister's study group, those LDP members sympathetic to the banks acknowledged that a preponderance of the party's members were on the side of the postal system.[74]

On September 30 Miyazawa, Yamanouchi, and Watanabe agreed, in very vague terminology that only sounded harmonious, to continue disagreeing for the time being. The Ministry of Finance and the Ministry of Posts and Telecommunications would simply continue to consult before changing interest rates. By October 1981 MPT bureaucrats and commissioned postmasters were thanking the members of the LDP Postal Affairs Group for their successful sponsorship. The postal system escaped without so much as a single cabinet ordinance inhibiting its activities, and in fact the MPT went ahead with its individual pension program in September 1981 as specified in the earlier bargain with the MOF.[75]

[73]"Seikai Yūcho Sensō," *Tōyō Keizai*, September 19, 1981, pp. 16–17.
[74]"Yūseiha vs. Ōkura-Kinyūha," *Tōyō Keizai*, October 15, 1981, pp. 36–41.
[75]"Yūchokon Kankakuryō Gōi wa Nennmatsu Kessen no Hidane ni," *Kinyū Zaisei Jijō*, October 12, 1981, pp. 10–11; Moriyoshi Satō (secretary, LDP Postal Operations Study Group [*Yūsei Jigyō Konwakai Jimukyokuchō*]), "Yūchokon Tōshin no Shūsen o Sengensuru," *Kinyū Zaisei Jijō*, October 19, 1981, p. 28.

Savings Tax Back on the Docket

As loath as the members of the LDP Postal Affairs Group were to alienate their postmaster friends by imposing interest rate or tax limitations on their operations, the growing government deficit had generated strong demands from industry for administrative reform in the desire to avert a future hike in corporate income tax. This administrative reform movement brought questions about the postal system before the public again and, eventually, back onto the floor of the Diet.

In 1981 Prime Minister Suzuki commissioned a group of businesspersons and academicians under the leadership of former Keidanren chairman Toshio Dokō to find ways to cut back the size and role of the government. Dokō's conditions for chairing the Administrative Reform Council (Rinchō) were that the government not attempt to solve its fiscal difficulties by raising taxes (*zōzei naki zaisei saiken*).[76]

On January 17, 1983, the Fourth Committee of the Ad Hoc Administrative Reform Council issued a report that wholly reaffirmed the recommendations the five-man Study Group on the Role of Government in Finance had issued two and a half years earlier: the scale and scope of the MPT's financial operations should be limited, and the MOF should control interest rates. But as before, the Ministry of Posts and Telecommunications vehemently rejected the suggested changes.[77]

The LDP's Postal Affairs Group still was opposed to curbing the postal system, either for the sake of administrative reform or for the banks. As the administrative reform movement gained momentum with growing support from the business sector, however, it became increasingly difficult for the LDP to resist change altogether. The LDP was soon confronted with the prospect of taxing the interest

[76]"Rinchō Daiyon Bukai ni Okeru Yūchō Mondai no Setsumei," *Kinyū*, April 1982, pp. 37–38; Gerald Curtis, *The Japanese Way of Politics* (New York: Columbia University Press, 1987), pp. 76–79.

[77]Kiyoshi Tsuchiya (member of the five-man study group), "Yūchō Mondai o Kiru," *Kinyū Zaisei Jijō*, February 14, 1983, pp. 20–24; "Rinchō Naibu no Fukyō-waon de Nagareta Yūcho Mineika Kōsō," *Kinyū Zaisei Jijō*, March 21, 1983, pp. 16–17; Yūseishō, "Kinyū Seido Chōsakai Koiinkai Hōkoku ni Taisuru Yūseisho no Kangaekata," *Kinyū Zaisei Jijō*, May 16, 1983, p. 73.

on savings. For though the primary goal of the Administrative Reform Council was to eliminate pockets of governmental inefficiencies that cut into tax revenue, this group was most concerned to cap the corporate income tax, and they had concluded that raising some form of tax revenue would be necessary.[78] Meanwhile, the Ministry of Finance had charged its Tax Council to consider alternative sources of government revenue, including taxation of value added and savings income.[79]

To the chagrin of the other members of the Postal Affairs Group, their dean, Shin Kanemaru, who was also chairman of the LDP Executive Committee, suggested in May 1984 that at least temporary abandonment of the tax-free savings system was inevitable, given the government's tight fiscal situation. Kanemaru's change of posture was probably due to his appointment as party secretary in 1984, a post that demands consideration of the LDP's wide-ranging and often conflicting interests.[80] Encouraged, the MOF submitted a plan to the Diet in November 1984 for a 10 percent taxation of all interest income, along with an alternative bill that would have strengthened the existing framework for monitoring savers in excess of their tax-free allotment. The first bill, clearly the MOF's preferred choice, would bring in an estimated additional tax revenue of 1.2 trillion yen. The alternative bill represented the controversial Green Card idea without the card itself. Post offices and banks would rely on identification presented by the depositor and check on their computers for duplication.[81]

Large banks were pleased with neither option: an across-the-board interest income tax would scare money into securities, and a self-check system provided no guarantee of fairness as long as the

[78]The corporate sector's concern about the corporate tax rate in Japan increased as campaigns got under way in both Britain and the United States to reduce corporate taxes to levels below those of Japan.

[79]"Maruyū Haishiron no Haikei," *Asahi*, October 6, 1982; Tsuchiya, "Yūcho Mondai o Kiru," pp. 20–24; "Maruyū o Tenaoshi Sonzoku," *Mainichi*, April 13, 1984; "Rishi Haitō Kazei Kaikaku de Sanan," *Tokyo Shimbun*, April 14, 1984; "Hikazei Chōchiku Minaoshi no Sūjimichi," *Yomiuri*, May 14, 1984.

[80]"Kanemarushi no Maruyū Teishiron," *Asahi*, May 27, 1984; "Jigen Rippō de," *Asahi*, November 9, 1984; "Nerai wa Takeshita Ijime?" *Kinyū Bijinesu*, July 1985, pp. 72–73.

[81]"Maruyū wa Nanaan Heiretsu," *Asahi*, September 12, 1984; "Maruyū Kaikaku," *Asahi*, November 7, 1984.

post offices kept the tax authorities off their premises. Remembering the Green Card scare, banks were concerned about how the taxation would differentially affect the popularity of postal and bank accounts, since the ten-year postal deposit did not pay interest income until maturity. Or worse yet, banks alone might be saddled with an interest income tax were they to give in to the tax before the MPT agreed to go along. The large banks' opposition to the interest income tax was largely a public relations stunt.[82]

The small banks were less sure of what position to take, because their single greatest rival was the postal system and because the current system was costly for them to maintain. Payment of taxes on behalf of customers, when tax evasion was discovered by the tax authorities' spot checks, represented a sizable expense for small banks. To recoup the cost from their tax-evading customers, they feared, would be to surrender too much business to the postal system. Their resistance to a 10 percent interest income tax weakened when the Ministry of Finance promised to temper the tax audits in the event of a tax on savings income. The Federation of Bankers Associations, however, was led by large banks and voiced its opposition to both bills.[83]

The postmasters also struck swiftly. On December 7, 1984, the Association of Commissioned Postmasters assembled in the lecture hall of LDP headquarters for a Rally against Postal Taxation (Yūbin Chokin e no Kazei Hantai Sōkekki Shūkai). In attendance were 240 Diet members and another hundred or so personal representatives of other Diet members. As the name of each Diet member was called, the member stood to acknowledge the postmasters' applause. This appreciation was a token of considerable significance, for those LDP members who fought for the postmasters' cause would be rewarded at election time.[84]

[82]"Maruyū Kaikaku do Ketchaku," *Asahi,* November 11, 1984; "Ryōan ni mo Hantai," *Asahi,* November 21, 1984; "Zenginkyō Kaichō Aratamete Hantai," *Asahi,* December 5, 1984; "Yūchō no Minaoshi Nuki ni Ketsuron wa Midasenai," *Kinyū Zaisei Jijō,* April 7, 1986, pp. 24–28.

[83]"Yūchō Kazei de Kakehiki," *Asahi,* November 23, 1984. The smallest banks derive about three-fourths of their total deposits from individuals, placing them in closest competition with the postal system. Individuals supply 52 percent of regional banks' deposits and 39 percent of city banks'. "Maruyū Haishi Sansei," *Asahi,* November 20, 1985.

[84]Kishiro, *Jimintō Zeisei Chōsakai,* pp. 25–36.

Table 7. Rate of growth of various personal savings
instruments (in trillions of yen and percentage increase)

	1983	1984	Rate of increase
Savings deposits			
Banks[a]	80	85	6.7%
Small financial institutions[b]	58	62	6.6
Agricultural cooperatives	33	35	6.2
Workers' credit unions	3	4	9.3
Postal savings	77	85	10.7
Subtotal	251	271	7.3
Other			
Trusts	21.	23	10.9
Bonds	35	38	10.1
Investment trusts	8	12	58.5
Insurance	65	74	14.2
TOTAL	380	419	10.0

[a]Banks includes twelve city banks, the Bank of Tokyo, three
long-term credit banks, and sixty-four local banks.

[b]Small financial institutions includes 69 mutual banks, 456
credit associations (*shinkin*), and 448 credit cooperatives (*shinyō kumiai*).

Source: "Deregulation of Finance and Internationalization of
the Yen," *Fuji Bank Bulletin*, September–October 1984, p. 9.

Mutsuki Katō, chairman of the LDP Tax Committee, was in a
difficult position. Although he was an influential member of the
Postal Affairs Group, he would also have to demonstrate his ability
to forge workable settlements for the party as a whole if he was to
advance farther in party ranks. Furthermore, he had been appointed
to the post by one of his (Fukuda/Abe) faction's leaders, PARC
chairman Masayuki Fujio, and Fujio was a known detractor of the
Postal Affairs Group, complaining that they were narrowly self-
serving. Katō suggested, as a more modest goal, adoption of the
MOF's second draft. In exchange for the continued tax exemption
of interest on savings, the postal system would submit to regular
scrutiny of the tax authorities to eliminate tax evasion. The Tax
Committee ratified Katō's plan.[85]

Since there were still sharp divisions within the party, the final
decision was left to the top five posts (Goyaku Kyōgi) in the LDP:
party secretary Shin Kanemaru, PARC chairman Masayuki Fujio,

[85]"Maruyū Shushō Saidan no Hōkō," *Asahi*, December 10, 1984; "Ōkura Tei-
ritsu Kazei o Dannen," *Asahi*, December 16, 1984; "Maruyū wa Gendo Kanri,"
Asahi, December 17, 1984; "Maruyū Seido wa Fukōhei," *Asahi*, December 18,
1984; "Maruyū no Ōsuji Ketchaku," *Asahi*, December 19, 1984.

Executive Council chairman Kiichi Miyazawa, vice-president of the LDP Susumu Nikaido, and Masaharu Gotōda, chairman of the LDP caucus in the House of Councilors. At their meeting on December 19, 1984, the five diluted the compromise further, replacing admittance of tax authorities into postal accounts with a self-check system. The Ministry of Finance and the Ministry of Posts and Telecommunications were charged with working out the details for a mutually satisfactory monitoring system.[86]

The LDP Tax Committee printed up its final outline for the 1985 tax proposal on the afternoon of December 19. Keizō Obuchi, secretary of the Postal Affairs Group, scanned the pages and found to his dismay that, beginning in fiscal 1985, the MPT was obliged to pay taxes on interest earned on the amount of savings in excess of the limit or for accounts for which the depositor's address could not be verified. This was not part of the Group of Five's decision. After further debate, Katō agreed to amend the provision in the tax draft to read, "Taxation of savings will be decided in negotiations between the MOF and the MPT."[87]

Although the LDP had given its imprimatur to stricter monitoring of savings accounts, the MOF-MPT talks to determine specifics for implementation were arduous. Banks had guessed right that the MOF would not be able to impose tax scrutiny on the MPT, since the LDP had been vague and noncommittal on that point. Finally, on February 1, 1985, the MOF announced that a new monitoring system would be introduced on January 1, 1986, at which time individuals would have to present personal identification with a birthdate in order to open a new account or to make deposits in old accounts. But at the MPT's insistence, savers would be able to hold their existing deposits until maturity or earlier withdrawal, without presenting identification. In short, new tax evasion would be more difficult after a grace period of one year.[88]

[86]Kishiro, *Jimintō Zeisei Chōsakai*; "Okura no Nerai Zasetsu," *Asahi*, December 19, 1984; "Gendo Gensei Kanri de Ketchaku," *Asahi*, December 19, 1984; "Maruyū Kaikaku Aimai Ketchaku," *Asahi*, December 20, 1984; "Yūbinkyoku ni Tsūchi Gimu," *Asahi Yūkan*, December 24, 1984.

[87]Kishiro, *Jimintō Zeisei Chōsakai*, pp. 37–40; "Maruyū Kaikaku Kōshite Kotsunuki," *Asahi*, February 26, 1985; "Nerai wa Takeshita Ijime?" *Kinyū Bijinesu*, July 1985, pp. 72–73; Masao Oka, "Yūbin Chokin Seido no Hizumi to Jishu Unyō," *Zaikei Shōhō*, September 9, 1985, p. 7.

[88]"Kakekomi Maruyū Okotowari," *Asahi*, February 2, 1985; "Seinen Gappi no

For all the opposition, the Ministry of Finance had not abandoned its plan for taxing interest income. On February 22, 1985, the MOF announced its outline for fiscal 1986, which included a flat tax of 5–10 percent of income from savings deposits and stock dividends.[89]

Fortunately for the MOF, support began to grow within the LDP for some form of taxation, albeit for reasons not necessarily shared by the MOF. First, plans for individual and corporate income tax cuts in the United States, West Germany, Britain, and even France would leave Japan with one of the highest corporate tax rates in the industrialized world. Big business urged that sales and/or interest income taxes be used as a means to cut back the corporate tax rate.[90] Second, the demands from the corporate sector, small and medium-sized businesses in particular, for government relief in the wake of the yen's rapid appreciation in 1985 could not be answered without raising additional revenue or burdening the government with more debt. Big business was strongly opposed to more government debt, fearing a future corporate tax hike.[91]

Third, though more of an excuse for taxation than a reason, there were foreign allegations that Japan's tax incentives to save were contributing to Japan's current account surpluses. Prime Minister Nakasone's hand-picked Study Group on Economic Structural Adjustment, or the Maekawa Group, reported in April 1986 that although the tax exemptions for interest income probably did not have much effect in promoting savings given low interest rates to begin with, Japan should nonetheless change its tax structure to promote consumption rather than savings.[92]

Meki ga Jōken," *Asahi*, April 7, 1985; "Kanzen na Nayose Muri," *Asahi*, May 17, 1985.

[89]"Ichiritsu Kazeian ga Chūshin," *Asahi*, February 23, 1985.

[90]"Maruyū Haishi de Gensei no Zaigen ni," *Asahi*, July 10, 1985; "Maruyū Minaoshi," *Asahi*, July 18, 1985; "Ōgata Kansetsuzei wa Hitsuyō," *Nikkei*, June 21, 1986; "Kojin Shōhi Shūdōgata Keiki Kakudai o Hakaru Beiō," *Kinyū Zaisei Jijō*, December 1, 1986, p. 6.

[91]"Keidanren ga Gyōzaisei Kaikaku Zeisei Kaikaku ni Tsuite Teigen," *Kinyū Zaisei Jijō*, April 7, 1986, p. 29; "Raigetsuchū ni Endaka Kinkyū Taisaku," *Nikkei*, April 25, 1986; "Hōsei Yosan mo Fukume Kōryō," *Nikkei*, May 16, 1986; "Kokka Ginkō," *Sankei Shimbun*, May 27, 1986.

[92]Keikoken no Maruyū Haishi Hōkoku ni Tsuyoi Hanpatsu," *Kinyū Zaisei Jijō*, April 21, 1986, p. 6; "Minaoshi Hantai o Tsuranuku Zenginkyō no Sakusen,"

However, as the prospect that there would be elections in the summer of 1986 for both houses of the Diet became increasingly certain, politicians began speaking out against tax increases. Still within recent memory was the LDP's diastrous showing at the election polls in 1979 following Prime Minister Masahiro Ōhira's campaign pledge to levy a general consumption tax. This time Prime Minister Nakasone did not forsake the tax idea altogether, but opted for a revenue-neutral tax plan that would match tax cuts with tax increases. Individual and corporate income tax cuts would be announced before the election; once safe on the other side of the election hurdle, he would grapple with how to raise revenue through savings and/or value-added taxes.[93]

Sharp criticism during the election campaign from the opposition parties of the LDP's proposed tax increases left only the most stalwart pledging their implementation. Masayuki Fujio, chairman of the LDP PARC, was one of the few politicians who continued to support both the interest income tax and value-added tax right up until the election.[94] LDP secretary general Shin Kanemaru, who had once advocated a tax on savings income, now publicly expressed his doubts on its wisdom.[95] Even Prime Minister Nakasone pledged not to introduce a "large" value-added tax and promised that interest income would continue to be tax exempt for the elderly and widowed.[96]

It is important to note, however, that the opposition to the value-added tax was greater than the resistance to taxation of income on interest. Small and medium-sized businesses in Japan, which figure largely in the LDP's support base as well as that of the Democratic

Kinyū Zaisei Jijō, May 5, 1986, pp. 38–39. The Maekawa Report was conveniently timed for publication just prior to the Tokyo Summit in May 1986, so that Nakasone could point to concrete measures designed to bring Japan into line with foreign expectations.

[93]"Maruyū Kaikaku 62-nen Jisshi o Meguru Tatemae to Honne," Kinyū Zaisei Jijō, December 2, 1985, pp. 12–13; "Maruyū Shukushō ni Katamuku ka," Kinyū Bijinesu, June 1986, pp. 12–13.

[94]"Maruyū Teppai ga Gensoku," Nikkei, June 6, 1986; "Maruyū Haishi, Ōgata Kansetsuzei mo Dōnyū," Asahi, June 6, 1986.

[95]"Maruyū Haishi wa Kimeteinai," Asahi, June 12, 1986; "Maruyū Haishi ni Shōkyokuteki," Nikkei, June 13, 1986.

[96]"Ōgata Kansetsu Zei Shushō Kasanete Hitei," Nikkei, July 1, 1986; "Maruyū Haishi Meguru Kinyūkai no Rakkan to Iradachi," Kinyū Zaisei Jijō, July 21, 1986, pp. 14–15.

Socialist party, would lose the ability to shield large segments of unreported income from the Tax Agency's view if the value-added tax were instituted. The LDP feared the loss of votes and financial support of the small and medium-sized business sector, particularly since the DSP and all the other opposition parties were campaigning vigorously against the value added tax. Opposition to the tax on interest income, on the other hand, was led primarily by the approximately twenty thousand commissioned postmasters who, though politically influential, are not in the same league with the millions of small-enterprise proprietors.

When the Diet reconvened after the July 1986 election, the LDP occupied 308 of 512 seats in the Lower House. And yet even with the largest LDP majority since 1969, Prime Minister Nakasone was unable to push through the value-added tax legislation that he had once supported so ardently. Nakasone dropped the value-added tax from his agenda, but the LDP finally forced a version of the value-added tax through the Diet in late autumn 1988 after making adjustments to soften the opposition of the DSP and Kōmeitō. The DSP and Kōmeitō, on their side of the compromise, sat in the Diet and voted against the tax reform bill rather than join the JSP's boycott designed to discredit the LDP's handling of the matter.[97]

The battle for the interest income tax, though intense, was largely within the party, for many LDP members had accepted the campaign assistance of postmasters' networks in exchange for pledges to support the continued tax exemption of postal savings interest.[98] In November 1986 postmasters invited LDP members to a rally such as the one in December 1984, hoping to repeat their past success.[99]

The LDP's proposed final solution on the taxation of interest

[97]The LDP won 304 seats out of the 512 Lower House seats. Four seats were added to the LDP's number when most members of the New Liberal Club returned to the LDP after ten years of separation. See also Shinji Itō, "Lower House Approves Modified Tax Reform Bills," *Japan Times*, November 17, 1988, p. 1.

[98]"Maruyū Haishi ni Hantai," *Asahi*, July 25, 1986; "Ōgata Kansetsu Zei Yori Muzukashii Maruyū Haishi," *Tōyō Keizai*, July 26, 1986, pp. 66–69; "Maruyū wa Kenji," *Asahi*, August 19, 1986; "Higan Maruyū Haishi no Shinario ni 304 Giseki no Jūatsu," *Kinyū Zaisei Jijō*, September 1, 1986, pp. 14–15; "Maruyū Kaikaku no Chakujiten," *Kinyū Zaisei Jijō*, October 13, 1986, pp. 30–31.

[99]"Ninen Mae no Saigen Sakusu," *Kinyū Zaisei Jijō*, November 1986, pp. 40–43.

income—signed on December 5, 1986, by party secretary Noboru Takeshita, Executive Committee chairman Shintarō Abe, PARC chairman Masayoshi Itoh, Tax Committee chairman Sadanori Yamanaka, Administrative and Fiscal Reform Group chairman Tokuo Yamashita, cabinet secretary Masaharu Gotōda, Minister of Finance Kiichi Miyazawa, and Minister of Posts and Telecommunications Yasujirō Karasawa—contained concessions to both banks and the postal system. Interest on all savings deposits, with exceptions for those over sixty-five years of age, the physically handicapped, and single mothers, would be taxed at a flat rate of 20 percent, reducing the tax-reporting work for financial institutions.[100] The same rate would apply to interest from postal and bank deposits.[101]

To compensate the postal system for the taxation of savings income, the ceiling on postal deposits was raised from 3 to 5 million yen, though the deposit ceiling for tax exemption for those qualifying remained 3 million.[102] Second, the postal system would be allowed to keep 2 trillion yen of its deposits to invest; half would be earmarked for central government bonds, and the remainder could be used to purchase local government bonds, public corporation bonds, financial debentures, financial trusts, specified corporate bonds, foreign government bonds, or, from 1989, corporate equity.[103] The 2 trillion yen of postal funds not handed over to the MOF's FILP would increase by 500 billion yen every year until 1991. For the first year, the postal system would be permitted to sell

[100]The alternatives were (1) taxation of interest income along with the rest of personal income, and (2) two rates of interest income taxation depending on the amount of the deposit. The MOF favored the second alternative because it would have generated more revenue, but it would also have meant more checking and documentation work for the banks. "Chakuten Miezu," *Kinyū Bijinesu*, October 1986, pp. 38–39.

[101]The Postal Affairs Group had made a last-ditch effort to have only bank savings, not postal savings, taxed. "Yūsei Giinzoku no Gorioshi," *Tōyō Keizai*, October 4, 1986, p. 77.

[102]"Shin Rishi Kazei Seido Seishōrei no Jitsumu Pointo," *Kinyū Zaisei Jijō*, December 21, 1987, p. 20.

[103]The MPT commissioned the trust banks to manage the investment of 200–300 billion yen in equities beginning in 1989. One of the MPT's goals is apparently to reduce the resistance of financial institutions to the MPT's control over its funds by affording them some commission income. "Yūchō Shikin, Kabushiki de Unyō," *Nikkei*, April 10, 1988.

a total of 1 trillion yen of the government bonds in its portfolio to postal savings clientele. Third, the statement reaffirmed the existing practice that the interest rate paid by the FILP for postal funds would be determined by the two ministries. And finally, a vaguely worded clause urged the MOF and MPT to consult whenever necessary to ensure that the taxation of savings income did not impair the operations of the postal savings system or the FILP.[104]

The terms of the agreement reflected a strong desire on the part of the LDP to accommodate both the postal savings system and the banks. But the banks were vexed by the statement's last point. For while they were relieved that the savings tax would apply equally to the postal system and the banks, and though they were not troubled that the postal system would be purchasing government bonds, banks most wanted the LDP to address the postal system's various unfair advantages in attracting customers. Specifically, banks hoped the LDP would force the MPT to amend the ten-year, fixed-amount deposit (*teigaku chokin*).[105]

Not only did the LDP fail to pressure the postal system to reduce the attractiveness of the ten-year fixed-deposit, but it looked the other way as the postal system began offering savers a new "government bond fixed-amount deposit" (*kokusai teigaku chokin*). This account pays semiannual interest on long-term government bonds, up to one thousand yen of which the post office places into the customer's non-interest-bearing transactions account, transferring any interest over one thousand yen into a ten-year fixed-amount deposit. The MOF and the banks objected strongly to this innovation by the postal system for fear savers would abandon their bank accounts for the postal system. But so far their protestations have borne no results.[106]

[104]"Yūbin Chokin Hikazei Seido no Kaitei ni Saishite no Seifu, Tōgōi," *Asahi,* December 5, 1986; "Jimin Zeichō, Zeisei Kaikakuan Kettei," *Yomiuri,* December 5, 1986. For the MPT's requests, see "Jishu Unyō o Montomeru Yūseishō Gaisan Yōkyū," *Kinyū Zaisei Jijō,* September 8, 1986, p. 9.

[105]"Maruyū Haishi wa Hitsuka," *Kinyū Zaisei,* August 14, 1986, p. 9; "Jimintō Zeiseizoku," *Kinyū Bijinesu,* September 1986, pp. 64–67; "Shikin Shifuto Bōshisaku ni Daitō no Kinyūkai," *Kinyū Zaisei Jijō,* December 22, 1986, pp. 14–15.

[106]"Kokusai Teigaku Chokin de Hanabi," *Nikkei,* April 10, 1988; "Yūchō no Kokusai Teigaku Chokin," *Nikkei,* April 17, 1988, p. 5; "Hanbai Miokuri Yōkyū e," *Nikkei,* April 17, 1988, p. 3; "Koguchi Kinri Jiyūka ni Hamon," *Nikkei,* April 21, 1988, p. 5.

The MOF has been unable to convince the MPT to abandon the ten-year fixed-yield deposit.[107] As the next-best option, the MOF and MPT agreed to permit banks and post offices to begin issuing relatively high-yield money market certificates (MMCs) in June 1989 in denominations as small as 3 million yen (about $25,000 at 120 yen to the dollar). The interest rates on small-denomination MMCs are fixed below interest rates on larger-denomination or longer-maturity instruments to limit competition for these funds. For example, three-year MMCs bear an interest rate fixed at 0.5 percent below the coupon on ten-year government bonds. The issuance of these MMCs to small savers unquestionably raises the cost of capital for the banks, but the alternative was to watch the postal system continue to expand at the expense of bank deposits. At least the cap on MMC interest rates, though higher than on ordinary bank savings deposits, limits for the time being the competition between banks and the postal savings system.

An Exception to the Theory of Regulation

Unlike the examples of financial regulation and deregulation discussed in previous chapters, many of the events in retail banking recorded in this chapter cannot be explained by the theory of regulation. In retail banking we would expect the interests of banks in low-interest rates to prevail unequivocally over the desire of individual savers for high-yield deposits, for two reasons. First, banks are a well-organized group and individual savers are not. Second, individuals, unlike corporations, do not have easy access to competitive foreign banking services, and it is not in the interests of the domestic banks to offer higher yields to individuals.

Retail banking in Japan deviates from the theory of regulation's model of policy making in that there are two bureaucratic agencies regulating two separate groups of small deposit takers. Instead of providing uniform regulation in the interests of the deposit takers,

[107]In March the MOF announced an indefinite postponement of the first step in liberalizing small-denomination deposits originally scheduled for autumn 1988. The MOF cited lack of agreement with the MPT. "Koguchi Kinri no Jiyūka Enki," *Nikkei,* March 6, 1988.

the two regulators make efforts on behalf of their clients that result in arduous interministerial discussions, political intervention, and some degree of competition in the marketplace. The messy policy-making process in retail banking more closely resembles what we would expect from pluralist models.

Of the two grievances the banks had against the postal system—tax evasion and interest rate independence and hence competition—the 1987 tax reform would seem to take care of the first. The tax authorities found numerous tax evaders among bank depositors as well, but banks had been willing to pay the avoided taxes from their own earnings rather than lose their customers to the postal system. Alternative scenarios that banks had been most concerned about were, first, a lower rate of taxation for deposits under a specified sum, which would have left open the possibility of incomplete reporting by the post offices or, worse yet, full tax exemption for postal accounts only. The banks' problem was finally resolved with the imposition of a flat-rate 20 percent tax that applied evenly across institutions.

Why did the LDP, if so solicitous of the goodwill of postmasters, agree to the interest income tax? At first, the LDP was not interested, and the success of the tax bill owes much to Prime Minister Nakasone's political leadership. As director of the Administrative Agency in Zenko Suzuki's 1981 cabinet, Nakasone successfully utilized what was considered a second-class cabinet post to garner support for administrative reform, first from big business and then from the public at large. Many members of the LDP, closer to small business than to large, were leery of Nakasone's enthusiasm for the Administrative Reform Council, but Nakasone's strong support from big business was instrumental in overriding the opposition within the LDP both to his leadership and to the administrative reform movement.

The prime minister's influence, however, was only the proximate cause for tax reform. LDP politicians ultimately adopted the interest income tax not so much to get government finances back in order but to raise revenue for promised tax cuts, to increase government spending for pet projects, and because it was a way to answer banks' demands for "equal tax footing" with the postal system.

Moreover, there were many recommendations of the Administrative Reform Council which the LDP did not accept. Whereas the LDP acceded to the privatization of Nippon Telegraph and Telephone (though it remained under MPT jurisdiction) and Japan National Railways, it did not agree to curb the postal system's operations in any fundamental way. After the LDP rejected the recommendation of the five-man Study Group on the Role of Government in Finance that the postal system be checked by various means, the Administrative Reform Council took up the investigation of postal expansion. The council's March 1983 and April 1986 reports, concluding that the postal savings system had overstepped the bounds of prudent government and urging similar restraints, were likewise disregarded.[108]

The Policy-Making Process

The LDP is inexorably drawn into the bank–postal savings rivalry; for though it would prefer not to make alienating choices if at all possible, there is no other adjudicating body to which it can delegate. The difference between this and the bank-securities competition is not the intensity of the rivalry, because both are fierce, but in the overseeing regulatory structure. Although the Ministry of Finance has the will and the means within its own bureaus to equilibrate between the banking and securities industries, it has no ultimate authority over the postal system. Banks and postmasters alike have no choice but to take recourse with the politicians.

The Structure of Influence

Although the policy-making process varies along the lines of institutional structure, policy outcomes still depend, as much in the banking–postal system rivalry as in the banking-securities one, on how much political capital each side can muster. Weighing the sides in the postal savings debate is a difficult task for LDP politicians, particularly for those from rural areas where small banks are joined

---

[108]Chio Tanaka, "Yūcho no Kosuto wa Kashō ni Sugiru," *Kinyū Bijinesu*, May 1986, pp. 46–49; "Kan wa Min no Hokan," *Kinyū Zaisei Jijō*, May 19, 1987, p. 6; Hiroshi Takizawa, "Koguchi MMC no Shoshinsei to Yūcho Minaoshi e no Gutaian," *Kinyū Zaisei Jijō*, May 19, 1986, pp. 20–24.

by the financial arm of agricultural cooperatives against the expansion of the postal savings system. Many LDP members have attempted to ride the fence, signing the petitions of both sides, but this response leaves them open to censure from both sides.

Postmasters represent considerable political force, since politicians believe they command a large number of votes in nearly every election district. Their influence is generally weaker in urban areas, however, where the looser human networks render traditional authority less translatable into votes. Indeed, the postmasters' alleged ability to gather votes is remarkable given Japan's extensive urbanization. But some LDP Diet members have already abandoned the postmasters' base with impunity. One of these is Junichirō Koizumi, who was elected with the largest number of votes in his district in the July 1986 election, despite vows from the postmasters to hurt his campaign because he did not support the postal system within the LDP.[109]

Large banks have never been much involved in election campaigning and, until fairly recently, have not even apportioned their campaign contributions to individual politicians (though they have to factions) in exchange for support in policy matters. But as in the banking industry's intensifying battle with the securities industry, banks' struggle with the postal system has required a shift to a more discriminating political strategy. Sympathetic Diet members such as Koizumi are recompensed; others are not necessarily.

The LDP's position in December 1986, which permitted the taxation of savings and thus eliminated the possibilities of tax evasion through postal savings, while at the same time endorsing the postal system's wide financial reach, reflected a stalemate between the two plaintiffs. The postal system was compensated for its concession, and the banks were assured of being no longer disadvantaged on tax grounds. The real loser was the small saver, whose already low interest income is now taxed. Banks, after all, still have the MOF's implicit guarantee against failure. Moreover, banks will continue to resist further deregulation of interest rates on small deposits.

[109]Interviews with politicians, summer 1986, Tokyo.

208

7

The Political Context
of Japanese Finance

The preceding chapters describe how the banking industry battled the securities industry, the postal savings system, and even the Ministry of Finance in attempts to acquire and preserve policies favorable to itself. In some instances the banks "won," such as in fighting off the MOF's stricter bank disclosure rules and in gaining permission, albeit at a cost, to trade and deal in the government bond market heretofore monopolized by the securities industry. In other instances the banks fared less well, as when they failed to force the postal savings system to adopt the unified deposit interest rate applied to banks. In other examples the results were less clearly victory or defeat for the large banks: they lowered their resistance to a larger domestic corporate bond market because their obstinacy no longer fueled their loan business; and they agreed to foreign demands for a Euroyen market not only to avert retaliation but also because they had no compelling reason not to.

The underlying theme of the preceding chapters has been that the success or failure of a particular group in the Japanese polity, in this case the banks, to obtain its desired policy decisions is a function of its political resources relative to those of its opponent. Regardless of whether or not the dispute ultimately involves politicians, the political arena is the recognized locus of ultimate decision making and, as such, delimits the benefits that either disputant could hope to gain or fear to lose. The apportionment of costs and benefits must mirror the distribution of political resources, or the settlement will be

209

challenged until it does. That both banks and securities firms chose to abide by the MOF's compromise in their row over the government securities market speaks not of MOF omnipotence but of the MOF's sensitivity to political reality. Both industries made a reasoned judgment that the cost of a full-scale political battle would be greater than the income lost in compromising. The industries accepted an MOF-enforced settlement rather than expend additional sums in competitive campaign contributions for a political resolution that would, in any case, more or less parallel the MOF's scheme.

Profit and market share, not deregulation per se, are the desired goals of every group in the financial sector. Only when these coincide with deregulation do financial institutions become champions of market forces and competition. Banks favored "liberalization" of the government bond market but want to limit competition from the postal savings system in the retail deposit market. The securities firms decried bank protectionism in the corporate bond market but cling tenaciously to their own fixed commissions in securities underwriting and trading. And yet financial deregulation continues in Japan. Because the alternative of freer financial markets abroad exists for at least the top tier of Japanese corporations, Japanese financial institutions must match the better terms or lose their clientele. Although the tempo is dampened marginally by the historically close ties between corporations and their banks, the strongest firms have little need for a main bank at excessive cost.

Because the administration of private finance is central to the economic health of a nation, it is easy to see why observers have expected the Ministry of Finance to take leadership in this area of policy making.[1] If the state were ever to formulate national goals independently of society and attempt to implement these goals, it would be on an issue for which sound administration is vital to the rest of the economy. As the case studies have shown, however, Ministry of Finance policies are not formulated, much less implemented, autonomously. A more fruitful line of inquiry would be to ask which parts of society are reflected in governmental policy, to what degree, and why.

[1]See, for example, John Zysman, *Governments, Markets, and Growth* (Ithaca: Cornell University Press, 1983), pp. 296–97.

The Political Context of Japanese Finance

The supply-and-demand theory of regulation espoused by George Stigler and others predicts that, all things being equal, policy benefits will accrue to concentrated interests and costs to diffused interests. Because consumers are numerous, widely dispersed, and hence have small per capita stakes in how a particular issue is resolved, they are systemically disadvantaged. Other social scientists have conceded the importance of the public goods and free rider problem but go on to specify how variations in the *ceteris paribus* qualification could turn the course of events. Martha Derthick and Paul Quirk recount numerous examples in recent U.S. political history in which the consumer has benefited at the expense of highly concentrated interest groups: witness the reluctance of the airlines, trucking, and telecommunications industries to undergo deregulation.[2]

It is important, then, to delineate the circumstances under which widely dispersed general voter interests might prevail. Chapter 1 outlined three structural dimensions that reinforce or modify the logic of collective action. In summary, decentralized state authority, flexible and competitive or encompassing political parties, and fragmented producer interests are most conducive to the incorporation of consumer interests in policy decisions. By contrast, centralized state authority, rigid political parties, and concentrated producer interests tend to exclude unorganized interests. In other words, these are the domestic conditions under which the theory of regulation predicts outcomes most accurately.

First, as a proxy of decentralized state authority, we examined the structure of the overseeing bureaucracy. When the regulating bureaucracy has a comprehensive mandate, or a monopoly over administration in a particular issue area, there is less likelihood of a consumer orientation because of the bureaucracy's uniform interest in maintaining a peaceable equilibrium among the industries within its jurisdiction. The bureaucracy will seek to limit the competition among the industries to maintain order in both the economic and political markets—that is, to make its job easier.

If the Ministry of Finance prefers to preside over a quiescent, easily regulated financial sector, its industrywide jurisdiction and capacity to equilibrate the subsectors make this possible. And solici-

[2]Martha Derthick and Paul Quirk, *The Politics of Deregulation* (Washington, D.C.: Brookings, 1985).

211

tousness of financial institutions means smaller returns to the consumers. As the struggles with the banks over disclosure and mergers suggest, the MOF has had difficulty streamlining the financial industry as much as it would like, but its troubles with political intervention would be far greater if its bureaus were separate entities with no coordinating mechanism among themselves. Finance would be as highly politicized and competitive as in the United States, where there are multiple regulators of the same sector. In retail banking, over which the MOF and the MPT share jurisdiction, politicians do indeed intervene frequently, and banks and post offices do compete to some extent in the marketplace.

Second, the nature of the political party system affects the incentives of individual politicians to assume leadership of unorganized causes. Clearly, the combination of political parties wed to specific interest groups and strong party discipline bodes least well for consumers. As in all parliamentary democracies, Japanese political parties are characterized by strong voting discipline. Of course political entrepreneurship need not be limited to one or a few mavericks who forge new coalitions for themselves. An entire party may alter its policy program, as the LDP has from time to time in response to the demands of interests heretofore outside the party's coalition. Indeed, this pragmatic flexibility is an important reason for the LDP's long years as the dominant party in Japanese politics.[3] Nevertheless, strong party discipline inhibits the incorporation of "outsider" interests in the absence of the threat of massive retaliation at the election polls. Although the LDP represents a large number of organized groups, many with conflicting goals, the usually unorganized interests of the consumer are the least inviting politically.

To depict parties in Japan as thoroughly beholden to interest groups would be an overstatement. Yet it is true that there have been relatively few successful consumer or general voter movements at the national level, and of those that are notable in their achievement, such as the environmental protests in the mid- and late 1970s,

[3] Gerald Curtis, *The Japanese Way of Politics* (New York: Columbia University Press, 1987); Michio Muramatsu and Ellis S. Krauss, "The Conservative Policy Line and the Development of Patterned Pluralism," in Kozo Yamamura and Yasukichi Yasuba, eds., *The Political Economy of Japan*, vol. 1: *The Domestic Transformation* (Stanford: Stanford University Press, 1987).

few were politically sponsored at the outset. The most likely political parties to mobilize consumer groups, the Japan Socialist party and Democratic Socialist party, were actually in many cases reluctant to support citizens' movements against established industries because the industry unions, their supporters, would have been hurt at the same time.[4] If at all, opposition politicians became involved in the environment movement only after citizens' advocates had mobilized support for the cause. The LDP itself was also able to absorb much of the more moderate environmental protection orientation into its own platform and was thus able to hold its electorate without alienating industry.[5]

Private finance, a less visible and ordinarily less personally threatening issue than environmental pollution, has attracted far less attention from voters in Japan. Even if the average voters were aware that their bank was paying them a far smaller yield on their account than the bank was getting for its loans to industry, the loss of potential income to simple depositor/voters is too small to incite them to devote time, money, and energy to organize or even be a part of a political campaign for more interbank competition. Perhaps if nominal personal income in Japan had been growing more slowly, or if inflation had been higher, citizens would have been more vocal about yields on their savings accounts. But this was not the case, and as in the environmental pollution cases, the opposition parties have sought to protect the labor unions even if at the expense of the consumers. The LDP politicians have therefore been free to sponsor bank-oriented policies with impunity from the electorate. Only competition from the postal savings system has finally led to higher deposit yields, at least for those with 3 million or more yen (about $25,000) to spare in illiquid MMCs.

An example of political entrepreneurship in Japanese finance did occur in the loan shark (*sarakin*) business. The "consumer finance industry" had been a supporter of the *Seiyūkai* (Political Friends

[4]Ellis S. Krauss and Bradford L. Simcock, "Citizens' Movements: The Growth and Impact of Environmental Protest in Japan," in K. Steiner, E. Krauss, and S. Flanagan, eds., *Political Opposition and Local Politics in Japan* (Princeton: Princeton University Press, 1980), pp. 187–227.

[5]John C. Campbell, "Policy Conflict and Its Resolution within the Governmental System," in E. Krauss, T. Rohlen, and P. Steinhoff, eds., *Conflict in Japan* (Honolulu: University of Hawaii Press, 1984), p. 302.

213

Financial Politics in Contemporary Japan

Association) and the Jiyūtō (Liberal party) since its prewar origins in the pawn shop business.[6] To complicate matters, large banks provide loan sharks with sizable amounts of funds through the back door. But in the late 1970s the loan sharks became the subject of splashy news coverage and were charged with driving hapless individuals who could not pay the legally maximum annual 109.5 percent interest rate on their loans to despair and sometimes suicide.[7] For the LDP to do nothing would have been to appear irresponsible to an angered public. In 1983 the Diet passed a consumer loan law (*Kashikin Gyōhō*) which would lower the interest rate ceiling in three steps, to 40 percent by November 1986.[8] Though interest rates were now far better than before, this was hardly a bonanza for the average borrower. For the LDP, however, the new law successfully quieted the public outrage while allowing all but the least respectable "consumer lenders" to stay in business. This, then, was political entrepreneurship in the sense that the LDP moved strategically, if only partially, against the interests of an industry to benefit a wider group of users.

Affecting a politician's or a party's incentive to take up causes on behalf of the public is the degree of voter awareness of issues that affect them. The orientation and reach of the mass media are key to establishing an environment in which politicians have reason to fear voter arousal and retaliation at the election polls on a national scale.

Citizens in Japan are reached more uniformly by the mass media than in nearly any other country in the world. The five most popular newspaper dailies have a combined circulation of roughly 25 million and almost every Japanese home has a television, receiving programing from four national networks. But two factors militate

[6]"Taikin Gyōhō Enmeiki," in Kinyū Zaisei Jijō Kenkyūkai, ed., *Sengo Kinyū Zaisei Rimenshi* (Tokyo: Bunshodō, 1980), pp. 65–72.

[7]For example, "Ginkō no Sarakin Yūshi," *Kinyū Zaisei Jijō*, October 30, 1978, p. 6; Kazuo Iwasaki, *Sarakin no Subete* (Tokyo: Shio Shuppansha, 1978), pp. 186–92; Shōzō Ueda, "Akushitsu Sarakin no Kamen no Hagu," *Ekonomisuto*, July 28, 1981, pp. 79–83; Kinji Hasegawa, "Jittai Chōsa ni Miru Taikingyō no Genkyō," *Kinyū Zaisei Jijō*, August 24, 1981, pp. 28–35.

[8]Akira Hiyoshi, "Kashikingyō Kiseihō no Seitei to Shōhisha Kinyū Gyōsei no Kongo no Kadai," *Kinyū Jānaru*, September 1983, pp. 51–56; Etarō Iwara, "Nanzan no Kashikingyō Kiseihō," *Kurejitto Sangyō Tokushū*, March 17, 1983, pp. 59–63; Kazuo Iwasaki, "Shōhisha Shinyō Sangyō," *Kinyū Bijinesu*, May 1986, pp. 82–85.

214

against the mass media playing a large role in raising consumer consciousness in financial matters. First, the personnel structure of newspaper companies has not favored the coverage of finance from a consumer's point of view, though this has begun to change in recent years with the growth in interest in personal income management. Until recently, finance reporters covered business finance to the exclusion of personal finance. Second and more important, reporters covering a particular issue rely heavily on official information: reporters on the MOF beat report and analyze MOF reports, and so on. Reporters are therefore more likely to repeat the bureaucracy's rhetoric, which couches the regulation of the financial system in terms of "stability" and "consumer protection."[9] There is relatively little investigative reporting, not because the reporters are not capable of it but because to irk the source of information would be disastrous for the reporters', and possibly their companies', future access to that information.

The third feature we examined is the structure of the industry in question. The more concentrated, cohesive, and intense the interest of the industry, the easier it is to mobilize for collective action and avert unfavorable political entrepreneurship. Admittedly, there is something of a cause-and-effect problem here, because those interest groups that have succeeded in obtaining favorable regulation will have limited new entry, thus maintaining their small numbers, and will have limited their intraindustry competition, thus maintaining their cohesiveness. But the banking industry has two additional advantages: as with other businesses that are government-licensed, there is a ready-made throttle under bureaucratic control which with bank pressure can be used to restrict new entry; and because banks are entrusted with the public's funds, the regulator itself has some incentive to restrict intraindustry competition as a way to avert bank failure and financial panics even though there are other ways to protect the public trust.[10]

[9]For an example of how the bureaucracy's rhetoric is used in another policy area, see J. Mark Ramseyer, "Lawyers, Foreign Lawyers, and Lawyer Substitutes: The Market for Regulation in Japan," *Harvard International Law Journal* 27 (1986), 534–35.

[10]If there is an inherent tension between protecting the two consumer interests of deposit safety and yield, then limiting competition among financial institutions is probably an inefficient way to go about it. Limited competition results not only in

Financial Politics in Contemporary Japan

In Japan, the large, politically unwieldy banking industry was thinned out by the financial crash of 1927. In spite of two categories of new entry since then—the incorporation of the mutuals (*mujin* or *tanomoshikō*) and credit associations (*shinyō kinko*) into the banking industry (broadly defined) in 1951—commercial banks have maintained their small number. And until recent years the banks have also supported a policy of strict jurisdictional division (market segmentation) among the different types of financial institutions to limit the competition among themselves. Although the weaker institutions still favor that policy, the stronger city banks have been trying increasingly to diversify into assorted areas of financial operations. Nevertheless, to date the loss of bank industry consensus on large questions has been minimal. The larger banks, for example, theoretically could afford to offer considerably better yields on individual deposits and thus force the smaller banks out of business. But as long as the postal savings system could raise the returns to depositors higher still, the larger banks cannot afford to lose their allies in their ongoing political battle with the postal system. Second, the larger banks would probably be compelled to absorb the weaker banks even if a shake-out were to occur. The small depositor will have to wait.

The first conclusion from these observations is that the bureaucracy does not control any group in society; rather, it orchestrates according to a score it did not compose. The bureaucracy engages in continual negotiations to reach what Richard Samuels calls "reciprocal consent" with the private sector, because it must rely heavily on the private sector for voluntary compliance.[11] Policy making in Japan often resembles what John Zysman terms the "negotiated model of adjustment," in which "the distributional questions of the economy are explicitly confronted and resolved by a political bargain rather than through marketplace conflict."[12]

---

low interest rates on savings deposits but also in the lack of provision of a wide range of other financial services such as twenty-four-hour cash machines. Consumers pay economically unjustifiable rents for the benefit of weak financial institutions.

[11] Richard J. Samuels, *The Business of the Japanese State* (Ithaca: Cornell University Press, 1987).

[12] Zysman, *Governments, Markets, and Growth*, p. 311. Zysman is speaking here about German, not Japanese, policy making. But this characterization is more apt than the strong state model he uses to depict Japan.

The second is that, although distinct possibilities exist for ordinary voters to register their concerns with the Japanese state, it is clear that organized, and usually producer, interests retain a powerful advantage. The economic ministries, including the MOF, are more directly accountable to the private-sector industries they regulate than to the general public by dint of the relative weight of these groups in the political process.

How might the structural features surrounding financial policy making in Japan change significantly? Constitutional rules and state structure are most likely to persist, but Japan may face a new external economic environment that renders its state structure less agile than before. Second, the political opposition in Japan might, in a burst of unaccustomed pragmatism, reformulate their platforms to reflect the interests of a broader segment of the population and thereby gain power of governance, perhaps in coalition with the LDP. This would bring new groups into the ruling coalition and would circumscribe the role of informal bureaucracy-business negotiations. Most Japan experts, however, discount the possibility of a resurgent opposition in the near future, given its demonstrated policy inertia. Third, the interests of the private sector may diverge increasingly as Japan's economy becomes more open to international market forces. It is the drive to compete for profits and market share in an increasingly interdependent world market that will ultimately exert the greatest impact on the nature of financial regulation in Japan.

A U.S. Comparison

A comparison with the United States is apt for two reasons. Certain of the basic attributes of the Japanese financial system were patterned after the American model during the Occupation. An examination of structurally similar systems in different national contexts will illuminate contrasts in the political environments in which they operate. Second, the United States is characteristically labeled a "weak state" in distinction to Japan, which is considered a "strong state." The comparison will demonstrate why the dichotomy is inadequate and misleading.

The American banking industry, likes its Japanese counterpart, is government-licensed to manage the public's funds, but there are over 14,500 commercial banks in the United States, over five times the number per capita in Japan.[13] The American banking industry has not been as successful as the Japanese industry in enacting regulations that limit new entry and competition, though it had been successful until recently in preventing banking across state lines.

The primary reason for the large number of U.S. banks relates to a second aspect of the American context: the fragmentation of the banking regulatory structure. There are federal and state chartering authorities independent of one another, and until the collapse of the banking system in the 1930s these authorities competed vigorously for charters to enlarge their own jurisdictions. This competition led to "overchartering," resulting in some thirty thousand banks by the late 1920s. Placing partial blame for the financial collapse on the excessive number of banks, the 1935 Banking Act sought to rectify the situation by establishing a "needs" criterion for new bank entry. Although the new regulation has indeed limited the number of banks, there has not been a total blockout as in Japan, and banks are still chartered both by the Federal Reserve Board and state banking authorities.[14] This is not to say that there is free competition in American banking; indeed, the unit banking rule that prevents banks from operating in more than one state restricts competition while allowing large numbers of banks to survive.

In addition to two-tier chartering, other types of bank regulation are also dispersed among multiple agencies. The Federal Reserve Board, the Comptroller of the Currency, the Federal Deposit Insurance Corporation, the Federal Home Loan Bank Board, the Federal Savings and Loan Insurance Corporation, the Federal Bureau of Credit Unions, the Securities and Exchange Commission—all are major agents of regulation and supervision at the federal level, and all are accountable to various committees in Congress.[15] State au-

[13] Arnold A. Heggestad, ed., *Regulation of Consumer Financial Services* (Cambridge: Abt, 1981), p. 12.

[14] Sam Peltzman, "Entry into Commercial Banking," *Journal of Law and Economics* 8 (1965), 11–50.

[15] Neil Skaggs and Cheryl Wasserkrug argue that the Federal Reserve Board attempts to protect its scope for discretionary action by keeping banks satisfied and out of the corridors of Congress. See "Banking Sector Influence on the Relationship

thorities, moreover, are responsible for regulating state-chartered financial institutions and are accountable to state legislatures.[16]

This diffusion of regulatory responsibility has had an unmistakable effect on the course of financial regulation in the United States. American banks, like Japanese banks, benefited from ceilings on deposit rates, though the limits were of little effect until 1966, when inflation left the authorized rates below the market price. The periodic attempts in the 1970s by competitive banks to have the ceilings raised were blocked by the other banks.[17] Whereas a change in regulation allowed banks to give higher returns to large-scale depositors (on amounts in excess of $100,000) after 1970, the small saver had no alternative to the closely regulated accounts at depository institutions.[18]

What occurred next in the United States could not have happened in Japan because of the MOF's encompassing jurisdiction over commercial and investment banking and because of Japanese courts' reluctance to rule on administrative matters. Securities firms began offering money market mutual funds at higher yields than banks were permitted to provide. Predictably, depository institutions proposed that rates on competing unregulated investments be reduced to match their own; instead of making savings deposits more attractive, the industry wanted to make the alternative less so, as in Japan. But mutual funds were under a different regulatory umbrella from the depository institutions, and in the absence of a coordinating mechanism among regulatory agencies the dispute fell to the courts to resolve. The courts ruled that the mutual funds should be free to issue market-rate instruments, putting banks at a competitive disadvantage under the existing interest rate regulations.[19]

---

of Congress to the Federal Reserve System," *Public Choice* 41 (1983), 295–306. But the Fed's efforts are seriously hampered by the limits of its jurisdiction.

[16]Thomas F. Cargill and Gillian G. Garcia, *Financial Reform in the 1980s* (Stanford: Hoover Institution Press, 1985), pp. 35–36; Thomas F. Cargill and Shōichi Rōyama, *The Transition of Japanese Finance and Money in Comparative Perspective with the United States* (Stanford: Hoover Institution Press, 1987).

[17]A. S. Carron, "The Political Economy of Financial Regulation," in Roger Noll and Bruce Owens, eds., *The Political Economy of Deregulation* (Washington, D.C.: American Enterprise Institute, 1983), pp. 71–72.

[18]Ibid., p. 73.

[19]Banks brought suits and undertook expensive lobbying campaigns to fight the legality of money market mutual funds in a number of states. See Frederick Karr, "Is

Financial Politics in Contemporary Japan

In the new Depository Institutions and Monetary Control Act of 1980, Congress ordered interest rate ceilings on deposits to be lifted by 1986. The stronger commercial banks were delighted because they could weather the stiffer competition; the thrift institutions were beset by a drop in profits though they received certain concessions.[20] Small deposits, long held at low yields in the United States and still so in Japan, were deregulated in America not because of greater consumer consciousness, or organization in the United States but because the regulatory authorities could not work out a solution among themselves that protected their regulated groups. In Japan the MOF and the MPT disagreed over small-deposit interest rates, but the two ministries reached a compromise in setting an interest rate ceiling on money market certificates, thus averting all-out competition between banks and post offices in the marketplace. The political entrepreneurship in the United States on the part of congressional proponents of the new law was more in response to the new demands of the competitive commercial banks given the courts' decision than to consumers of financial services in search of higher yields on their deposits.

The disposition of the Glass-Steagall wall between the banking and securities industries, another area of controversy, has fallen to the marketplace and to the courts for lack of bureaucratically enforced compromises and because of congressional reluctance to enact legislative changes that are likely to incite at least as much anger as gratitude.[21] Unlike in Japan, the American legislature does

the Cash Management Account Innovative Brokerage or Unlawful Competition for Smaller Banks?" *Banking Law Journal* 96 (1979), 307–12; John Adams, "Money Market Mutual Funds: Has Glass-Steagall Been Cracked?" *Banking Law Journal* 99 (1982), 4–54.

[20]Thrifts' liability portfolios are in large part locked in to low-interest, long-term mortgage loans. Carron, "Political Economy," p. 74; Cargill and Garcia, *Financial Reform in the 1980s,* pp. 58–60.

[21]Franklin Edwards, "Banks and Securities Activities: Legal and Economic Perspectives on the Glass Steagall Act," in L. G. Goldberg and L. J. White, eds., *The Deregulation of the Banking and Securities Industries* (Lexington, Mass.: Lexington Books, 1979), pp. 273–74; Nathaniel Nash, "Financial Legislation, Perhaps," *New York Times,* January 8, 1987; P. Zweig and J. Yang, "New York Fed's Chief Makes Proposal to Revamp Financial Services Industry," *New York Times,* January 30, 1987; Nathaniel C. Nash, "Bank Powers and the Fed's Role," *New York Times,* February 2, 1987; "Bankers and Financiers Square Off at the Fed," *New York Times,* February 4, 1987.

not have the option of delegating the matter to the bureaucracy for resolution.

Because American financial authorities have a narrower scope of jurisdiction and are thus less able to protect their regulated groups from competition, the relationship between the regulator and the regulated is less cordial than it ordinarily is in Japan. Faced with the continual threat of changes in the marketplace or unfavorable decisions from the courts or Congress, the orientation of U.S. banks is conspicuously more antigovernmental than that of their Japanese counterparts. David Vogel has pointed out that the U.S. business sector is therefore leery of leaving too much regulatory authority to bureaucratic discretion and prefers for rules to be specified clearly in legislation.[22]

The political party system is the third factor affecting the likelihood and character of political entrepreneurship. Because party discipline is relatively weak in American politics, the generally pro-business posture of the Republican party and pro-labor orientation of the Democratic party are not as rigid as they might otherwise be. The flexibility of individual campaigns translates into a wider reach from politicians of both parties for the median voter, or at least for the powerful local constituencies.[23]

Although the Republican party traditionally has supported and been supported by the big banks, politicians of all stripes have bowed to the combined strength of the numerous small, local financial institutions in their districts which have fought to preserve their niches from the encroachment of larger banks. Over 80 percent of the commercial banks in 1982 had total assets of less than $100 million, and over 50 percent had less than $50 million.[24] Under heavy pressure from Congress, the Federal Home Loan Bank Board announced in February 1987 a new policy that would permit beleaguered savings and loan institutions to continue operating even

[22] See David Vogel, "Why Businessmen Distrust Their State: The Political Consciousness of American Corporate Executives," *British Journal of Political Science* 8 (1978), 61–63.

[23] Richard Berke, "PAC's Aided Legislators on Banking Panels," *New York Times,* August 4, 1987; Gary Jacobson and Samuel Kernell, *Strategy and Choice in Congressional Elections* (New Haven: Yale University Press, 1981), p. 85.

[24] D. R. Fraser and J. W. Kolari, *The Future of Small Banks in a Deregulated Environment* (Cambridge: Ballinger, 1985), p. 19.

with net worth near zero.[25] The political power of small financial institutions in the United States is not very different from that in Japan; the greater difference is in the regulatory structures, the American one being too fragmented to coordinate ex ante the interests of competing or overlapping groups of financial institutions. The American policy response to interest group demands, therefore, tends to be ad hoc, coming after a problem has already occurred.

The American mass media are not unlike their counterparts in Japan, and their effect on financial regulation is probably similar. Even the media are to some extent susceptible to symbolic reassurances that public policies are indeed in the public interest.[26] But as in Japan, the failure of consumers in the United States to protect their interests against those of the banks probably had less to do with inadequate information about the interest rate ceiling than with the lack of incentive to put political pressure on Congress.

At the very least, politicians' fear of exposure to the public has probably curbed the natural apathy toward unorganized consumer interests.[27] At best, the expectation of wide media coverage and national approbation has encouraged a number of Congresspersons to take up otherwise risky anti-organized-interest, pro-consumer positions, such as on the deregulation of the railroad, trucking, airlines, and telecommunications industries.[28] In finance, however, consumers got what they wanted only when the mutual funds exploited a crack in the regulatory structure to meet latent public demand for higher-yield instruments.[29]

One key difference between financial policy making in the two countries is that the United States has been the world's dominant economy with the largest market for goods and services, and it has

[25]Nathaniel Nash, "Bank Board to Ease Net-Worth Rules for Ailing Thrift Units," *New York Times,* February 26, 1987; Nash, "Wright in FSLIC Reversal," *New York Times,* April 29, 1987; Nash, "Senate Accepts Compromise Bill on Bank System," *New York Times,* August 5, 1987.

[26]See Murray Edelman, *Symbolic Uses of Politics* (Urbana: University of Illinois Press, 1964), pp. 22–43.

[27]Michael Hayes, *Lobbyists and Legislators: A Theory of Political Markets* (New Brunswick, N.J.: Rutgers University Press, 1984), p. 95.

[28]Theodore Keeler, "Theories of Regulation and the Deregulation Movement," *Public Choice* 44 (1984), 104–5.

[29]It was actually not until the high inflation period of 1978–80 that the gap between the ceiling on deposits and the market rate became very large.

been the key architect of most of the rules of the world's financial system. American economic might, moreover, is backed by military power and political influence in the world second to none. We would therefore expect the United States to be the one who makes the rules, not follows them, in financial policy making. Regulatory changes in the United States have far greater bearing on financial regulation in the rest of the world than do regulatory changes elsewhere affect U.S. markets and policies.

The structure of the bureaucracy represents a second stark contrast between the American and Japanese regulatory environment. In the United States, any given financial policy is less clearly embedded in an interlocking web of policies. American solutions in the administration of private finance tend to be ad hoc and disjointed. For despite congressional oversight, the myriad routine bureaucratic decisions and numerous court cases relating to financial regulation bear the imprints of a wide range of players, at least in the short run.[30]

In Japan, by contrast, because the Ministry of Finance has wide jurisdictional reach, it can forge "in-house" solutions that have met with the approval of the regulated groups. The various groups in the Japanese financial sector continue to jostle among themselves for market share and regulatory advantage, but the MOF can usually address the disputes before they move into the political and public spheres.

Even in Japan, however, the political resources of the various groups nevertheless remain the standard by which the feasibility of a policy is measured, since any group retains the last-resort option to bring its case up for a political hearing. In the words of John Haley, the "consistent pattern of compromise both in making and

[30]*Confusion in the Legal Framework of the American Financial System and Service Industry,* Hearings, U.S. Congress, House Committee on Government Operations, July 12–20, 1983, pp. 12–13; "Competitive Equity in the Financial Services Industry," U.S. Congress, House Committee on Banking, Housing, and Urban Affairs, January 16, 1984, pp. 203–12. In the wake of the stock market's plummet on October 19, 1987, the Brady Commission called for greater centralization of regulatory oversight of the financial markets, but entrenched bureaucratic interests stand in the way of major reorganization. See Nathaniel Nash, "Reagan Group Is Likely to Back Broad Proposals on Stock Crash," *New York Times,* April 26, 1988.

Financial Politics in Contemporary Japan

implementing government policies ... can only be characterized as a
reflection of failure on the part of the economic bureaucracies to
achieve their original goals."[31] The two countries' different bureaucratic structures thus have more bearing on the financial policy-
making *process* than on what types of resources are honored and
what types of groups are rewarded in the policy outcomes.

Jurisdictions with fragmented regulatory authority, such as the
United States and the Euromarket, have set the global deregulatory
process in motion. Countries with encompassing, protective banking regulation, such as Japan and West Germany, have had no
choice but to deregulate domestic markets to the extent that domestic industries can avail themselves of more competitive financial
services abroad. This dynamic leads to a convergence of international financial markets, at least in wholesale banking. In retail
banking, where customers have little access to foreign alternatives,
domestic factors are more salient. In general, then, the theory of
regulation more accurately characterizes the policy-making process
in countries where the bureaucracy has encompassing jurisdiction
than it does in countries with fragmented state authority.

Interest Representation in Japanese Finance

The combination of Japan's slower growth and the trend toward
direct financing methods in global markets has diminished the traditional preeminence of banks in the Japanese economy. Yet even as
market forces are taking from the banks, the political process gives
them back at least part of what they lose. The Ministry of Finance,
following political cues, is redrawing the jurisdictional boundaries
to allow banks gradual entry into the more lucrative securities
business.

Small banks are the most decisive winners in the political game,
since they would be the most serious losers in a laissez-faire economy. The Liberal Democratic party's attentiveness to small banks,
along with its concern for small businesses, has become even keener

[31]John O. Haley, "Governance by Negotiation: A Reappraisal of Bureaucratic
Power in Japan," in Kenneth Pyle, ed., *The Trade Crisis: How Will Japan Respond?*
(Seattle: Society for Japanese Studies, 1987), p. 184.

224

since the 1974 Election Campaign Law, which placed a low upper limit on a corporation's contributions to politicians. The LDP's shift to a "shallow and wide" fund-raising program necessitates greater dependence on local bases of support. Although the LDP's simultaneous dependence on the Commissioned Postmasters League for election support impedes the party from favoring the small banks' requests to curb the postal savings system, the LDP at least shields small banks from the MOF's designs to streamline the financial sector.

As is generally the case even in representative democracies, the public barely even appears on the political map in routine policy decisions.[32] The Ministry of Finance is not in the business of meting out "collective benefits" to a "universalistic constituency," as Martin Shefter might suggest, but rather particularistic, divisible benefits based on the logic of politics.[33] Consumers of financial services are given last priority because they are not mobilized as a political force. The MOF's rhetoric about protecting consumer interests serves the function of slippers with which to tiptoe past the silent majority.

We have noted in the preceding chapters that there are certain pressures on politicians to become increasingly involved in financial regulatory policy making in Japan. First, foreign governments dissatisfied with the bureaucracy's slow consensus-building approach may take their cases to politicians for speedier resolution. Second, the media or the opposition may incite the public to take action on otherwise latent political issues. Third, the MOF is less able to supply banks with protective regulation. Many large Japanese corporations now have access to the Euromarket for capital and have lessened their dependence on loans from their Japanese banks. As the banks' loan spread decreases, they are all the more eager to

[32] Alessandro Pizzorno, "Interests and Parties in Pluralism," in Suzanne Berger, ed., *Organizing Interests in Western Europe* (Cambridge: Cambridge University Press, 1981), pp. 273–74. See Kozo Yamamura, "Caveat Emptor: The Industrial Policy of Japan," in Paul Krugman, ed., *Strategic Trade Policy and the New International Economics* (Cambridge: MIT Press, 1986), p. 183, for another example in the Japanese context.

[33] Martin Shefter, "Patronage and Its Opponents: A Theory and Some European Cases," Cornell Western Societies Program Occasional Paper no. 8 (Ithaca, N.Y., May 1977), pp. 14–15.

protect their low deposit rates, but the MOF is incapable of forcing the postal savings system to accept a uniform low deposit rate ceiling. Fourth, making a profit in Japanese banking used to be a function of the quantity of deposits and loans, since a healthy spread was virtually ensured. Now loan spreads are more variable and bank performance depends increasingly on skillful asset-liability management. This shift from "quantity to quality banking" weakens the MOF's ability to effect adjustments among groups in the financial sector.

Nevertheless, change in the policy-making process is not likely to be drastic. The MOF, also eager to diffuse foreign vexation at the continued closure of Japanese markets, has shown itself capable of responding with considerable speed. Second, rarely have either the general public or the opposition parties pressed the demands of the financial consumer in the political arena. When public arousal has occurred, such as in the case of the loan shark interest rates, direct involvement by the politicians has been limited in time and scope. Third and most important, the MOF is capable of acting preemptively to equilibrate among groups in the financial sector, rewarding them in proportion to their political resources. Through negotiation with the private sector, the MOF preserves its procedural autonomy at the expense of its substantive independence, the latter of which it could not in any case hope to keep.

Japan in the International Arena

Strong market forces have deeply penetrated the financial systems in both the United States and Japan. Large financial institutions of both countries, for example, have had to respond to the global standard of competition in corporate finance to retain the patronage of their client firms. But the Japanese financial institutions' ability to react in a more measured pace, shielding themselves where possible as change proceeds, has engendered a new set of problems for the Japanese financial community. Foreign financial institutions and manufacturing firms claim they are at a disadvantage in competing against the Japanese and demand that Japanese financial markets be "opened." The Japanese have found that foreign governments cannot always be mollified by the step-by-step pattern of financial reform that the Japanese would prefer.

The Japanese financial system adapted to competition from the Eurobond market by gradually deregulating its domestic bond market, while compensating the banks with a larger role in underwriting privately placed bonds. While banks have made their loans and large-scale deposits more attractive to prime customers, the MOF has helped ease the banks' transition to a more competitive financial market by granting banks limited access into the new growth areas in the securities business through a series of compromises with the securities industry.

As we have seen, however, the MOF's ability to foster the competitiveness of Japan's financial sector is constrained by the political power of the small, in many cases hopelessly uncompetitive, local banks. A two-tier market of coexisting competitive and uncompetitive banks works well enough in a closed economy, but not when foreigners lose patience with Japanese financial market protectionism and threaten retaliation.

Foreign retaliation, or the fear of it, has prodded Japan to move more quickly in lifting restraints on the Euroyen market, on foreign bank licensing to engage in securities operations in Japan, on foreign bank entry into the domestic trust bank market, and on foreign membership in the Tokyo Stock Exchange. Japanese financial institutions, the LDP, and the MOF concur on the need to avert massive foreign retaliatory action if at all possible. Japanese banks, because of the enormous success of their operations abroad, would pay a heavy price for punitive measures directed at them.[34] The LDP is held publicly responsible for a major rift in foreign relations, particularly in the case of Japan's largest trading partner and defense benefactor, the United States. And for the MOF foreign retaliation would mean loss of credibility with its domestic financial sector as well as troublesome questioning and interference from the Diet. The opposition may incite the public to take action on otherwise latent political issues. Third, the MOF is less able to supply banks with protective regulation. Many large Japanese corpora-

[34] Japan's current account surplus generates a large stream of funds that have to be invested abroad in some form; much is handled by foreign subsidiaries of Japanese financial institutions.

227

tions now have access to the Euromarket for capital and have lessened their dependence on loans from their Japanese banks. As the banks' loan spread decreases, they are all the more eager to protect their low deposit rates, but the MOF is incapable of forcing the postal savings system to accept a uniform deposit rate ceiling. Fourth, making a profit in Japanese banking used to be a function of the quantity of deposits and loans, since a healthy spread was virtually ensured. Now loan spreads are more variable and bank performance depends increasingly on skillful asset-liability management. This shift from "quantity to quality banking" weakens the MOF's ability to effect adjustments among groups in the financial sector.

The MOF has been deregulating Japan's financial markets, even without foreign pressure, in those areas where domestic clients have access to a global standard of competition. In a second category of cases where domestic responses and foreign demands differ, the MOF has responded by allowing foreign institutions to tread even where comparable domestic institutions do not. Foreign banks, but not Japanese banks, are licensed in the Japanese trust business; affiliates of foreign banks, but not of Japanese banks, are permitted to operate in the Japanese securities market. Third, in pockets where few alternatives exist for the customer and foreign pressure is still weak, such as in retail banking, the banks will stall as long as possible. The MOF may attempt to use the threat of foreign retaliation to promote the consolidation of the banking sector through mergers, which it has desired all along. But more likely, the MOF will be compelled to appease foreign banks by other means before small deposits are completely deregulated. Resistance from Japanese banks will be fierce, not only to avoid loss of privilege, but because the postal savings system makes it difficult for banks to minimize the cost of change through coordinated rate setting.

Japan will continue to respond through a variety of means, combining defensive efforts to protect its domestic structure and positive moves of genuine change.[35] As Takashi Inoguchi has pointed out, disparate views about Japan's role in the international system,

[35] For an interesting delineation of the alternative adjustment strategies states choose among, see G. John Ikenberry, "The State and Strategies of International Adjustment," World Politics 39 (October 1986), 53–77.

from spoiler to free rider to supporter, are likely to persist because "these three images reflect the enigmatic reality Japan poses to the rest of the world."[36] Japan is not a rising hegemon, eager to grasp the reins of the free trade regime. Too many powerful domestic interest groups are still enjoying the fruits of protection. And as long as domestic constituencies have the greatest bearing on a politician's fate, liberalizing schemes without domestic support are unlikely to be more than gestures.

[36]Takashi Inoguchi, "Japan's Images and Options: Not a Challenger, But a Supporter," *Journal of Japanese Studies* 12, no. 1 (1986), 96.

Index

Abe, Shintarō, 128–130, 186, 203
Abegglen, James, 71
administrative guidance (*gyōsei shidō*), 21–23, 129
Administrative Reform Council, 195, 206–207
Allison, Gary, 34n
Arisawa, Hiromi, 113n, 114n, 139n, 142, 143n, 190

balance of payments, and Japan's financial policy, 3, 50, 54–55, 69. *See also* capital flows
Bankers Acceptance (BA) market, 155
Bank for International Settlements (BIS), capital-asset ratio, 92
Bank of Japan, 41n, 46, 51, 63–64, 66, 74, 79, 99–100, 103, 114, 119–120, 143
Banking Act of 1982, 44, 46, 96–136; bank entry into government bond secondary market, 96–112; battle over cost of protection, 112–131. *See also* section 65 of the Securities Exchange Act of 1948
banks, 23–24, 51–53; and the Banking Act of 1982, 96–136; city banks, 23–24, 80–81, 101, 107; Industrial Bank of Japan, 104, 140, 151–152, 170; in international loan market, 55; and the Japan Offshore Market, 86; long-term credit banks, 64, 80, 85, 94–95, 104, 161; "main bank," 42, 150; mutual

banks, 24, 118, 123, 124–126; National Federation of Bankers Associations, 25, 102, 104, 109–111, 117, 120, 126, 154, 156, 175, 192; and Occupation, 114–118; political influence of, 25–37, 131; and postal savings system, 167–208; small banks, 23–24, 47, 118, 120–128, 133–135, 197, 207, 224; trust banks, 64–80, 85, 94–95, 161; trustee banks (*jutaku ginkō*), 39, 140, 160; wartime control, 112–114, 141. *See also* Bond Arrangement Committee; government bond market
Bentley, Arthur, 6
Bergsten, C. Fred, 68–69. *See also* yen-dollar exchange rate
Bond Arrangement Committee or Bond Issuance Committee (Kisaikai), 39, 40, 55, 83, 100, 140–141, 144–145, 159–161, 164–166
bond market: bond rating, 147, 160–163; Bond Study Group, 159; convertible bonds, 149; deregulation in Japan, 56, 138, 157–166; Euromarket and, 147–166; Occupation and, 142–144; postwar development, 145–147; prewar history of Japan's corporate bond market, 138–147; prewar politicians and, 139. *See also* government bond market
Brittain, Alfred, 62
business sector (small- and medium-sized), 118, 121, 124, 139, 186, 200, 224

231

Index

233

Index

Nakatani, Iwao, 147n
"national treatment" in U.S. commercial policy, 51, 58; reinterpreted, 72, 76, 93. *See also* retaliation
Nikaido, Susumu, 199
Niskanen, William, 18
Noguchi, Yukio, 41n, 44n
Noll, Roger G., 6n, 21n, 80n

Obuchi, Keizō, 199
Occupation of Japan (after World War II), 37–42, 141–145
Ōhira, Masayoshi, 128, 201
oil shocks, 55, 57, 129; and government bond market, 99–100; and shift in corporate finance strategies, 97, 147, 157, 182. *See also* "securitization"
Okimoto, Daniel, 8, 19n, 23n
Ōkita, Saburō, 142, 190
Olsen, James P., 20n
Olson, Mancur, 6n, 34n
opposition parties. *See* Democratic Socialist party; Japan Communist party; Japan Socialist party; Kōmeitō
"overloan," 120

Packer, Frank, 42n
Patrick, Hugh T., 71n, 113n, 114n, 145n, 169n
Pauly, Louis, 58n, 59n, 76n, 77n
Peltzman, Sam, 6n
Pempel, T. J., 4n, 28n
Pension Fund Association (Kōsei Nenkin Kikin Rengōkai), 77
political entrepreneurship, 145, 212–215, 221–222
Posner, Richard A., 6n
postal savings system, 27; competition with banks, 213; Green Card, 180–187; interest income tax (abolition of *maruyū*), 196–205; interest rate setting, 187–194; origins, 168–172; and tax evasion, 174, 180–183, 187, 199, 206; *teigaku chokin*, 175, 187, 197, 204; wartime control, 172. *See also* Ministry of Posts and Telecommunications
"preemptive equilibration." *See* Ministry of Finance
Prindl, Andreas, 53n, 57

Ramseyer, Mark, 12, 215
Reagan, Ronald, 73
Reconstruction Finance Bank (Fukkō Kinyū Kinko), 115–116
Regan, Donald, 73–77

regulation, theory of, 6, 9–13, 48, 96, 205–208, 211
Rengō (National Federation of Private Sector Unions), 33
retail financial markets, 10, 95, 134, 167–208. *See also* postal savings system
retaliation against Japanese trade and financial policies, 14, 52, 75, 91–94, 227. *See also* international pressures
Riker, William, 26
Rōyama, Shōichi, 2n

Samuels, Richard, 8, 216
Satō, Ichirō, 130, 194
Satō, Seizaburō, 4n, 9, 29n, 30n, 34n
Schmiegelow, Michèle, 57n
section 65 of the Securities Exchange Act of 1948, 40, 46–47, 77, 84, 85, 150; and Banking Act of 1982, 97–136; drafted by Occupation officials, 142; and Japan Offshore Market, 85–91. *See also* Banking Act of 1982; Glass-Steagall Act; Ministry of Finance: Three Bureaus Agreement
securities firms, 25–26, 51; and Banking Act of 1982, 96–136; "Big Four," 25, 100, 145–156, 161–162, 166; and bond market, 150, 166; Council of Securities Organizations (Shōken Dantai Kyōgikai), 26; interest in offshore market, 86; political influence of, 37–38, 129; Securities Industry Association, 107, 111, 156
"securitization," 86, 100, 182
Sekiguchi, Sueo, 53n, 54n, 55n
Sheard, Paul, 42n, 147n
Shepsle, Kenneth A., 26n
Solomon-Murchison Report, 70–71, 79
Sprinkel, Beryl, 64, 69
state structure, 15–16, 211–212, 216–217, 219, 224. *See also* Ministry of Finance
Stigler, George, 6n, 9, 211
Study Group on a Free Economy (Jiyū Keizai Konwakai), 194
Study Group on the Role of Government in Finance (Yūchokon), 190–193. *See also* postal savings system
Sumita, Satoshi, 122
Suzuki, Yoshio, 2n, 54n, 129n
Suzuki, Zenkō, 104, 195, 206

Tachi, Ryūichirō, 2n
Takeshita, Noboru, 73, 193, 194, 203
Tanaka, Giichi, 139

234

Recent Studies of the
East Asian Institute

Perspectives on a Changing China. Joshua A. Fogel and William T. Rowe, eds. Boulder, Colo.: Westview Press, 1979.

The Memoirs of Li Tsung-Jen. T. K. Tong and Li Tsung-Jen. Boulder, Colo.: Westview Press, 1979.

Unwelcome Muse: Chinese Literature in Shanghai and Peking, 1937–1945. Edward Gunn. New York: Columbia University Press, 1979.

Yenan and the Great Powers: The Origins of Chinese Communist Foreign Policy. James Reardon-Anderson. New York: Columbia University Press, 1980.

Uncertain Years: Chinese-American Relations, 1947–1950. Dorothy Borg and Waldo Heinrichs, eds. New York: Columbia University Press, 1980.

The Fateful Choice: Japan's Advance into South-East Asia. James William Morley, ed. New York: Columbia University Press, 1980.

Tanaka Giichi and Japan's China Policy. William F. Morton. Folkestone, England: Dawson, 1980; New York: St. Martin's Press, 1980.

The Origins of the Korean War: Liberation and the Emergence of Separate Regimes, 1945–1947. Bruce Cumings. Princeton: Princeton University Press, 1981.

Class Conflict in Chinese Socialism. Richart Curt Kraus. New York: Columbia University Press, 1981.

Education under Mao: Class and Competition in Canton Schools. Jonathan Unger. New York: Columbia University Press, 1982.

Private Academies of Tokugawa Japan. Richard Rubinger. Princeton: Princeton University Press, 1982.

Japan and the San Francisco Peace Settlement. Michael M. Yoshitsu. New York: Columbia University Press, 1982.

New Frontiers in American–East Asian Relations: Essays Presented to Dorothy Borg. Warren I. Cohen, ed. New York: Columbia University Press, 1983.

236

Studies of the East Asia Institute

The Origins of the Cultural Revolution: II, The Great Leap Forward, 1958–1960. Roderick MacFarquhar. New York: Columbia University Press, 1983.

The China Quagmire: Japan's Expansion on the Asian Continent, 1933–1941. James William Morley, ed. New York: Columbia University Press, 1983.

Fragments of Rainbows: The Life and Poetry of Saito Mokichi, 1882–1953. Amy Vladeck Heinrich. New York: Columbia University Press, 1983.

The U.S.–South Korean Alliance: Evolving Patterns of Security Relations. Gerald L. Curtis and Sung-joo Han, eds. Lexington, Mass.: Lexington Books, 1983.

Japan and the Asian Development Bank. Dennis Yasutomo. New York: Praeger Publishers, 1983.

Discovering History in China: American Historical Writing on the Recent Chinese Past. Paul A. Cohen. New York: Columbia University Press, 1984.

The Foreign Policy of the Republic of Korea. Youngnok Koo and Sungjoo Han, eds. New York: Columbia University Press, 1984.

Japan Erupts: The London Naval Conference and the Manchurian Incident. James W. Morley, ed. New York: Columbia University Press, 1984.

Japanese Culture. 3d ed. rev. Paul Varley. Honolulu: University of Hawaii Press, 1984.

Japan's Modern Myths: Ideology in the Late Meiji Period. Carol Gluck. Princeton: Princeton University Press, 1985.

Shamans, Housewives, and Other Restless Spirits. Laurel Kendall. Honolulu: University of Hawaii Press, 1985.

Human Rights in Contemporary China. R. Randle Edwards, Louis Henkin, and Andrew J. Nathan. New York: Columbia University Press, 1986.

The Manner of Giving: Strategic Aid and Japanese Foreign Policy. Dennis T. Yasutomo. Lexington: Lexington Books—D. C. Heath, 1986.

Security Interdependence in the Asia Pacific Region. James W. Morley, ed. Lexington: Lexington Books—D. C. Heath, 1986.

China's Political Economy: The Quest for Development since 1949. Carl Riskin. London: Oxford University Press, 1986.

Anvil of Victory: The Communist Revolution in Manchuria. Stephen L. Levine. New York: Columbia University Press, 1987.

Library of Congress Cataloging-in-Publication Data

Rosenbluth. Frances McCall.
  Financial politics in contemporary Japan/Frances McCall Rosenbluth.
    p. cm.—(Studies of the East Asian Institute)
  Includes bibliographical references and index.
  ISBN 0–8014–2274–4 (alk. paper)
  1. Financial institutions—Japan—Deregulation. I. Title. II. Series.
HG187.J3R67 1989   332.1′0952—dc19   89–30074